The Adaptation of History

The Adaptation of History

Essays on Ways of Telling the Past

Edited by LAURENCE RAW
and DEFNE ERSIN TUTAN

Forewordist James M. Welsh

McFarland & Company, Inc., Publishers
Jefferson, North Carolina, and London

ALSO OF INTEREST

Character Actors in Horror and Science Fiction Films, 1930–1960, by Laurence Raw (McFarland, 2012)

LIBRARY OF CONGRESS ONLINE CATALOG DATA

Raw, Laurence.
   The adaptation of history : essays on ways of telling the past / edited by Laurence Raw and Defne Ersin Tutan ; foreword by James M. Welsh.
      p.   cm.
   Includes bibliographical references and index.

   ISBN 978-0-7864-7254-3
   softcover : acid free paper ∞

   1. Historical films—History and criticism.   2. Film adaptations—History and criticism.   3. History in motion pictures.   4. Motion pictures and history.   I. Raw, Laurence. II. Tutan, Defne Ersin.
PN1995.9.H5 A43 2013
                                                      2012039326
BRITISH LIBRARY CATALOGUING DATA ARE AVAILABLE

Front cover images: background atomic bombing of Japan (Wikimedia Commons); film graphic © 2013 Shutterstock

Manufactured in the United States of America

McFarland & Company, Inc., Publishers
   Box 611, Jefferson, North Carolina 28640
      www.mcfarlandpub.com

Table of Contents

v

Acknowledgments

The seeds for this collection were planted one very hot summer day on Başkent University's campus as Laurence and Defne were discussing the possible ways they could join their personal fields of interest to produce collaborative academic work. Laurence had an undying interest in adaptation studies and Defne in history, and the overlap provided a fruitful site of discussion that they could not even begin to exhaust within the boundaries of this collection.

Laurence's interest in the nature of history was inspired many years ago in high school, when he took classes from E. N. Williams, author of such magisterial works as *The Ancien Regime in Europe: Government and Society in the Major States, 1648–1789*, *The Eighteenth Century Constitution; 1688–1815: Documents and Commentary*, *Dictionary of English and European History; 1485–1789*, and *A Documentary History of England; 1559–1939*. It was Williams who introduced him to E. H. Carr's *What Is History?* Defne's questioning of history, on the other hand, reached its peak while she was working on her Ph.D. dissertation, focusing on "alternative histories" being created in the postmodern postcolonial context. She is ever grateful to Serpil Oppermann, her thesis advisor at Hacettepe University, Department of English Language and Literature, who has always been a mentor and motivator. Yet perhaps no specialization in history would make the same sense if it were not for Laurence under whose guidance Defne was initiated into the broader field of cultural studies about sixteen years ago.

The idea for the collection ripened at a conference, "The Poetics of Love: Theory and Practice in Film and Television," held in Milwaukee in 2010. We are grateful to the Center for the Study of Film and History at the University of Wisconsin-Oshkosh for organizing the event, and to Loren P. Q. Baybrook, director of the center and editor-in-chief of *Film and History*, and Cynthia J. Miller, associate editor-in-chief of the same journal, for providing an opportunity to discuss the issue of "history" and its representation. Peter C. Rollins, former editor-in-chief of *Film and History* and a leading authority on "history" and the media, provided valuable input, as did A. Bowdoin Van Riper. We are fortunate that both Miller and Van Riper have contributed to this collection.

Many of the ideas discussed in the introduction previously appeared in different form in articles mentioned in the introduction. Laurence is grateful to the respective book review editors Paul M. Cohen (*Film and History*) and Monika Pietrzak-Franger (*Adaptation*) for commissioning them. Laurence also had the chance to raise some of the issues in this collection at "Adapting Historical Narratives," a conference held at Centre for Adaptations, De Montfort University, Leicester, United Kingdom. He is grateful to Claire Monk, reader in film and culture, and Deborah Cartmell, director of the centre, for organizing the event, as well as chairing extremely suggestive sessions. Others whose input helped to shape this collection include Alan Munslow — whose recent work on history's futures should be read by anyone interested in the discipline — Sarah Gilligan, Isobel Johnstone, Ashley Polasek and Martine Cuillerier. He is also grateful to Tony Gurr, consultant, polymath, and humanist, for consistently fruitful beer o'clock discussions on Sunday afternoons — preferably in a comfortable hostelry. Fuat Altunkaya, currently chair of the Department of English at Başkent University, consistently provides an amenable working environment. Şeref Mirasyedioğlu, dean of the Faculty of Education in the same university, offers unstinting support. And Laurence's current officemate, Nehir Sert, offers patient yet sound criticism of most of his ideas.

Defne would like to further acknowledge the support of the members of the Department of American Culture and Literature at Başkent University, namely Himmet Umunç, Özlem Uzundemir, Meltem Kıran-Raw, Pürnur Uçar-Özbirinci and Berkem Gürenci-Saglam for always being there and encouraging innovative thinking. Moreover, if it were not for the technical support provided by A. Esin Ağaoğlu, department secretary, we would never be able to master the technology required to put together a publication.

We thank James M. Welsh, professor emeritus of English at Salisbury University and founding editor of *Literature-Film Quarterly*, for writing the foreword.

Last but not least, we are both indebted to our families for believing in us forever.

Foreword: Adapting Cinema + History (= Cinematic History?)

James M. Welsh

This is a book of trends. Twenty years ago, Oliver Stone made several films touching on historical topics (though, in truth, most of them were biographical or autobiographical), so an historian decided to call Stone a "cinematic historian," then went on to propose that history films somehow constitute a "genre" (Rosenstone, "Oliver" 26–39). Now, *there* was a trend, though perhaps not a promising one, for "history" surely lacked the classic components of a time-honored genre, such as the western: predictable elements involving certain definable character types, a set number of plots that could be endlessly reassembled and combined interestingly and entertainingly, and an elegant landscape upon which the action could be played out. Oliver Stone rejected this label, however, because he *knew* he was a writer and director, and not really an "historian." After all, *he made things up*! Who *was* that character "Jack Jones" anyway, that fictional Texan in Stone's *Nixon* (1995), for example, played by Larry Hagman of *Dallas* fame? *Real* historians are not allowed to do that. But we now live happily in postmodern times, so I reckon almost anything is forgivable. Absurdity sticks!

A second trend has also arisen to kiss the first one and perhaps marry it, involving a new-found "discipline" called "adaptation studies," and Laurence Raw is one of its leaders and pioneers. Initially the field was rather narrowly defined and sadly limited to literary things—plays, novels, short stories—that had been adapted to film; nothing as significant as history. That kept the presses busy for a decade and fattened the tenured ranks of colleges and universities. But Laurence Raw preferred to think in broader terms. Adaptation, after all, is an ongoing process, probing into unnoticed corners

1

of human endeavor. Examples of adaptation are all around us, if we look for them.

One example from this book would be the essay by Manjree Khajanchi wonderfully entitled "Adapting Archaeological Landscapes: Re-Presenting Ireland's Heritage," a piece that appealed to me as an expatriate Irish half-breed; it is about the touristic "adaptation" of "heritage" sites in Ireland, where tourism seems to be a major source of GNP after the Celtic Tiger got sick and died. Newgrange, a spectacular Neolithic monument near the Boyne River north of Dublin, used to be merely a roadside attraction you could drive right up to, *roadside*. Now, you are taken into a coachpark, then made to walk to a tourist center, with slide shows for the ignorant, where you purchase tickets (and food concessions), before walking further to catch the minibus that takes you to the well-manicured Neolithic monument, where you wait your turn to be escorted up to the illuminating passageway. Of course the best time to visit Newgrange is on the morning of the winter solstice, at just the hour the rising sun hits the opening of the ancient passage tomb and penetrates, however briefly, the interior. But this only happens once a year, and you need to win the lottery to gain entry, so gullible tourists are led into the dark and mysterious passage to see it tricked up with electric lights. They tell you, "You haven't really seen Newgrange until you've seen the solstice," so *there*, tourists, you've just been sucker-punched. But the Boyne Valley is certainly "historic" enough, and green, too, and pastoral (like most of the Emerald Isle). Other follies follow in this essay, but I won't go there.

The indefatigable Walter C. Metz finds an intertextual "project" lurking behind Martin Scorsese's *Shutter Island* (2010), an adaptation of Dennis Lehane's best-selling 2003 novel, that involves "the relationship between violence and a specifically American masculinity" (pushing another trend button). This film, Metz argues, is a counter-argument to journalist Tom Brokaw's simplistic, feel good mantra about the "greatest generation." It all comes down to *Shutter Island*'s "status as a film about the Holocaust," but, more than that, Metz sees *Shutter Island* as "an inter-textual adaptation of *The Cabinet of Dr. Caligari*." As usual (I say fondly), Metz can be counted on to rile things up. In contrast, Cynthia J. Miller calms things down as she channels Florenz Ziegfeld, who just *knew* that "a pretty girl is like a melody," and that a pretty melody is like a narcotic, like "No clouds of gray on that great whiteway," pounded over and over again into the national consciousness in *The Broadway Melody* (1929), America's first (and, arguably, most boring) movie musical. We learn from Miller that although God may have created women, Ziegfeld "invented" them. Are they really "the stuff that dreams are made of" (or "on," to quote the Bard truly)? Did Flo Ziegfeld really "invent" American girlhood, or simply *exploit* it? Cynthia will tell you.

A. Bowdoin Van Riper's contribution on Hollywood's depictions of the Manhattan Project broaches a topic that is both "scientific" and world-changing, certainly in its impact on war, diplomacy, and politics. He isolates six films for discussion, including a Showtime miniseries and two made-for-television films—*Enola Gay* (1980) and *Day One* (1989). That only leaves three feature films, so to enrich his "project" he might have considered *The Day After Trinity*, the J. Robert Oppenheimer documentary that was nominated for an Academy Award for Best Documentary of 1980, that is both "scientific" and philosophical. The title comes from Oppenheimer's response to Robert Kennedy asking President Lyndon Johnson to initiate talks to stop the spread of nuclear weapons: "It's twenty years too late. It should have been done *the day after Trinity*" (*Day After Trinity*) (italics mine). This documentary would certainly cover what the author calls "The Manhattan Project and 'Big Science.'"

Other contributions range from the practical to the theoretical. Gerald Duchovnay, the founding editor of the journal *Post Script*, takes a pedagogical stance, for example, explaining how three courses involving the "history" of the 1960s and 1970s were taught at Texas A & M University, classes where "most of the learners had epiphanies," we are told. Anecdotal information is shared. In one graduate course, almost everyone could identify Gandhi and Malcolm X and Bob Dylan, but—for shame!—almost no one had heard of the Gulf of Tonkin or Daniel Elsberg. Beyond basic content, the goal was to go "beyond mere narrative—to understand how form relates to content...." Testimonials follow from fellow teacher Eric Gruver and from graduate student Charles Hamilton, who remembers Mike Nichols' *The Graduate* (1967) as a sort of life lesson, and undergraduate student Hayley Hasik.

On the other hand, Clare Foster's essay raises the old-fashioned but sensible question of "authenticity" in historical adaptation, citing as examples films purporting to treat antiquity, such as Ridley Scott's *Gladiator* and Oliver Stone's *Alexander*, and, perhaps, Wolfgang Petersen's *Troy* to what may seem to be mere action-adventure spectacles like Zack Snyder's *300*. Packaging for the cineplex and, later on, video games, would seem to take precedence over "authenticity," meaning what, exactly? For directors, she opines, "authenticity is at once unimportant yet important in the way their products are consumed." Just as Joe McGinnis was interested in "the selling of the President" decades ago, Hollywood is now interested in the marketing and selling of history. Foster does bring historiography to the fore, and key historians such as Hayden White into her discussion. White, a distinguished professor at the University of California, was the author of *Metahistory: The Historical Imagination in Nineteenth-Century Europe* (1973) and *The Content of the Form: Narrative Discourse and Historical Representation* (1987). Hayden White spoke in a lecture series commissioned by the American Film Institute at UCLA on April 8, 1992, and that lecture was then converted into an essay, "The Modernist Event," later presented in Vivian Sobchack's collection, *The Persistence of History* (1996). White was concerned about the relationship between literature and history and between fact and fiction, between fact and "faction," docudramas, and "historical metafiction." White's thinking led him to issues such as postmodernist docudrama and historical metafiction, resulting in what Getrude Himmelfarb called "History As You Like It" (qtd. in White, "Modernist" 19). Hayden White could therefore be considered a posterboy for postmodern relativistic historiography.

The Persistence of History set an important precedent for film scholars interested in history films. But this effort lagged behind interest taken up by historians themselves. Pioneering efforts by my friend, John E. O'Connor, and Martin A. Jackson, who founded The Historians Film Committee and the journal *Film & History*, resulted in a booklet under the umbrella of the American Historical Association entitled *Teaching History with Film* (1974).

O'Connor was also a founding member of an ambitious group effort, the International Association of Media and History (IAMHIST), which instituted its own *Historical Journal of Radio, Television, and Film*, edited first by Ken Short, then by David Culbert. IAMHIST member Pierre Sorlin, a professor at the University of Paris and the Universite de la Sorbonne Nouvelle, published *The Film in History* (1980), and others would soon follow his lead. John O'Connor's successor as editor of *Film & History*, Peter C. Rollins, edited *The Columbia Companion to American History on Film* in 2003, so let it not be said that historians themselves have not been attentive to cinema. That same year Rollins and O'Connor edited *Hollywood's White House: The American Presidency in Film and History* (2003). The latest book to appear (as of this writing) also comes from the IAMHIST camp, including essays by David Culbert, David Eldridge, and IAMHIST President Nicholas J. Cull, entitled *Hollywood and the American Historical Film* (2012), edited by J. E. Smyth of the History Department of the University of Warwick (UK). The anthology includes Robert Rosenstone's essay "Inventing Historical Truth," and opens with a reprinted groundbreaking essay written by the highly regarded Warren Susman (1927–1985), "Film and History: Artifact and Experience."

So the present volume has a lineage tracing back to historians who may have been film enthusiasts, cinema studies scholars who may have been history buffs, and the adaptation studies tribe as well. What this present collection suggests about film director Ridley Scott's Crusade film *Kingdom of Heaven* (2005) is surely on target. Traditional historians may have criticized it for being "inaccurate" or even "irresponsible," but Scott nonetheless recreates a vivid, imaginative impression that has powerful resonance with contemporary Near East tensions and conflicts.

In our own recent study of director Oliver Stone, Donald Whaley and I consider three major phases of history: (1) Pre-Modern History or Mythic History (as practiced by Homer in his treatment of the Trojan Wars, or perhaps by Richard Slotkin in his extended discussion of the "Frontier Myth" in American history, as defined by Frederick Jackson Turner and the Turner thesis; (2) Modern History, treating the "facts" objectively as "evidence," a "scientific" approach leading to the obsessions of historians to extrapolate all sorts of meanings from past events (supposing that the historians among us are as "scientific" and as "objective" as they might believe themselves to be); and (3) Post-Modern History, moving away from the "scientific" evaluation of "factual" matters back towards the Truth of the Mythic. We believe Oliver Stone belongs in this latter category of the historian as mythmaker (Welsh and Whaley). Stone's inclination is to emphasize the "story" of "history." Modernist historians would of course object to his making things up, of being "inaccurate" and inventing characters; but the distinctions that apply here are not so much between "fact" and "fiction" as between "fact" and "truth" and between "fiction" and "truth." In our opinion that which is fictional may also speak to a larger "truth," a mythic truth that deserves careful attention. And so it may be with Ridley Scott. The discussion continues in the pages that follow.

Works Cited

Alexander. Dir. Oliver Stone. Perf. Colin Farrell, Anthony Hopkins, Rosario Dawson. Warner Bros., 2004. Film.

The Broadway Melody. Dir. Harry Beaumont. Perf. Bessie Love, Anita Page. MGM, 1929. Film.

The Cabinet of Dr. Caligari. Dir. Robert Wiene. Perf. Hans Janowitz, Carl Meyer. Decla-Bioscop AG, 1919. Film.

The Day After Trinity. Dir. John Else. Perf. Hans Bethe, Holm Bursom, Haakon Chevalier. KTEH, 1981. Documentary.

Day One. Dir. Joseph Sargent. Perf. Brian Dennehy, David Strathairn, Michael Tucker. Spelling Entertainment, 1989. TV Film.

Enola Gay. Dir. David Lowell Rich. Perf. Billy Crystal, Kim Darby, Patrick Duffy. Viacom Productions, 1980. TV Film.

Gladiator. Dir. Ridley Scott. Perf. Russell Crowe, Richard Harris, Oliver Reed. Dreamworks SKG/ Universal Pictures, 2000. Film.

The Graduate. Dir. Mike Nichols. Perf. Dustin Hoffman, Anne Bancroft, Katharine Ross. Embassy Pictures, 1967. Film.

Kingdom of Heaven. Dir. Ridley Scott. Perf. Russell Crowe, Orlando Bloom, Eva Green. Twentieth Century–Fox, 2005. Film.

Nixon. Dir. Oliver Stone. Perf. Anthony Hopkins, Joan Allen, Powers Boothe. Hollywood Pictures, 1995. Film.

O'Connor, John E., ed. *Image as Artifact: The Historical Analysis of Film and Television.* Malabar, FL: Robert E. Krieger, 1990. Print.

_____, and Martin A. Jackson. *Teaching History with Film.* Washington, DC: American Historical Association, 1974. Print.

Rollins, Peter C., ed. *The Columbia Companion to American History on Film: How the Movies Have Portrayed the American Past.* New York: Columbia University Press, 2003. Print.

_____, and John E. O'Connor, eds. *Hollywood's White House: The American Presidency in Film and History.* Lexington: University Press of Kentucky, 2003. Print.

Rosenstone, Robert A. "Oliver Stone as Historian." *Oliver Stone's USA.* Ed. Robert Toplin. Lawrence: University Press of Kansas, 2000. 26–39. Print.

Shutter Island. Dir. Martin Scorsese. Perf. Leonardo DiCaprio, Emily Mortimer, Mark Ruffalo. Paramount Pictures, 2010. Film.

Smyth, J. E., ed. *Hollywood and the American Historical Film.* Basingstoke and New York: Palgrave Macmillan, 2012. Print.

Sorlin, Pierre. *The Film in History: Restaging the Past.* Totowa, NJ: Barnes and Noble, 1980. Print.

Susman, Warren. "Film and History: Artifact and Experience." *Hollywood and the American Historical Film.* Ed. J. E. Smyth. Basingstoke and New York: Palgrave Macmillan, 2012. 1–12. Print.

300. Dir. Zack Snyder. Perf. Gerard Butler, Lena Headey, David Wenham. Warner Bros., 2006. Film.

Troy. Dir. Wolfgang Petersen. Perf. Brad Pitt, Eric Bana, Orlando Bloom. Warner Bros., 2004. Film.

Welsh, James M., and Donald M. Whaley. *The Oliver Stone Encyclopedia.* Lanham, MD: Scarecrow Press, 2012. Print.

White, Hayden. *The Content of the Form: Narrative Discourse and Historical Representation.* Baltimore: Johns Hopkins University Press, 1987. Print.

_____. *Metahistory: The Historical Imagination in Nineteenth-Century Europe.* Baltimore: Johns Hopkins University Press, 1975. Print.

_____. "The Modernist Event." *The Persistence of History: Cinema. Television, and the Modern Event.* Ed. Vivian Sobchack. New York and London: Routledge, 1996. 17–38. Print.

James M. Welsh, *professor emeritus of English at Salisbury University in Maryland, was the founder of the Literature/Film Association and a founding editor of* Literature/Film Quarterly. *In 1997 he organized with Peter Lev the XVII International IAMHIST Congress, held at Salisbury University and at the National Archives in Washington, D.C. His latest books are* The Oliver Stone Encyclopedia *(with Donald M. Whaley) and* The Francis Ford Coppola Encyclopedia *(with Gene D. Phillips and Rodney Hill).*

Introduction: What Does "Adapting" History Involve?

DEFNE ERSIN TUTAN and LAURENCE RAW

The inspiration for putting this collection together originated from several sources. The first was a sequence of talks broadcast in BBC Radio 3's *The Essay* series in November 2011 entitled "What Is History, Today?" Produced by Katherine Godfrey to commemorate the fiftieth anniversary of the publication of E. H. Carr's seminal work *What Is History?*, it comprised the personal views of five historians of different generations. Richard J. Evans, regius professor of English at Cambridge University, believed that Carr was one of the first historians to question "objectivity"; speaking for a younger generation, Elizabeth Buettner of the University of York treated *What Is History?* as a product of its time. She was particularly interested in how the book's questioning of the nature of history mirrored the larger questions being raised about Great Britain's future in world politics in the postcolonial era, thereby covertly signaling the idea that one's adaptation of history actually tells more about the present than the past. Amanda Foreman was somewhat more critical of Carr's arguments; she believed that he failed to acknowledge the importance of lived experience. By probing people's lives— through interviews, or reading autobiographies, diaries or other firsthand accounts— the historian can discover how societies work and how they impinge on people's lives. Niall Ferguson, the Yale historian and *Newsweek* columnist, had little time for Carr, who overlooked the presence of "counterfactual" history — in other words, the kind of history prompting people to ask "what if" questions. The series ended with Michael Cox of the London School of Economics, who insisted that Carr was not a professional historian, but someone more preoccupied with international relations— particularly in his earlier books on the growth and development of Soviet Russia. *What Is History?* should be treated as a meditation on the Cold War, and how East and West construct one another's subject positions in relation to one another ("What Is History, Today").

Two things struck us most about the series. All five speakers were preoccupied with the issue of relevance, without defining either what the term actually meant, or speculating on its imagined readership. We wondered exactly which kind of audience Carr's *What Is History?* "related" to—historians, publishers, the producers of the Radio 3 program, or the listeners at large. Secondly, and perhaps more significantly, we noticed the way in which all five speakers implied that professional historians were best qualified to comment on the past for present-day readers. Little attempt was made to acknowledge the contributions made by others interested in the past—filmmakers, fiction writers, or individual people sharing their autobiographies either orally, in print or through blogs. This kind of analysis might have proved suggestive as a means of shedding light on the important issue of whether "history" as an autonomous field of study has a future, or whether it should be rethought in comparative, transcultural or transdisciplinary terms.

The second inspiration came from two review essays that Laurence Raw wrote on the relationship between film and history. The first, "Retelling European History on Film," published in *Film and History*, took up E. H. Carr's point that history can be used to tell different stories in different periods. It suggested that the experience of an historical film comprises several different histories: the history told on the screen by the director, actors and other creative personnel; and the histories of individual audience members witnessing the film, either in the movie theater, on television or online. The only way we can make sense of an historical film is to look at the ways it affects us: "the past represents different things to different generations" (Raw, "Retelling" 65). In an attempt to elaborate on this democratic view that everyone constructs their own histories, the second review essay for *Adaptation* surveyed the ever-expanding canon of critical literature on medieval film, from Richard Burt's *Medieval and Early Modern Film and Media*, to Bettina Bildhauer's *Filming the Middle Ages*. Raw argued that many of these texts draw no distinction between filmmakers and historians: both make use of similar interpretive processes as they try to make sense of limited primary sources. Despite their claims to the contrary, the majority of historians of the medieval period draw on the kind of evidence that might be termed "disputable" or "circumstantial," and have to create their own narratives to make sense of it (Raw, "Imaginative History" 2–3). Filmmakers exploit similar freedoms to create works operating according to their own historical and dramatic logic that "mock our desire for origin, for truth, for stability, for history" (Finke and

Schichtmann 286). Since the Enlightenment we have become accustomed to approaching history in terms of temporal logic, factual coherence and genre specificity (social history, oral history, political history, and so on). Medieval filmmakers present imaginative worlds where such distinctions no longer exist; and by doing so encourage each one of us to reflect on what comprises an "accurate" or "reliable" view of the past, and its relationship to the present and the future (Raw, "Imaginative History" 6–7).

Alun Munslow has recently described these contrasting approaches to constructing historical narrative as "interpretive" and "adaptive" (Munslow, "Adapting"). Interpreters insist that their views are independent of any self-serving theory or master narrative forced on the evidence; their role is primarily to establish the veracity and accuracy of the evidence, and then put it all into an interpretive focus through organizing concepts (for example, Niall Ferguson's "counterfactual history"). The interpretive historian works on the evidence and infers its most likely meaning — "unlike non-historians [...] [they] are blessed with the intellectual capacity to overcome the gravitational pull of [their] earthly tethers" (Munslow, "Reappraisal"). Adapters, on the other hand, are not likely to be professional historians, but rather filmmakers, novelists, readers, filmgoers or television viewers. They are not so much concerned with veracity and accuracy; what matters to them is the desire to make sense of the past in terms of the present. They are thus more likely to create imaginative approaches, involving the kind of speculation that might be dismissed as "inaccurate" by the professional historian. An example of this might be Ridley Scott's film *Kingdom of Heaven* (2005), which was lambasted by Thomas F. Madden, director of the Center for Medieval and Renaissance Studies at the University of St. Louis, for its irresponsible view of the medieval world:

> Given events in the modern world it is lamentable that there is so large a gulf between what professional historians know about the Crusades and what the general population believes. This movie only widens that gulf. The shame of it is that dozens of distinguished historians across the globe would have been only too happy to help Scott and [screenwriter William] Morahan to get it right [Madden].

The fact that Scott and Morahan felt no desire to incorporate a "right" view of history in their adaptive text has been conveniently overlooked.

While this distinction might serve to distinguish the work of what Munslow elsewhere describes as "conventional historians" (i.e., those who profess to tell "the truth" about history) from others interested in more creative treatments of the past (Munslow, *Future* 34), it does not allow for the fact that the meanings of "interpretation," "adaptation," "truth" and "fiction" are culturally and historically determined. The Turkish novelist Orhan Pamuk alludes to non-western novelists of the twentieth century who used fictionality "as a shield against the repression of the state (perhaps saying, 'Do not accuse me — my novels are products of the imagination')." At the same time they boasted about the way in which they revealed the truth about human behavior. These apparently contradictory statements represented one of several "practical solutions to oppressive and political conditions"—especially in the Republic of Turkey (Pamuk 39). Pamuk likens the novel to "a play of mirrors": neither reader nor writer can disentangle truth from fiction. This willful confusion is the driving force of all novels (52). Such was the case of *The Satanic Verses* (1988), for instance, in which Salman Rushdie amalgamated elements of Indian and British history, as well as of Islam. He was not claiming to be either truthful or accurately historical, but he was accused of being unsuccessful in both. That is, the *fatwa* issued in his name revealed more about human behavior outside of the novel than it did about the novel *per se*, as it did not provide any "practical solutions to oppressive and political conditions" of the time. Although the *fatwa* constituted the most forceful of the accusations, Rushdie was accustomed to the fact that such human behavior was not constrained to bringing religion into literary scrutiny. Following a visit to Nicaragua in 1984, Rushdie stated that

> [t]he modern world lacks not only hiding places, but certainties. There is no consensus about reality between, for example, the nations of the North and of the South. What President Reagan says is happening in Central America differs so radically from, say, the Sandinista version, that there is almost no common ground. It becomes necessary to take sides, to say whether or not one thinks of Nicaragua as United States' "front yard." (Vietnam, you will recall, was the "back yard.") It seems to me imperative that literature enter such arguments, because what is being disputed is nothing less than *what is the case*, what is truth and what untruth. If writers leave the business of making pictures of the world to politicians, it will be one of history's great and most abject abdications [Rushdie 100].

In this respect, unless any interpretation of the past is accepted, as well as welcomed, as *adaptation*, there would never be a consensus on the ways in which history should be treated.

Rather than engaging in debates about the way history should be approached (either adaptively or interpretively), we propose that all historical documents should be treated as *adaptations*. We approach this concept in Darwinian terms as a process of making sense of the world around us: "daily and hourly scrutinizing [...] rejecting that which is bad, preserving and adding up all that is good; silently and insensibly working, whenever and wherever opportunity offers at the improvement of each organic being in relation to its organic and inorganic conditions of life" (Darwin, *Origin* 143). In his *Recollections*, published between 1876 and 1881, Darwin emphasized that this process of "scrutinizing" was the means by which all species, including human beings, "gradually become modified" by adapting to the world around them. They engage in "a struggle for existence [...] under these circumstances favorable variations would tend to be preserved & unfavorable ones to be destroyed. The result of this would be the formation of new species" (Darwin, *Recollections* 401). Everyone conducts "a daily and hourly" scrutiny of the past in relation to their "organic and inorganic conditions of life" in the present; by doing so they create a series of "favourable variations" that help them make sense of the present and determine their future. As a result, they are transformed into "new species" with a broader understanding of the world around them and their place within that world.

This view of adaptation was further developed by the psychologist Jean Piaget, who argued in *The Origin of Intelligence in the Child* (1953) that children enrich their understanding of things in the present by acting and reflecting on the past. They learn to adapt to a new environment, and as a consequence, reorganize their knowledge to make sense of increasingly complex structures. The process of contrasting past and present helps children develop a sophisticated awareness of the "rules" that underpin every social and behavioral interaction — for example, identifying the difference between right and wrong. For Piaget, adaptation comprises a process of incorporating past experience in a framework defined by the present (accommodation), and reconstituting that experience in one's own terms (assimilation). Once children come to appreciate the difference between accommodation and assimilation, they indulge in "experimental behavior [...] the discovery of new means through active experimentation." This provides a way of negotiating their future (Piaget 330).

This view of history-as-adaptation values individuals as creative talents who not only come to terms with the world around them, but possess the capacity to transform that world through experimental behavior. More significantly we can move beyond questions of historical accuracy and concentrate instead on *narrative representation*, a process that can be broken down into four components: (i) *story* (in Piagetian terms, the outcome of the processes of accommodation); (ii) *narrating* (the mode of expression an individual chooses to tell their story); (iii) *narrative* (the structure of that story); and (iv) *mode of expression* (Munslow, *Future* 155). Like the novel, as described by Pamuk, an historical narrative comprises an idiosyncratic combination of "truth" and "fiction." In the words of Roseanne, the protagonist of Sebastian Barry's *The Secret Scripture* (extensively analyzed by Gülden Hatipoğlu in this collection), "no one has the monopoly on truth. Not even myself" (134).

The major advantage of this approach lies in the way it *democratizes* the process of creating history. Narrating the past is no longer the preserve of the professional historian; everyone—filmmakers, novelists, sociologists, as well as those recounting their lives to an interviewer— participates on a level playing-field as witnesses to the past and how it relates to the present or future. In explicating the Bakhtinian notion of "dialogism," Arthur Asa Berger suggests that "[f]irst, there is the past, which has an impact on our ideas and what we create. Second, there is the future and the responses we anticipate from our audience (real or imagined), which affect what we do [...] Texts, then, are suspended between the past and the future" (35–6). Viewed from the dialogical perspective, one's interpretation of the past becomes more suggestive of the ways in which that person has adapted to the present for purposes of determining the future.

On this view "history" consists of a series of conflicting stories that reveal how individuals have adapted to a particular event, or series of events. Throughout his lengthy academic career, Ray B. Browne championed the cause of popular history and popular culture "as a window to the human condition [...] popular culture is often a more truthful picture of what the people were thinking and doing at any given time than artistic creations are [...] in the arts the forms and shapes, and ideas, that last, come up from the people, or at least last longest among them" (Browne 25). While understanding Browne's point, we would argue that the high/popular culture opposition is a construction often invoked by those who try to preserve their disciplinary territory (in Browne's terms, those who favor "artistic creations" rather than analyzing "what people were thinking and doing"). Bearing this in mind, we would extend Browne's point by arguing that *all* forms, shapes and ideas about history "come up from the people." Whether such forms survive or not depends on a process that Darwin described long ago as natural selection: "man can produce and certainly has produced a great result by his methodical and unconscious means of selection" (Darwin, *Origin* 142).

Focusing on history in this way also encourages an interdisciplinary, or rather a transdisciplinary, view of the subject, with the emphasis placed on the *processes* by which historical narratives are adapted, rather than valuing knowledge for its own sake. We can investigate how a literary scholar, a filmmaker, or a professional historian approaches a similar subject, and how they are influenced by their respective conditions of production. It might be instructive, for instance, to look at the ways in which the Gallipoli campaign of 1916 has been represented by former poet laureate John Masefield, or contemporary historians Alan Moorehead and Nigel Steel; and compare their adaptations with those of Australian filmmaker Peter Weir and the American-educated Turkish director Tolga Örnek. This kind of approach is a good example of what Munslow describes as "experimental history," where we explore "how to 'tell the past' in genres that reflect upon the needs of representation [....] History henceforth speaks in new ways—first person, the language of fiction and poetry, of tarot cards, mystery, entertainment, and brevity" (Munslow, *Future* 193). Such languages are not conventionally associated with writing "history," but belong to other disciplines—literature, film, detective fiction, and the like. When these new ways of speaking are accepted, and when the distinction between so-called "good" and "bad" history is negated, we end up with relativity in the place of value judgments. In this respect, in the words of Linda Hutcheon, "intertextual dialogism" offers a "multilaminated" experience (Hutcheon 21).

More importantly, by drawing on the Darwinian concept of the survival of the fittest, we can understand why some adaptations assume more significance than others at particular points in time. Weir's film *Gallipoli* touched a nerve in early 1980s Australia, as it brought back memories of how the Anzacs suffered at the hands of incompetent British officers. Mel Gibson's Frank Dunne and Mark Lee's Archy Hamilton became cult figures—representatives of the youth of a nation that were quite literally cut down in their prime fighting on behalf of the Empire. Twenty-four years later, Örnek's documentary on the same campaign was one of the first adaptations to adopt an evenhanded view, by suggesting that Anzac, British and Ottoman troops experienced similar horrors in the Gallipoli trenches. His film emphasized the importance of mutual understanding of the past: different cultures shared similar memories of a long-forgotten conflict. Both films achieved far more recognition, both financial and critical, than the BBC drama *All the King's Men* (1999), a fictionalized account of the mysterious disappearance of the Norfolk Regiment during the Gallipoli campaign. The main explanation for this was the BBC's insistence on drawing on familiar orientalist stereotypes to portray the Ottoman forces. They misjudged the temper of the times; by the late 1990s the prevailing mood was one of reconciliation: Anzac veterans and their descendants were welcomed by their Turkish hosts, whenever they visited the battleground.

This mode of analysis, drawing on historical enquiry, film studies, anthropology as well as trans- or cross-cultural studies might best be defined as interdisciplinary; an attempt to highlight the issues—political, social, personal, as well as historical—that matter to members of specific cultures in the past, present and future. Rather than examining historical specificities, the emphasis is placed on what Augsburg and her fellow-authors term "real world relevance and [...] the chance to contribute to the understanding of complex issues" (Augsburg et al. 241). These issues of "real world relevance" encompass the search for identity, individual or collective, the importance of self-determination and tolerance of others, and the capacity to adapt to prevailing ideologies, or perhaps adapt them (in the Darwinian sense).

A focus on history as adaptation also offers a suggestive framework for cross-cultural analysis, focusing, for instance, on the relationship between past and present in different contexts. As an example, we might consider the filmmaker Derviş Zaim, whose 2006 film *Cenneti Beklerken* (*Waiting for Heaven*) is set in the seventeenth century Ottoman Empire, and explores the career of Eflâtun (Serhat Tutumluer), a miniaturist summoned to the vizier's palace in Istanbul and ordered to travel to the center of the country to make a portrait of the rebel leader Danyal (Nihat İleri), so that the Ottoman leaders can verify the leader's identity. Zaim reflects on the process of historical adaptation (Eflâtun insists he can draw the portrait from memory, without having to meet Danyal in the flesh), while concentrating on the intricacies of the miniaturist's art. Danyal captures Eflâtun and orders him to make a miniature by deliberately distorting a western painting — a pastiche of Velázquez's "Las Meninas" ("The Maids of Honor") (1656). The newly-created picture will help fulfill Danyal's dream of becoming the new Muslim messiah. Zaim creates this sequence to demonstrate how historical adaptation can incorporate "different realms, times and spaces" (to quote Danyal's phrase).

On one level, we are invited to compare our (mostly western-inspired) knowledge of the Velázquez painting with the adapted version in Zaim's film. Both contain the image of the artist reflected in the mirror working on the image we see before us. On a second level, we observe an Ottoman–inspired historical image of a ruler (cut out from one of Eflâtun's older miniatures) being pasted over the artist's image at the back of the Velázquez pastiche, thereby producing a palimpsestic adaptation combining western and eastern motifs. On a third level, we are invited to speculate on who has appropriated the new picture: does it still belong to the artist or has it now become public property? Danyal is in no doubt that his visual image can be adapted by artist and viewers alike: whether they are the viewers involved in Zaim's story, or those witnessing the film in the movie theater, on DVD or online. W. J. T. Mitchell emphasizes how viewers across all historical periods engage in a process of active adaptation that not only "'mediates' knowledge of a particular culture and its particular preoccupations, but also extends, obstructs, fragments, and negates that knowledge" (Mitchell 17). Zaim shows how past and present are interconnected by inviting us to reflect on the ways in which we interpret historic artifacts. This impression is reinforced through the costumes, which Zaim claims were "the production of a present-day filmmaker looking back on the past" (qtd. in Raw, *Exploring* 296).

This kind of adaptive approach enables Zaim to explore the relationship between power and appropriation. Every viewer of the Velázquez picture throughout history has "colonized" it, in the sense that they interpret it according to their received opinions. Whereas this process can often be empowering for individuals, it offers the perfect opportunity for rulers to impose their ideas on their subjects. This is clearly what happens when the Ottoman image is pasted over the artist. This same image of power and appropriation is evident in the quadrangle of the Museum of Anatolian Civilizations in Ankara, the architectural style of which is a direct adaptation of the Covered Bazaar in İstanbul, where "long wall reliefs" from the "late Hittite period," from "Charchemish 920–900 B.C." are displayed. Four panels depict the war between the Hittites and the Egyptians. The Hittite figures are atop a chariot, crushing their Egyptian adversaries underneath the wheels. It is astonishing to find out that the exact same wall reliefs are also on display in the Cairo Museum, with one *minor* difference: in that *adaptation*, the Hittites are the ones being crushed underneath the chariot with Egyptians atop. In this reconstruction, power relationships are reversed: this testifies that coming to terms with the present necessitates an adaptation of the past, and thus, of the present and future.

The contributions included in this book all look at the question of adapting history from a Darwinian perspective, with the emphasis placed on the ways in which individuals and/or communities make sense of the world around them, and subsequently transform it. Our authors originate from a variety of disciplinary backgrounds: literature specialists such as Tanfer Emin Tunç and Gülden Hatipoğlu compete for our attention with film studies scholars Walter C. Metz and Cynthia J. Miller; historians such as A. Bowdoin Van Riper and Dunja Dogo vie with anthropologists such as Manjree Khajanchi and a classicist like Clare Foster. The choice of subject-matter is refreshingly varied: topics include Irish history ancient and modern; Hollywood films past and present; recent Zimbabwean politics; German children's literature since the 1930s; British documentaries; a theater production based on the classic David Lean film *Brief Encounter* (1945); and a study of contemporary native Indian poetry. We have spread our net wide in an attempt to show how adapting history can help to promote interdisciplinary and intercultural perspectives.

For the sake of convenience, this book is divided into two parts comprising "mainstream" and "alternative" historical adaptations. While realizing that such terms are contested, invoking the kind of binary oppositions which are characteristic of those who try to fence in their academic agenda rather than expand it, we use them as a means of differentiating the processes by which different individuals (or institutions) throughout history have adapted to the world around them.

The first part, titled "Mainstream History," kicks off with Cynthia J.

Miller's fascinating analysis of how the early twentieth century impresario Florenz Ziegfeld established a cultural icon—"the Ziegfeld Girl"—which became "a Broadway brand," foregrounding idealized images of femininity. While Ziegfeld recognized no differences, whether racial, national or sexual, he expected his girls to be tall, long-limbed and graceful, "creating a standard of beauty that the impresario claimed glorified women." For audiences of the time, Ziegfeld's musicals offered dreams of wealth and prosperity; the kind of life that anyone could embrace, so long as they worked at it. Miller also shows how the Ziegfeld Girl has penetrated other areas of American popular culture, adding glamor to everything from blogs to home décor, bath towels and bowling shirts. The image celebrates feminine sensuality, independence and possibility—qualities that remain as significant today as they were a century ago. In spite of major shifts in the ways women perceive themselves as individuals, the Ziegfeld Girl image continues to encourage them to adapt to more prosperous ways of life.

Walter C. Metz reviews the ways in which Martin Scorsese adapts the topic of the Holocaust in *Shutter Island* (2010). Scorsese reshapes his source-text, Denis Lehane's best-selling novel of the same name (2003), to such an extent that the film resonates with explorations of American masculinity and historical trauma. Metz discusses how Scorsese positions *Shutter Island* in an intertextual (as well as historical) dialogue with *Vertigo* (1958), relying on Alfred Hitchcock's late 1950s construction of masculinity as the basis for the central character Teddy's (Leonardo DiCaprio's) perception of "reality." Teddy has not yet learned to adapt imaginatively to changed social, moral and personal circumstances. Scorsese also stresses the continuities of historical adaptation by linking the Holocaust to Robert Weine's expressionist classic *The Cabinet of Dr. Caligari* (1919), a study of the relationship between destroyed masculinity and the political destabilization of Germany.

Continuing the German historical theme, Anne Klaus analyzes how successive governments policed the production of children's literature during the Nazi era and beyond. From the early 1930s onwards the Nazis reinvented history for young people by foregrounding the achievements of the Aryan race and consciously denigrating other ethnic and social groups—Jews, gypsies, homosexuals. In the post–1945 era the East German authorities undertook similar ideological work: in their adaptation of history the communists were represented as heroes struggling against the pernicious effects of Nazism and fascism. What is perhaps more intriguing, however, is that West German authors found it difficult to adapt to the changed political landscape: Klaus argues that they seldom confronted issues such as the Holocaust with conviction and/or honesty. Even in the post-unification period, there has only been a gradual movement towards acknowledging the past and its implications for the future of German society. The task of adapting to changed conditions can often prove painful.

Claudia Georgi's discussion of Kneehigh Theatre's production of *Brief Encounter* takes as its point of departure the landmark David Lean film of 1945, as well as the Noël Coward play *Still Life* (1936), the source-text for the filmscript written by Lean, Ronald Neame and Anthony Havelock-Allan. Georgi analyzes a 2008 performance at London's Cinema Haymarket of Emma Rice's stage adaptation of the film (a play of a film of a play), and shows how the director pays tribute to the wartime setting, even while emphasizing the modernity of her version. She deliberately appeals to the British audience's popular memories of the film, while simultaneously creating a vividly contemporaneous version of World War II social history. By doing so she unites past and present, looking at the past through the lens of the present.

Marco Grosoli takes up this theme of continuity by comparing Mario Martone's *Noi Credevamo* (*We Believed*) (2010) with a milestone of Italian cinema, Luchino Visconti's *Senso* (*Sentiment*) (1954). Grosoli is interested in the ways filmmakers have approached a turbulent moment in national history — in this case, the series of violent conflicts leading to Italian unification in 1861, known as Risorgimento. Grosoli shows how Visconti and Martone draw on melodramatic conventions, that divide the characters according to a simplistic moral schema — the good versus the bad. However Martone adapts the material to prevailing historical conditions; he departs from the linear plot-structure characteristic of the genre — denoting an inevitable progression of events — in an attempt to negotiate the kind of "cynical fatalism" that Grosoli believes is typical of Italian audiences. *Noi Credevamo* is an optimistic adaptation, hinting at the possibility of change — not only politically but economically — in the midst of crisis. It endorses the Darwinian view that individuals have a perpetual capacity to adapt themselves to changing circumstances.

Dunja Dogo examines a similar adaptive process at work in Soviet Russia immediately after the 1917 Revolution. However the emphasis here was not on individual self-fulfillment but collective security. Dogo analyzes two films, Aleksandr Ivanovskij's *Dekabristy* (*The Decembrists*) (1927), and Leonid Trauberg and Gregorij Kozincev's *Sojuz Velikogo Dela* (*The Union for the Great Cause*) (also 1927), both of which offer contemporary historical adaptations of the uprising against the Tsar that took place between December 1825 and January 1826. Despite some negative publicity from the Party press, both films were box-office successes. *Dekabristy* celebrated the heroic deeds of those leading the uprising, while *Sojuz Velikogo Dela* transformed the entire story into a melodrama combining politics and romance. Dogo argues that both adaptations were part of a deliberate strategy by the Party to adapt Russia's past to emphasize Marxist principles. They built on the success of previous cultural events dedicated to the uprising—for example, an exhibition held at the Museum of Revolution in Petrograd (now St. Petersburg).

A. Bowdoin Van Riper looks at cinematic adaptations of another government-sponsored project—the so-called "Manhattan Project," that introduced nuclear weapons to the world. After July 16, 1945, the day of the first explosion over a desolate patch of the New Mexican desert, it seemed no longer important to refer to "Great Powers." The world was dominated by two superpowers—the United States and Soviet Russia. In a penetrating analysis of six Hollywood films released between 1947 and 1995, Van Riper shows how the Manhattan Project was adapted to suit different social and political landscapes. In the Cold War years of the 1940s, the Project was perceived as a symbol of security; if properly administered, it could help preserve the American way of life against the threat of communism. As the Cold War waned, so the Project was reimagined as a cautionary tale of what might happen if scientists wielded too much power. Van Riper's piece proves the truth of Piaget's contention that history is invariably adapted imaginatively, as individuals try to come to terms with a perpetually changing world.

Clare Foster addresses the whole question of adapting history in relation to the logic of contemporary Hollywood film. Using Wolfgang Petersen's *Troy* (2004), and Zack Snyder's *300* (2006) as examples, she argues that producers deliberately address different target audiences; those with no knowledge of the classical period, and those who go to see such epics to see the extent to which directors have adapted the source material. She also questions the whole idea of historical 'truth' by showing how it was a concept developed during the nineteenth century, when the concept of 'originality' evolved as a means of judging the worth of cultural artifacts.

Sabelo J. Ndlovu-Gatsheni suggests that the Mugabe government has re-emphasized the kind of Marxist ideology characteristic of post–1917 Soviet Russia, by adapting two culturally-specific concepts—*Chimurenga* and *Gukurahundi*. *Chimurenga* operates according to the doctrine of permanent revolution against nationalism and imperialism, dating from the liberation war fought against the British colonizers in 1896–7. Mugabe's ZANU-PF party has re-invoked the concept to justify the nationalist cause—even if that involves annihilating some fellow-Zimbabweans who had fought alongside them for independence in the 1970s. *Gukurahundi* literally translates as "the storm that destroys everything;" in the ZANU-PF interpretation it was used to justify violence as a legitimate political tool in the annihilation of political opponents. While recent years have witnessed the emergence of new adaptations of Zimbabwean history, favoring pluralism and tolerance, the old order continues to dominate the political and adaptive landscape.

The book's first part concludes with Manjree Khajanchi's essay on "heritage" sites in Ireland. While the subject-matter — the preservation and representation of Ireland's historic sites — seems a world away from Ndlovu-Gatsheni's discussion of Zimbabwean history, the methodological framework remains strikingly similar. Based on her own fieldwork as a member of a group sponsored by the University of Lampeter, North Wales, Khajanchi shows how those responsible for the upkeep of these sites have consciously favored past-centered adaptations of history. While some efforts have been made to show how these sites changed through time, Khajanchi argues that they consciously shy away from promoting contemporaneous interpretations or recording new memories in the present. Visitors do not have the freedom to construct their own adaptations; they cannot "breathe in the [historic] landscape, and experience the site without the feeling of claustrophobia." Khajanchi calls for a more pluralistic approach to site management, enabling visitors to create their own adaptations and thereby forge a close link between themselves and Ireland's ancient past.

The second part of this collection, "Alternative History," looks at the ways in which different groups or individuals have adapted their histories in an attempt to challenge dominant ideologies. Following on from Khajanchi's discussion of ancient Irish sites, we move forward to the twenty-first century to Gülden Hatipoğlu's discussion of the way in which Barry deals with Irish history in *The Secret Scripture*. Following the creation of the Free State in 1922, the Church and State collaborated in the creation of an 'official' discourse concerning family life and sexuality. Anyone challenging what they perceived as the norm — in which women were expected to assume secondary roles within a civil marriage partnership and have children as soon as possible — was deemed "deviant." Barry understands the significance of (re-)telling their stories and thereby adapting Irish history to accommodate more pluralist discourses, as well as imagining what Hatipoğlu describes as "alternative futures."

However the process of creating such futures is not as easy as it might seem. Following on from Dogo's and Ndlovu-Gatsheni's analyses of twentieth century Soviet and Zimbabwean history, Yuki Obayashi demonstrates that this task can prove as traumatic for the victims of war as for the aggressors. The essay shows that the Vietnamese have experienced considerable mental trauma — especially when they have settled down to new lives in the United States. They have not only been scarred by the experience of war, but have experienced racism — both conscious and unconscious — from their American hosts. Obayashi suggests that their adaptations of recent history have been suppressed by mainstream Hollywood representations of the Vietnam War in the Rambo films or *Good Morning, Vietnam* (1987), where the Americans are either portrayed as heroic or sympathetic, while their Vietnamese adversaries are aggressors or victims, unable to communicate coherently in English. Obayashi suggests that this dominant adaptation has been challenged (or "re-scripted") recently by Vietnamese–language films, but more work needs to be done to accommodate the Vietnamese experience both during the conflict and beyond.

Rose Gubele offers a suggestion as to how this process of developing alternative adaptations might be accomplished through a study of the poetry of Deborah Miranda. A member of the California–based Ohlone-Costanoean-Esselen Nation, Miranda's poetry deals with what Gubele terms "buried history"—the kind of history suppressed by a century and a half of internal colonization in the United States. Miranda proposes alternative adaptations of history that acknowledge Native America and its impact on the country's past and present. To deny the power of these adaptations will only perpetuate "the culture of violence" that continues to suppress Native peoples. Gubele argues that Miranda's poetry is preoccupied with the idea of adaptation-as-change; once Native histories (or herstories) are foregrounded, then her people can create new selves, as well as inscribing their own futures. We are left with the belief that "writing is [...] a manifestation of [adaptive] power."

Staying in the American context, Tanfer Emin Tunç's study of the Agrarian novelist Caroline Gordon highlights a similar struggle for self-expression. Her books *Penhally* (1931), and *None Shall Look Back* (1937) revolve around conflicts between history and memory: many southerners find it difficult to adapt to the present, as they are over-burdened by the past. Gordon offers a way out by adapting the past in an attempt to preserve (or revive) the Lost Cause myth, and thereby restore the glory days of the south. While this task might be difficult to accomplish in practice, the idea offers a way forward for any southerner imprisoned by a sense of regret for what might have been. Tunç sums up this mood of optimism with a quotation from one of Gordon's lectures delivered over four decades after *Penhally* was first published: "Everything that rises must converge but everything that converges must have risen. Hold [on to] your Confederate money, boys! The South [will] rise again!"

Heather Norris Nicholson likewise concentrates on the adaptation of the past in the present — this time through digitization. She is particularly concerned with the preservation of amateur film footage recording ordinary people's lives. Sometimes those entrusted with the responsibility of preserving this film accommodate it into dominant adaptive discourses, rather than letting viewers see it for themselves—for example, by showing clips rather than the completed film. However Norris Nicholson argues that digitization processes are so diverse these days that opportunities exist for communicating "the pluralities of texts" as well as encouraging a plurality of responses from viewers. Film restorers should be sensitive to the complexities of the adaptive process.

Our collection rounds off with a fascinating case study by Gerald Duchovnay, Eric Gruver, Charles Hamilton and Hayley Hasik — faculty members and learners in the Honors College of Texas A&M University in Commerce. They were involved at the undergraduate and graduate levels in creating courses devoted to "The Sixties," designed not only to investigate the decade's significance to an understanding of contemporary American history, but to develop critical reflection on a variety of texts. Rather than adopting a fact-based methodology, Duchovnay and Gruver — as faculty members — created a course based around a variety of films produced during that period, as well as films about the period such as *Mississippi Burning* (1988). As learners, Hamilton and Hasik were encouraged to discuss their reactions to these films, and subsequently make sense of such reactions through written assignments; this proved a fascinating task, as both of them came from very different backgrounds and generations. Their responses were fascinatingly diverse: Hamilton in particular, as someone who had grown up in the 1960s, found that the task of revisiting the decade as a learner turned out to be a voyage of self-discovery, as well as an exercise in collaborative learning. The contribution as a whole offers a fascinating analysis of the power of education to shape both learner and educator perceptions of one another, as well as demonstrating how historical adaptations are continually constructed, deconstructed and reconstructed over time: nothing remains stable. This process is something shared by everyone — as Piaget suggests, adaptation is predominantly psychological. At the end of the piece, all four contributors admit that their views of the 1960s and their individual relationship to the decade had changed beyond recognition: the course forced them to rethink what was significant about America's past and how it affected their views of the present. This piece sums up in microcosm what the collection as a whole is designed to prove: adapting history is not just the preserve of professional historians, but something undertaken by everyone, regardless of age, race, gender or class, as a means of coming to terms with their particular worlds. Once this basic point has been understood, then perhaps we can go beyond the kind of binary oppositions (between "facts" and "interpretation," or "accurate" and "inaccurate" history), which sometimes inhibit the development of interdisciplinary and cross-cultural approaches to adapting history. The future could prove fascinating.

Works Cited

All the King's Men. Dir. Julian Jarrold. Perf. David Jason, Maggie Smith, William Ash. BBC/WGBH, 1999. TV Film.
Augsburg, Tanya, Stuart Henry, William H. Newell, and Rick Szostak. "Conclusion."

The Politics of Interdisciplinary Studies. Eds. Augsburg and Henry. Jefferson, NC: McFarland, 2009. 227–57. Print.

Barry, Sebastian. *The Secret Scripture.* London: Faber and Faber, 2008. Print.

Berger, Arthur Asa. *Cultural Criticism: A Primer of Key Concepts.* Thousand Oaks: Sage, 1995. Print.

Bildhauer, Bettina. *Filming the Middle Ages.* London: Reaktion Books, 2011. Print.

Brief Encounter. Dir. David Lean. Perf. Trevor Howard, Celia Johnson, Stanley Holloway. Rank, 1945. Film.

Brief Encounter. Dir. Emma Rice. Kneehigh Theatre Company. Cinema Haymarket, London. 20 Feb. 2008. Theatre Performance.

Browne, Ray B. *Ray Browne on the Culture Studies Revolution: An Anthology of his Key Writings.* Ed. Ben Urish. Jefferson, NC McFarland, 2011. Print.

Burt, Richard. *Medieval and Early Modern Film and Media.* Basingstoke and New York: Palgrave Macmillan, 2008. Print.

The Cabinet of Dr. Caligari. Dir. Robert Wiene. Perf. Hans Janowitz, Carl Meyer. Decla-Bioscop AG, 1919. Film.

Carr, E. H. *What Is History?* Intro. Richard J. Evans. Basingstoke and New York: Palgrave Macmillan, 2001. Print.

Cenneti Beklerken (Waiting for Heaven). Dir. Derviş Zaim. Perf. Serhat Tutumluer, Melisa Sözen, Mesut Akusta. Sarmasık Sanatlar/ Tivoli Film/ Hermès Film, 2006. Film.

Coward, Noël. *Still Life.* 1936. *Plays Three — Design for Living, Cavalcade, Conversation Piece, Hands Across the Sea, Still Life, and Fumed Oak.* London: Methuen Drama, 1994. 335–381. Print.

Darwin, Charles. *On the Origin of Species by Means of Natural Selection. Evolutionary Writings.* Ed. James A. Secord. Oxford: Oxford University Press, 2008. 105–231. Print.

_____. *Recollections of the Development of My Mind and Character. Evolutionary Writings.* Ed. James A. Secord. Oxford: Oxford University Press, 2008. 355–426. Print.

Dekabristy (The Decembrists). Dir. Aleksandr Ivanovsky. Perf. Vladimir Maksimov, Yevgeni Boronikhin, Varvara Annenkova. Leningradkino, 1927. Film.

Finke, Louise A., and Martin B. Schichtmann. *Cinematic Illuminations: The Middle Ages on Film.* Baltimore: Johns Hopkins University Press, 2010. Print.

Gallipoli. Dir. Peter Weir. Perf. Mel Gibson, Mark Lee, Bill Kerr. Australian Film Commission, 1981. Film.

Gelibolu (Gallipoli). Dir. Tolga Örnek. Perf. Sam Neill, Jeremy Irons, Zafer Ergin. Ekip Film, 2005. Film.

Good Morning, Vietnam. Dir. Barry Levinson. Perf. Robin Williams, Forrest Whitaker, Tung Thanh Tran. Touchstone Pictures/Silver Screen Partners, 1987. Film.

Gordon, Caroline. *None Shall Look Back.* 1937. Nashville: J. S. Sanders, 1992. Print.

_____. *Penhally.* 1931. Nashville: J. S. Sanders, 1991. Print.

Hutcheon, Linda. *A Theory of Adaptation.* London and New York: Routledge, 2006. Print.

Kingdom of Heaven. Dir. Ridley Scott. Perf. Russell Crowe, Orlando Bloom, Eva Green. Twentieth Century–Fox, 2005. Film.

Lehane, Denis. *Shutter Island.* New York: William Morrow, 2003. Print.

Madden, Thomas F. "Kingdom of Heaven." *National Review Online*, 27 May 2005. Web. 6 Mar. 2012.

Masefield, John. *Gallipoli.* London: William Heinemann, 1916. Print.

Mississippi Burning. Dir. Alan Parker. Perf. Gene Hackman, Willem Dafoe. Orion Pictures, 1988. Film.

Mitchell, W. J. T. "Representation." *Critical Terms for Literary Study.* Eds. Frank Lentriccia and Thomas McLaughlin. Chicago: University of Chicago Press, 1990. 11–21. Print.

Moorehead, Alan. *Gallipoli.* Ware, Herts: Wordsworth Military Editions, 1997. Print.

Munslow, Alun. "The Adaptation of 'The Past-as-History.'" De Montfort University, Leicester, Centre for Adaptations. 28 Feb. 2012. Keynote Address.

_____. *The Future of History*. Basingstoke and New York: Palgrave Macmillan, 2010. Print.

_____. "Reappraisal of *What Is History?*" *History in Focus* 2, Nov. 1997. Web. 6 Mar. 2012.

Noi Credevamo (*We Believed*). Dir. Mario Martone. Perf. Luigi Lo Cascio, Valerio Binasco, Toni Servillo. Palomar/ Les Films d'Ici/ RAI Cinema, 2010. Film.

Pamuk, Orhan. *The Naïve and Sentimental Novelist: The Charles Eliot Norton Lectures 2009*. Trans. Nazım Dikbas. London: Faber and Faber, 2011. Print.

Piaget, Jean. *The Origin of Intelligence in the Child*. 1953. Trans. Margaret Cook. London and New York: Routledge, 1997. Print.

Raw, Laurence. "Derviş Zaim: To Return to the Past Means Embarking on a New Journey." *Exploring Turkish Cultures: Essays, Interviews and Reviews*. Newcastle-upon-Tyne: Cambridge Scholars, 2011. 281–99. Print.

_____. "Imaginative History and Medieval Film." *Adaptation* 5.2 (2012): 262–8. Print.

_____. "Retelling European History on Film: An Essay Review." *Film and History* 41.2 (Fall 2011): 64–8. Print.

Rushdie, Salman. "Outside the Whale." *Imaginary Homelands: Essays and Criticism, 1981–1991*. London: Granta/Penguin, 1991. 93–101. Print.

Senso (*Sentiment*). Dir. Luchino Visconti. Perf. Farley Granger, Alida Valli. Lux Film, 1954. Film.

Shutter Island. Dir. Martin Scorsese. Perf. Leonardo DiCaprio, Emily Mortimer, Mark Ruffalo. Paramount Pictures, 2010. Film.

Sojuz Velikogo Dela (*The Battle for the Great Cause*). Dir. Leonid Trauberg and Grigorij Kozincev. Perf. Emil Gal, Sergei Gerasimov, Konstantin Khokhlov. Sovkino, 1927. Film.

Steel, Nigel. *Gallipoli (Background Europe)*. Rev. ed. London: Leo Cooper, 1998. Print.

300. Dir. Zack Snyder. Perf. Gerard Butler, Lena Headey, David Wenham. Warner Bros., 2006. Film.

Troy. Dir. Wolfgang Petersen. Perf. Brad Pitt, Eric Bana, Orlando Bloom. Warner Bros., 2004. Film.

Vertigo. Dir. Alfred Hitchcock. Perf. James Stewart, Kim Novak. Paramount Pictures, 1958. Film.

"What Is History, Today?" *The Essay*. BBC Radio 3, 14–18 Nov. 2011. Radio.

PART ONE: MAINSTREAM HISTORY

"Glorifying the American Girl": Adapting an Icon

CYNTHIA J. MILLER

Over a century ago, impresario extraordinaire Florenz Ziegfeld created a cultural icon: the Follies Girl. Glamorous, beautiful, and unattainable, she posed, paraded, danced, and sang her way into the hearts of American theatergoers. Mainstays of the Ziegfeld *Follies* from 1907 until 1931, the Ziegfeld Girls, as these performers would come to be known, promoted an image of ideal American womanhood — graceful, refined, effervescent, young, and independent — an image that was a far cry from the corpulent, worldly, working-class character portrayed by their counterparts in dance halls, variety, burlesque and vaudeville, like the renowned Lydia Thompson. The Ziegfeld Girl celebrated twentieth-century American beauty and American excess, catering to the theatergoing public's ever-increasing appetite for spectacle. Through this elegant archetype, the lowly chorus girl was elevated to the status of "showgirl," and beyond, to a symbol of national identity — inextricably linked with images of idealized American womanhood. She was, as Ziegfeld, himself, would often say, "glorified."

Ziegfeld "turned his name into a Broadway brand;" one that used lavish displays to pay "tribute" to these beautiful women as "idealized images of femininity" (van der Merwe 39). Each year, a new production of the *Follies* reinvented the Ziegfeld Girl, adapting and revising themes and appearances though elaborate song-and-dance routines, extravagant costumes, and daring innovations in stagecraft. Even as public suspicions regarding the moral character of theatrical performers in other genres lingered, the "cult of the showgirl" sprung up in the wider American culture — from advice columns, to fashion houses, to talent entrepreneurs — offering hope to all young American women, that they, too, could participate in this archetype of extravagant, nationalized, high-culture success.

Ever the promoter, Ziegfeld adapted his trademark "brand" for the popular media of the day, partnering with producer Samuel Goldwyn for the production of the 1929 film *Glorifying the American Girl*, which featured actual *Follies* footage. He also transferred his highly visual stage spectacle to the airwaves for *The Ziegfeld Follies of the Air*, which aired on CBS radio until his death in 1932. But long after "the man who invented women" passed away, the reign — and cultural impact — of the Ziegfeld Girl continued. The vision she represented of the American woman would, in fact, be the impresario's most enduring legacy (van der Merwe 40). In 1934 and 1936, Ziegfeld's widow, Billie Burke, authorized the use of his name for posthumous productions of the *Ziegfeld Follies*, and his Follies Girl model was regularly adapted by other showmen (such as choreographer Busby Berkeley) for cinematic revues such as *Footlight Parade* (1933), The *Gold Diggers* series (1933, 1935, 1937) and *Fashions of 1934*. Cinematic allusions and homage to "the Great Ziegfeld" and his "glorified" girls may be found in other early films, ranging from *The Broadway Melody* (1929) and *Whoopee!* (1930), to the Academy Award–winning biopic *The Great Ziegfeld* (1936), and *Ziegfeld Follies* (1946). Whether directly, or indirectly, as Rick Altman and Randolph Carter suggest, the influence of Florenz Ziegfeld and the *Follies* can be felt "throughout the entire show musical tradition" in the first half of the twentieth century: "there is scarcely one of the scores produced that that does not stem to some degree from Ziegfeld's concepts" (Altman 204; Carter 152). Most significant among these "concepts" is the Ziegfeld Girl.

As an American icon, the power of the Ziegfeld Girl has not diminished with time, and in fact, has gained additional force in the new millennium as films, theatrical productions, and digital media have created contemporary venues for her preservation, appreciation, and appropriation. Adapted and re-adapted for more than a century, the web of historical meaning constructed around the image of the Ziegfeld Girl has grown even more intricate. While she retains her status as an icon of beauty and national identity, shifts in the conception of gender and nationalism over time have complicated her use and reception. She, like the Gibson Girl that preceded her,[1] serves merely as an icon of nostalgia; however, contemporary adaptations of the Ziegfeld Girl may benefit from closer examination. This essay will explore the history of this potent image of American beauty — her evolution from chorus girl to cultural icon to symbol of resistance — and the many ways in which her image has been invoked and appropriated over time and across genres of popular culture. As the image and idea of the Ziegfeld Girl has been adapted, so too have the values and ideals of the historical contexts from which she arose.

"The Man Who Invented Women"

In 1972, an article in the *Saturday Review* carried the headline "The Man Who Invented Women," signaling impresario Florenz Ziegfeld's self-proclaimed status as the originator of the American showgirl. According to the *Louisville Herald*, Ziegfeld had made the claim decades earlier, proclaiming, "I invented the showgirl," and taking credit for the phenomena of the grandiose gendered spectacle that took hold of American entertainment in the early twentieth century. As Linda Mizejewski notes:

> The publicity image of Ziegfeld as Zeus–like captain of industry, emitting show-girls from his forehead, typified the hype surrounding Ziegfeld himself, his Follies extravaganzas, and his high-profile Follies Girl [12–13].

The history of the Ziegfeld Girl is inextricable from the story of their creator. A showman, a promoter, and a purveyor of spectacle, Ziegfeld — often lauded as "the P. T. Barnum of the theater"—crafted an American archetype from a vision of beauty and the inspiration of single woman (Fishwick 51; see also Wolf). That woman was performer Anna Held.[2]

Ziegfeld first cast his eyes on Helene Anna Held in 1896, during her appearance at the Palace Theatre in London.[3] She was small in stature — only five feet tall — but her classic hourglass figure and large brown eyes were captivating (Charyn 33). Smitten by her highly acclaimed beauty and talent, the flamboyant Ziegfeld was relentless in his pursuit of Held, and finally lured her to New York with the promise of $1500 per week salary and $4000 to buy out her contract with Paris's Folies Bergères (along with an additional $4000 earmarked for repaying her then-husband's gambling debts).[4] In the ensuing months, Ziegfeld fiercely promoted his new star. Photographs and posters appeared in windows and newspapers across New York, exclaiming "Go to Held!"; when the singer finally arrived by steamer, she was the talk of the city. Her early performances met with great success, thanks to an effective combination of talent, effervescence, and compelling beauty, bolstered by Ziegfeld's outrageous publicity stunts.[5] Comedian Eddie Cantor wrote:

> For a generation, America succumbed to the Anna Held craze [....] She toured the country like a conqueror [...] Anna Held was the most buoyant and cheerful spirit that ever swept across our stage [qtd. in Golden 3].

After numerous increasingly extravagant and risqué productions, Ziegfeld had amassed all the elements necessary for a career breakthrough. Charyn relates that it was Held who gave Ziegfeld the idea for the *Follies*—"nagging him into producing a revue"— and at her suggestion he marshaled talent, experience in public relations, knowledge in costume design, and maturity as a entertainment manager for a new type of revue production (Charyn 33).

In 1907 he launched the *Follies*, which featured a line of beautiful chorines called the Anna Held Girls, and a tradition was born (Morris 269; Ziegfeld and Ziegfeld 39).

The sixteen chorus girls who were featured in the *Follies* that first year were little more than visual entertainment, but with each iteration of *The Ziegfeld Follies* (as the show would be called from 1911 onwards) the chorines' numbers grew, and they became increasingly essential to the spectacular effect of Ziegfeld's productions. They circulated on stage, paraded through the aisles, and in *Midnight Frolic*, moved among the tables.

> Chorus girls, dressed in playful and glorious attire [...] boldly presenting themselves as consumer objects, as symbols of adornment and success, advertising the body as a locus of desire and personal transformation [Taylor 164].

By the 1920s, the Ziegfeld Girls "made" the show; their spectacular costumes, elegance, and elaborate production numbers came to define the *Follies* as the pinnacle of entertainment (Ziegfeld and Ziegfeld 179). And it was that image that captured not only men's imaginations, but women's ambitions. In 1932, the writer J. P. McEvoy described the response whenever Ziegfeld held auditions at the New Amsterdam Theater. Long before the appointed time

> all the streets leading to the New Amsterdam would be blocked with flocks of girls all sizes, shapes, weights and ages. Shopgirls and home girls, girls from small towns and big towns, chorus girls, models, girls from burlesque, vaudeville and the movies, debs from Park Avenue homes and hostesses from taxi-dance halls—all the girls who ever worked for him before, and practically all the girls from all the shows then running in New York. For every girl in the show business or out wanted to be known as a Follies girl [n.p.].

But if Ziegfeld Girls made a show, what made a Ziegfeld Girl? An article attributed to Florenz Ziegfeld, Jr., appearing in the *Morning Telegraph* (1925) advised the following:

> Beauty, of course, is the most important requirement and the paramount asset of the applicant. When I say that, I mean beauty of face, form, charm and manner, personal magnetism, individuality, grace and poise. These are details that must always be settled before the applicant has demonstrated her ability either to sing or dance. It is not easy to pass the test that qualifies a girl for membership in a Ziegfeld production [qtd. in Kenrick].

Advertisements for *Follies* showgirls indicated no preference in terms of class or racial background, and Ziegfeld affirmed his belief in diversity: "All nations, and all parts of the country, have the beauty potentialities" (F. Ziegfeld, "What Becomes of the Ziegfeld Follies Girls?" 12–13). However, the chorines handpicked by Ziegfeld conformed to the "Nordic," fine-featured appearance of the Gibson Girl icon—an image he paid handsomely for the rights to use in

1907 — promoting the image of the American "New Woman" of the twentieth century (Erenberg 215). Far from the mature, world-weary "wicked" women of burlesque, Ziegfeld Girls were young — sometimes as young as fourteen — and wholesome-looking, symbols "of the modern, independent woman" (Ziegfeld and Ziegfeld 179). "Make her young and cute," the impresario would demand, and his staff of talent recruiters would do their best to comply (Wodehouse and Bolton 152). Tall, long-limbed, and graceful, successful *Follies* applicants met an exacting set of criteria of physical dimensions and proportions—from height and weight, to facial symmetry, to shoe size — creating a standard of beauty that the showman claimed "glorified" women. Posture was to be straight, bust and hips in just the right proportion (with hips measuring larger than the bust by a full two inches), and the legs tapered down evenly to the ankles:

> "I never diverge from these two rules [...] the shoulder-blades, the gluteus muscles of the back, and the muscles of the lower leg must be in direct line with each other" [qtd. in Parker 87].

Some of Ziegfeld's criteria were, as Parker notes, a bit eccentric: he would never employ a girl with gray eyes, as they were "too intellectual and belong only on a college girl." Even this, however, corresponded to his vision of the ideal girl — a girl embodied the promise of romance and excitement — "all the things a man dreams about when he thinks of the world girl" (87–88). As critics Gilbert Seldes and Edmund Wilson observed in 1924, this was an image bound up with American notions of innocence and idealism, a far cry from European sophistication:

> He does not aim to make them, from the moment they appear, as sexually attractive as possible, as the Folies Bergères, for example, does. He appeals to American idealism, and then, when the male is intent on his chaste and dewy-eyed vision, he gratifies him on this plane by discreetly disrobing his goddess [Wilson qtd. in Dabney 183–184; see also Seldes 140–141].

Ziegfeld's standard and execution of the notion of "beauty" rapidly became adapted to the cause of nationalism: "I try to choose the American type. There is a larger percentage of beauties in America than any other country" (F. Ziegfeld, "How I Pick Beauties" 160). From 1922 onward, every *Follies* theater program was inscribed with the motto "A National Institution — Glorifying the American Girl."

"The Stuff That Dreams Are Made Of"

Brimming over with symbolic meaning, the Ziegfeld Girl represented a constellation of historically situated ideas about nation and social class that were interpreted and projected through the lens of "woman." In order to communicate these notions effectively, Ziegfeld transformed his theater into a "cathedral of beauty"—a *sanctum sanctorum* of gendered spectacle where these notions of American idealism received their fullest expression:

> Ziegfeld's New Amsterdam Theatre became a temple in which audiences could worship youth and beauty. It became a place to dream and feel alive. But, most important, it became a place to feel young again [Hudovernik 21–22].

A Ziegfeld show was, indeed, "the stuff that dreams are made of": dreams carefully crafted by the theatrical artist Joseph Urban; designers such as Erté, Lady Duff Gordon, and Ben Ali Haggin; and some of the most well-known musicians of the day. The dreams worshiped in Ziegfeld's temple belonged to a particular ethnic group; as Robert C. Toll (1976) points out, "Of the some three thousand women he chose to be Ziegfeld Girls, there were no orientals [sic] and no Negroes" (317). The spectacular fantasies of the *Follies* Girls suppressed racial, ethnic, and economic differences beneath volumes of sequins, feathers, fur, and whiteness, in order to craft dreams that reflected the fantasies of highbrow Broadway audiences. Glamour, excess, consumption, and promise of possibility infused each edition of the *Follies*, fueled by lavish costumes, stunning jewelry, dazzling pageantry, and breathtaking tableaux. Each year, *Follies* productions rose to new heights of excess, creating a dream that shone just a bit more brightly than the year before.

For the patrons of Ziegfeld's *Follies*, these glamorous adaptations fueled their dreams—distinctly white American dreams—promoted through nationalist rhetoric and portrayed in patriotic revues. In 1909, Ziegfeld's showgirls saluted the Navy from beneath battleship headdresses that lit up as the stage lights dimmed; in 1913, a flood of chorines poured through the "locks" of the newly opened Panama Canal in tribute to the new icon of Army engineering; and with the United States' entry into World War I in 1917, Ziegfeld Girls supported the war effort with patriotic hearts, voices, and bodies. The *Follies* of 1917 and 1918, the two most unabashedly patriotic productions of the series, featured numerous wartime song and dance routines choreographed to tunes such as Victor Herbert's "Can't You Hear Your Country Calling?"; Gene Buck and Louis A. Hirsch's "We're Busy Building Boats" ("Ship Building Song"); and Irving Berlin's "I'm Gonna Pin a Medal on the Girl I Left Behind." Showgirls transformed into aviators in the "Aviator's Parade," and in a spectacular display of patriotic optimism, Ben Ali Haggin's 1918 tableau, "Forward Allies" ("The Road to Victory"); featured Ziegfeld Girls costumed to represent the Allied nations of the Great War.[6] After viewing the *Follies'* 1915 rendition of the national anthem, one reviewer commented that "not since Perry's men stripped and fought naked about the Lawrence has there been so much undressing on behalf of this sweet land of liberty" (Mizejewski 2).[7] More subtle displays of nationalism were woven into choral numbers throughout the show's history, with Ziegfeld Girls posing as Fourth of July sparkers and Revolutionary War minutemen, and supporting portrayals of figures of national pride, such as Paul Revere, the Wright Brothers, and Woodrow Wilson.

Along with those adaptations of nation and nationalism came dreams of prosperity. As Ziegfeld redeemed the chorus girl from the tarnished image of working-class sexuality found in burlesque, he simultaneously integrated her into bourgeois consumer culture.[8] By the 1920s, Ziegfeld's showgirls were following in their creator's footsteps as public experts on beauty, as they offered advice on make-up, skin care, diet, and exercise in countless newspaper and magazine articles; advocating slenderness, self-control, and the cultivation of a ladylike demeanor. Many publicly pledged the "Curves, Charm and Contour Club," vowing to choose clothing that enhanced their ability to be "at the same time graceful and dignified" (Mizejewski 99).

These affirmations marked a significant step in the evolution of the chorus girl. While the pre-war *Follies* were characterized as somewhat risqué or "a little sporty," Ziegfeld's productions became, by the Roaring Twenties, "eminently respectable and patronized by the best people" serving as the standard in upscale, trend-setting entertainment (Mizejewski 89). At the same historical moment when the emergence of the New Woman — with her defiant demeanor, playful independence, and greater social accessibility — stirred public controversy, the Ziegfeld Girl was the embodiment of elegance, affluence, and "good breeding," the epitome of style and poise. Ziegfeld's chorines adhered to a grace and movement, as Mizejewski notes, which was inextricably associated with classical "femininity": beauty and sensuality, combined with the discipline, restraint and control of traditional "ladies" (98). In their opulent — yet revealing — haute couture, the impresario's "glorified" showgirls served simultaneously as agents of both the excitement of social change and the certainty of tradition. They combined the allure and independence of the "new" woman of the Roaring Twenties with the dignity and propriety many feared was becoming a thing of the past. Issues of class, character, and individuality that prevailed in everyday life faded into the background, overshadowed by an air of homogenous beauty swathed in elaborate costumes— individual showgirls subsumed by an archetype of glamour and prosperity—creating an image that achieved unprecedented popularity and would endure for generations.

Imitation and Adaptation

In his preface to Will Page's *Behind the Curtains of Broadway's Beauty Trust* (1927), Jack Lait described the staggering popularity of the showgirl-centered follies and revues of the era:

The "girl revue," wonder child of the old "musical comedy," has become a gigan-
tic institution. Eight stupendous revues, and scores of lesser ones, blaze anew on
Broadway every autumn. The cost of producing one of them would have beg-
gared [the impresario] P.T. Barnum. Millionaires have gone bankrupt backing
them [....] The public, in return, pays millions to see them [i].

Ziegfeld parlayed his *Follies* success into numerous other "girl revues," such
as the *Midnight Frolics* (1915–1921) and the *Nine O'Clock Revue* (1918, 1920–
1921) held in the intimate rooftop theater of the New Amsterdam, and *The
Century Girl* (1917), which achieved two hundred performances, rivaling the
success of the *Follies*.[9] Theatrical and film producers and choreographers of
Ziegfeld's era rushed to capitalize on the desire for gendered spectacle created
by the *Follies*, each adapting both the lavish revue and the Ziegfeld Girl to
create their own niche in the "cult of the showgirl." George Lederer, Sydney
Rosenfeld, and Raymond Hitchcock all produced small showgirl-centered
revues. Lee and J. J. Shubert, of Broadway's famed theatrical family, offered
the elaborate *Passing Show* at the Winter Garden Theatre, from 1912 to 1924,
in direct competition with the *Ziegfeld Follies*, and George White also staged
his annual *Scandals* (1919–1939) closely following Ziegfeld's model.[10] Irving
Berlin and Sam Harris built The Music Box Theatre as a home for Berlin's
annual *Music Box Revue* (1921–1924). Earl Carroll added a dose of sexuality
to produce the racier *Vanities* (1923–1932, 1940), which, in its 1924 edition,
featured 108 showgirls, adorned only in peacock headdresses and carrying
fans made of peacock feathers. Film producer Samuel Goldwyn secured his
own stock company of Goldwyn Girls throughout the 1930s and 1940s, and
featured them in productions such as *Whoopee!* and *The Goldwyn
Follies* (1938). Perhaps the best known of these, however, were the cinematic
showgirls choreographed by Busby Berkeley for dozens of Hollywood musicals.

Berkeley's silver screen adaptation of the *Follies* brought a new dimension
to the visual wonder of showgirl production numbers, through his elaborate
geometric choreography and novel uses of cinematography (often making
use of an aerial camera, mounted on a crane) to create fantastic, synchronized,
graphic tableaux. The kaleidoscope effect, the "top shot," the "zipper effect,"
and the "parade of faces"; each transformed the beauty of showgirls into the
beauty of art — "glittering abstractions," as Peter Lev notes, and initiated traditions that would resound for generations in adaptations of the Ziegfeld Girl
archetype (3).[11] Each of these techniques, whether invented or appropriated
by Berkeley, enhanced the spectacle of the follies, and took full advantage of
cinematic technology to craft extravagant visual segments not possible within
the confines of live theater, creating a follies experience "conceived in filmic,
rather than theatrical terms" (Rubin 3). As Dugan notes:

One consideration of the dazzling spectacle of Berkeley's choreography is the grandness of its presentation, which can only be produced on film through unique camera moves and editing, allowing the audience to float through the bevy of beautiful women and be in the scene, with jump cuts to full screen shots of beautiful smiling faces [5].

Berkeley's cinematic adaptations of the Ziegfeld Girl and gendered spectacle made him not only one of the most sought-after choreographers in Hollywood, but also the advisor to numerous studio chiefs when it came to selecting beautiful girls for their musical productions. His biographer Jeffrey Spivak notes that the choreographer, like Ziegfeld before him, publicly went on record several times about the kind of girl he sought for his chorus lines. According to Spivak, from early in his career all the way into his seventies, Berkeley favored "regular girls—but they had to have "presence" (Spivak).

The chorine who embodied Berkeley's notion of the "perfect" showgirl image was "the girl with a face like the morning sun," Toby Wing (later Oliver). Although her Hollywood career only spanned one decade, Wing (born Martha Virginia Wing in 1915) was one of the most sought-after showgirls in the 1930s. Vivacious and poised, the platinum-haired dancer epitomized the image established and promoted by Ziegfeld, and was once described as "the most beautiful chorus girl in Hollywood" (Valiance n.p.). While she performed in numerous rival Goldwyn, Warner, and Paramount productions, Wing was best known for her performance in Berkeley's *42nd Street* (1933), where, clad in a white fox-fur brassiere, she was the object of actor Dick Powell's adoration as he sang "Young and Healthy" (composed by Harry Warren). As the legacy of the Ziegfeld Girl archetype continued into the second half of the twentieth century, and beyond, Wing's captivating portrayal of quintessential white American beauty—particularly as "The 'Young and Healthy' Girl"—would be one of its oft-cited representatives (Spivak). Echoes of the Ziegfeld Girl and the elaborate gendered spectacle of the *Follies* may be found in performances ranging from the black-and-white broadcasts of the June Taylor Dancers' kaleidoscopic opening sequences for *The Jackie Gleason Show*, to the acclaimed annual Radio City Music Hall revues featuring the Rockettes—a troupe of precision dancers that still perform today and which traces its origins to St. Louis's Missouri Theatre, where Russell Markert's showgirls, The Missouri Rockettes, debuted in 1925.

Ziegfeld's "glorified" girls remained the source of inspiration for reproductions and appropriations across media and generations, from lavish display volumes produced for collectors to collections of Ziegfeld Girl paper dolls and interchangeable costumes designed for children.[12] As the impresario and his iconic showgirls became increasingly interwoven in the histories of American spectacle, performance, and popular culture, cinematic and televisual portrayals both elaborated and mythologized the Ziegfeld Girl archetype. Productions such as *The Great Ziegfeld* (1936), *Ziegfeld Girl* (1941), *Ziegfeld Follies* (1945), *Funny Girl* (1969), the televised *Ziegfeld: The Man and His Women* (1978), and the theatrical production *Crazy for You* (1999) have all made substantial contributions to popular conceptions of the Ziegfeld Girl and the various myths and lore that surround her.

Ziegfeld was well aware that, as both a performer and a cultural icon, the Ziegfeld Girl was the embodiment of a dream — the stuff of imagination — and nowhere was that status more fully engaged than in the still images of the Ziegfeld Girls themselves. Alfred Cheney Johnston was the man who captured the light and shadow of such dreams, as Ziegfeld's "court photographer" from 1917 until the great showman's death. "It was Johnston's mandate as Ziegfeld's principal photographer to cast a spell of enchantment over the public, to draw them in to the beautiful sirens of the Ziegfeld Follies" (Hudovernik 36). Johnston's images captured the essence of the Ziegfeld Girl, transferring the magic of the stage to silent portraits that combined innocence, poise, sensuality, and that indefinable "it" that Ziegfeld sought in his showgirls.

During his fifteen years with Ziegfeld, Johnston created portraits, promotional photographs, and theatrical scene stills for the *Follies* and its "glorified" girls. In her memoir, *Midnight Frolic: A Ziegfeld Girl's True Story*, former chorine Marcelle Earle recalls that "Johnston was the photographer. Only selected beauties were sent to him" (196). It was Johnston's eye that provided the world with its most intimate glimpses of Ziegfeld beauty — still images no less choreographed than the most elaborate *Follies* routine — all bearing the unmistakable visual signature of their photographer. With smiles as demure and mysterious as the Mona Lisa, gazes averted from the intruding lens of the camera and bodies bared as if basking in complete privacy, Johnston's Ziegfeld Girls evidence little of the buoyant energy and effervescence of their performing counterparts. What do we make of this adaptive shift, this subtle, but critical recasting of theatrical history? Did Johnston's camera capture a facet of iconic American beauty that could not be articulated in a chorus line, or did he adapt its essential nature? It's possible that he accomplished both, and in so doing, played a critical role in the legacy of not only Ziegfeld's chorines, but of American notions of enduring beauty. It is these portraits that have articulated most closely with contemporary adaptations of the Ziegfeld Girl, creating a unified image of ethereal glamour and vulnerability. That unified image — of what Robert Hudovernik has termed "Jazz Age Beauty" (Hudovernik) — is found throughout twenty-first century popular culture, adding their charm to everything from blogs to home décor, complicating the meanings and interpretations of the "glorified" American girl, as its appropriations become increasingly diverse. These contemporary adaptations of the Ziegfeld Girl reflect those alterations and layers of meaning, as well as adding additional facets of their own to the images' contributions to discourses on gender, nation, and social history in America. While much of his work for Ziegfeld was lost, and even more only discovered after his death, Johnston's Ziegfeld portraits illustrate countless texts across media, are coveted as originals and collected as reprints, and have served as source material for subsequent adaptations in films, literary narratives and illustrations, portraiture and increasingly popular boudoir photography, costume and digital media creations.

It is, perhaps, through this last re-mediation that Johnston's photographs have been adapted with the greatest — and most revealing — degree of cultural creativity. The widespread availability of many of Johnston's Ziegfeld Girls in digital format has facilitated their use in such venues as online galleries; discussion forums on topics ranging from photography to philosophy, tributes to the *Follies*, glamour, and the Roaring Twenties, amateur and scholarly cultural historiography, and as both focal point and background visuals for YouTube.[13] Once serving as unique representations of unapproachable high-class spectacle, they may now be found on commodities ranging from bowling shirts to bath towels, while simultaneously reified in public and private galleries as valuable cultural artifacts. Ethereal, untouchable, and unmistakably representative of early twentieth-century high culture sophistication, these images, in their contemporary usages, blur the boundaries between eras and social classes, moving freely between highbrow and mass culture, even as they continue to engage with all of those in complex ways.

Eternal Beauty?

This convergence of media, ideologies, and historical moments creates space for adaptations and interpretations of the Ziegfeld Girl that both valorize and challenge the impresario's original conceptions of the "glorified" girl. Almost a century after the Ziegfeld name became associated with the promotion of a distinctly American beauty, notions of nationalism, portrayals of gender, and indeed, conceptualizations of beauty, itself, have shifted.[14] At the same time, the explosion of new media in the late twentieth and early twenty-first centuries has resulted in the creation of multiple platforms for the expression of those notions, leading to the marginalization of some and the reinforcement of others. Such platforms have allowed both individuals and institutions to adapt the image of the Ziegfeld Girl, endowing her with new meaning, yet never fully freeing her from the moorings of her historical moment.

Ziegfeld's Glorified American Girl arose at a time of shifting ideas about American womanhood, ranging from the physical, such as valued body types and physical abilities; to public displays, including fashion, demeanor, and even public presence; to social and economic concerns regarding sexuality, marriage and employment. Longstanding Victorian notions of gender, beauty, and appropriate gender roles existed in increasing tension with the emerging ideal of the sporty and sensual New Woman — with new celebrations of feminine sensuality, independence, and possibility asserting themselves against existing standards of reserve and gentility (Kibler 11). As the twentieth century got underway, the movement for women's suffrage was gaining momentum, and women were asserting their presence in the public sphere as never before, giving rise to a quiet panic in the wider society over gender-based morality.[15] "Public" women, especially those associated with entertainment, had long been stereotyped as women of low breeding and loose morals, but the Ziegfeld Girl — her dignified, elegant bearing always informing her role as the embodiment of explicitly sensual display — existed at the points of articulation between tradition and modernity, simultaneously contributing to, and aiding in the resolution of, that tension.

Conflicting perspectives on women's roles were not the only social tensions at play in the early decades of the twentieth century. Issues of race, ethnicity, caste, and class were also troubling middle and upper class Americans, particularly with the advent of World War I, as the demographics of immigration into the United States were radically altered. Similar questions of national origin had plagued urban areas in earlier times, as well, with anti-immigration campaigners and immigrants publicly clashing; even the theater community was not exempt.[16] By the 1830s, the American theater was already becoming a site where the drama of social and economic conflict and resentment was being played out alongside the scheduled entertainment (Allen 51).

In the wartime era, these tensions grew even more acute, as scores of new immigrants— whose presence challenged existing conceptualizations of what it meant to be American —flooded urban centers with difference. Fear, resentment, and class conflict gave rise to yearnings for a singular, Anglo-Saxon model of Americanism that would reaffirm the primacy of British and northern European heritage while separating middle and upper class culture from the working class in all its shadings.[17] One manifestation of those yearnings, as Mizejewski notes, was the attempt to reflect an archetype of the American Girl in popular media (115). Without question, the Ziegfeld Girl was the most successful of these.

How do such past adaptations of this politically, ethnically, and economically coded showgirl figure relate to contemporary ideas about gender roles, nationalism, and social hierarchies? How do we locate the Ziegfeld Girl as a symbol of beauty in a spectrum saturated with globalized references, where notions of a dominant archetype are increasingly contested or unclear? Twenty-first century constructions of social identity reflect many of the ideas prevailing over a century ago, yet incorporate them in a far broader array of competing and contesting ideologies. Dramatic shifts in the demographics of the United States, along with fragmented perspectives on nationalism and its expression, have subverted efforts toward an homogenous view of national identity.

Concerns regarding the objectification of women have complicated the use of female imagery for larger, symbolic ends. While the links between economics, social class, and body type are perhaps even more publicly articulated, the Anglo-Saxon archetype so highly prized and originally promoted by the impresario is no longer dominant in American society. The American Girl, once glorified through the magic of a showman's opulent spectacle, has transformed into a dynamic agent of social, political, and economic power, operating within a set of complex, continually negotiated gender roles. Similarly, the concept of femininity — once easily reduced to a formula of physical proportions and behavioral expectations — is, itself, now frequently critiqued and resists easy definition.

Even within this context, however, the Ziegfeld Girl retains her importance as an icon of beauty, elegance, and sensuality. The posthumous rediscovery of Johnston's Ziegfeld photographs, along with a previously unpublicized collection of showgirl nudes, have rendered images of Ziegfeld's Glorified American Girls widely available for adaptation, not only into familiar images of glamour, femininity, and innocence, but as signifiers of nostalgia for a bygone era. Among these, we find artifacts cited in homage to high fashion and sophistication; vibrant icons of gay culture; overlooked lives unearthed as lost histories; and as calls to return and reconnect with past constructions of femininity and power. Yet, the network of meanings in which the she participates is extensive and complex, spanning time, as well as entertainment genres and media. More than simply a nostalgic figure or an icon of halcyon days of patriotism and prosperity, her symbolism is adapted in ways that not only resonate with early twentieth-century meanings and values, but carry additional, intentional and unintentional, meanings as well.

This complex re-coding of the Ziegfeld Girl is, to varying degrees, the result of an increasingly participatory media culture that lends itself to multiple appropriations, from the personal to the public, and the affectionate to the political. While some of these adaptations echo Ziegfeld's intentions— glorifying an ideal feminine type and the constellation of ideologies it embodies— others range from chronicle to critique, from nostalgia to playful re-articulation. The media theorist Henry Jenkins explains that such adaptations are part and parcel of the process of media convergence — a cultural phenomenon that gives rise to new forms of exchange between the producers and users of media content — as consumers "make connections among dispersed media content," and meaning and the powers of creation are renegotiated (3). Thus we find images of Ziegfeld Girls Delores Costello, Louise Brooks, and Lilyan Tashman juxtaposed with an image of dancer Cyd Charisse portraying a Ziegfeld Girl, and embedded in a website devoted to "Life with a Parisian Flair."[18] Photographs of the showgirls Pearl Eaton, Marie Wallace, Lenore Baron, and Caryl Bergman are all appropriated in support of a discourse against vanity and cosmetic surgery, which cites the chorines, once considered willowy to the point of androgyny, as "real women: they have curves, hips, strong thighs, and they look confident in their own skins."[19] And while one anonymous Ziegfeld beauty creates the atmosphere for "The French Maid's Place" — an online meeting site for lovers of antiques — another gazes out from the title-page of a dissatisfied twenty-first-century blogger's lament:

> I wanta swallow up glitz and sip the edges of glamahh and do somethin' more with my life than slammin' down countless cups of joe with the stenographers and shopgirls of diamond rings and new linoleum kitchen dreams in the All Night Chock Full of Nuts Diner at 44th and Divine.[20]

These new consumer-created adaptations recur in countless other blogs, history sites, photo galleries, promotions for vintage and reproduction items, digital stories, music videos, and contemporary apparel. From glittery spectacle to ethereal waif, the Ziegfeld Girl brings the power of cultural memory to these adaptations, and endows them with an air of authenticity, grace, and elegance. Like a lightning rod, she attracts wonder and fascination, and in return, emits a bright glow that illuminates — and indeed, glorifies — the themes, ideologies, and values she is invoked to endorse. The Ziegfeld Girl, her glamour and spectacle, her association with the renowned impresario, and the cultural ethos of the early twentieth century from which she arose are all artifacts of the process of adapting history. Their meanings continue to respond to — and shape — contemporary notions of independence, grace, and distinctly American beauty.

Notes

1. Created by artist Charles Dana Gibson, the Gibson Girl was a fictionalized image of the American feminine ideal during the late nineteenth and early twentieth centuries. She is often thought to have served as the first national standard for feminine beauty.

2. Held's origins are the subject of some speculation, with sources differing on her place of birth — Warsaw, Paris — and birth date — March 18, 1873, is cited by Richard Ziegfeld; the performer's gravestone cites 1872; Golden suggests 1870. No birth certificate exists.

3. Called "The Palace Theatre of Varieties" at the time of Held's performance, the theatre reverted to its original name, "The Palace Theatre," in 1922.

4. See Golden 23–24.

5. Richard Ziegfeld relates one such instance, where Ziegfeld convinced the press that Held was taking milk baths. Held was quoted as saying, in her heavy French accent — "Ett eez for to take zee beauty bath"— thereby launching a craze that would sweep the country (R. Ziegfeld 30–31).

6. See van der Merwe 116–117 for a full discussion of these numbers.

7. An allusion to the Navy commodore Oliver Hazard Perry (1785–1819), who served with distinction in the Second War of Independence against Great Britain.

8. See Mizejewski for an extensive discussion of the Ziegfeld Girl and consumption.

9. The 1918 Nine O'Clock production was titled Ziegfeld's Nine O'Clock Frolic, after the successful Midnight Frolics.

10. White's Scandals were produced annually from 1919 to 1926, then 1928 to 1929, 1931, 1936 and 1939.

11. According to Spivak, although Berkeley did not invent the "top shot," which utilizes an aerial camera on a crane, poised directly over the chorus line's geometric choreography, he remained "its most successful artistic proponent" (Spivak). The "zipper effect" utilized this top shot to film lines of chorus girls or props (such as beds, in the 1934 production Dames) moving sequentially apart or together, like the functioning of a zipper.

12. See Hudovernik (2006) and Tierney (1985, 2004) for examples.

13. The following is only a small sample of the range of uses of Johnston's images online, from Ziegfeld tributes, to décor, to visuals for Charles Aznavour's popular song "She" (16 Feb. 2012): http://www.doctormacro.com/Movie%20Star%20Pages/Ziegfeld%20Girls/Ziegfeld%20Girls.htm; http://www.musicals101.com/ziegirls.htm; http://www.tfproject.org/tfp/tilted-entertainment/ 124941-ziegfeld-girls.html; http://www.shoeboxclassics.com/gallery.html; http://www.flickr.com /photos/ ghastlydelights/galleries/72157626027320128; http://www.youtube.com/ watch?v=GL_5 cIUvWDY; http://www.youtube.com/watch?v=fWlGyi8IJEM; http://www.youtube.com/watch?v =QAaWowviyfs; http://www.youtube.com/ watch?v=CjmbVr8feWc.

14. The Glorified American Girl became the official motto of Ziegfeld productions in 1922, but as early as 1914 promotional materials were associating the Ziegfeld "brand" with a distinctly "American" beauty.

15. See Peiss, 6–7; McGovern; and Rabinovitz.

16. For example, in the Astor Place riot of 1849, one of the deadliest immigration-spurred outbreaks of violence of its time occurred at the Astor Place Opera House.

17. See Mizejewski for an exceptionally thorough discussion of race, ethnicity, and eugenics in relation to the Follies.

18. http://parisatelier.blogspot.com/2011/02/ziegfeld-follies.html (8 Feb. 2012).

19. http://megaweapon-is-them.blogspot.com/2010/08/this-vain-world.html (9 Feb. 2012).

20. http://thefrenchmaidsplace.blogspot.com/2010/10/fabulous-flapper.html; http://at-the-bijou.blogspot.com/2010/01/i-wanta-be-ziegfeld-girl.html (9 Feb. 2012)

Works Cited

Allan, Robert C. *Horrible Prettiness: Burlesque and American Culture.* Chapel Hill: University of North Carolina Press, 1991. Print.

Altman, Rick. *The American Film Musical.* Bloomington: Indiana University Press, 1987. Print.

The Broadway Melody. Dir. Harry Beaumont. Perf. Bessie Love, Anita Page, Charles King. MGM, 1929. Film.

Carter, Randolph. *Ziegfeld: The Time of His Life.* 1974. Reprint, London: Bernard, 1988. Print.

Charyn, Jerome. *Gangsters and Gold Diggers: Old New York, the Jazz Age and the Birth of Broadway.* New York: Thunder's Mouth Press, 2003. Print.

Crazy for You. Dir. Mike Ockrent. Perf. Jodi Benson, Harry Greener, Bruce Adler. Angel, 1992. CD.

Dabney, Lewis M. *The Portable Edmund Wilson.* New York: Penguin, 1983. Print.

Dugan, Brian. "Busby Berkeley." Research Paper. Savannah College of Art and Design, 2009. Web. 14 Mar. 2012.

Earle, Marcelle. *Midnight Frolic: A Ziegfeld Girl's True Story*. Basking Ridge, NJ: Twin Oaks, 1999. Print.

Erenberg, Lewis A. *Steppin' Out: New York Nightlife and the Transformation of American Culture, 1890–1930*. Chicago: University of Chicago Press, 1984. Print.

Fashions of 1934. Dir. William Dieterle. Perf. William Powell, Bette Davis. First National Pictures, 1934. Film.

Fishwick, Marshall William. *Popular Culture in a New Age*. London and New York: Routledge, 2001. Print.

Footlight Parade. Dir. Lloyd Bacon. Perf. James Cagney, Joan Blondell. Warner Bros., 1934. Film.

42nd Street. Dir. Lloyd Bacon. Perf. Warner Baxter, Ruby Keeler, Bebe Daniels. Warner Bros., 1933. Film.

Funny Girl. Dir. William Wyler. Perf. Barbra Streisand, Omar Sharif. Columbia/Rastar, 1968. Film.

Glorifying the American Girl. Dir. Millard Webb. Perf. Eddie Cantor, Helen Morgan. Paramount Pictures, 1929. Film.

Gold Diggers of 1933. Dir. Mervyn LeRoy. Perf. Warren William, Joan Blondell. Warner Bros., 1933. Film.

Golden, Eve. *Anna Held and the Birth of Ziegfeld's Broadway*. Lexington: University Press of Kentucky, 2000. Print.

The Goldwyn Follies. Dir. George Marshall. Perf. Adolphe Menjou, The Ritz Brothers. MGM, 1938. Film.

The Great Ziegfeld. Dir. Robert Z. Leonard. Perf. William Powell, Myrna Loy, Luise Rainier. MGM, 1936. Film.

Hudovernik, Robert. *Jazz Age Beauties: The Lost Collection of Ziegfeld Photographer Alfred Cheney Johnston*. New York: Universe, 2006. Print.

Jenkins, Henry. *Convergence Culture: Where Old and New Media Collide*. New York: New York University Press, 2008. Print.

Kenrick, John. "Ziegfeld 101." *Musicals 101.com*. Web. 7 Feb. 2012.

Kibler, M. Alison. *Rank Ladies: Gender and Cultural Hierarchy in American Vaudeville*. Chapel Hill: University of North Carolina Press, 1999. Print.

Lait, Jack. "Preface." *Behind the Curtains of Broadway's Beauty Trust*. Ed. Will A. Page. New York: Edward A. Miller, 1927. i–viii. Print.

Lev, Peter. "Pin Up Girl, from Photograph to Feature Film." Literature/Film Association, University of Kansas, Lawrence, 9–11 Oct. 2007. Conference Paper.

McEvoy, J. P. "He Knew What They Wanted." *Saturday Evening Post* 10 Sept. 1932. Print.

McGovern, James R. "The American Woman's Pre-World War I Freedom in Manners and Morals." *Journal of American History* 55 (Sept. 1968): 313–33. Print.

Mizejewski, Linda. *Ziegfeld Girl: Image and Icon in Culture and Cinema*. Durham: Duke University Press, 1999. Print.

Morris, Lloyd. *Incredible New York*. New York: Random House, 1951. Print.

Oliver, Myrna. Obituary. "Toby Wing: MGM Dancer Appeared in 38 Films." *Los Angeles Times* 29 Mar. 2001. Web. 22 Dec. 2011.

Parker, Derek, and Julia. *The Natural History of the Chorus Girl*. Indianapolis: Bobbs-Merrill, 1975. Print.

Peiss, Kathy. *Cheap Amusements: Working Women and Leisure in Turn-of-the-Century New York*. Philadelphia: Temple University Press, 1986. Print.

Rabinovitz, Lauren. *For the Love of Pleasure: Women, Movies, and Culture in Turn-of-the-Century Chicago*. New Brunswick, NJ: Rutgers UP, 1998. Print.

Rubin, Martin. *Showstoppers: Busby Berkeley and the Tradition of Spectacle.* New York: Columbia University Press, 1993. Print.

Seldes, Gilbert. "A Tribute to Florenz Ziegfeld." *The Seven Lively Arts.* New York: Dover, 1924. 124–45. Print.

Spivak, Jeffrey. Personal Interview. 14 Dec. 2010.

Taylor, William. *Inventing Times Square.* New York: Russell Sage Foundation, 1991. Print.

Tierney, Tom. *Ziegfeld Follies Paper Dolls.* New York: Dover, 1985. Print.

_____. *Ziegfeld Girls Paper Dolls.* New York: Dover, 2004. Print.

Toll, Robert C. *On with the Show: The First Century of Show Business in America.* New York: Oxford University Press, 1976. Print.

Valiance, Tom. "Obituary: Tony Wing." *The Independent* (London) 28 Mar. 2001. Web. 15 Jan. 2011.

van der Merwe, Ann Ommen. *The Ziegfeld Follies: A History in Song.* Lanham, MD: Scarecrow Press, 2009. Print.

Whoopee! Dir. Thornton Freeland. Perf. Eddie Cantor. Samuel Goldwyn Co., 1930. Film.

Wodehouse, P. G., and Guy Bolton. *Bring on the Girls! The Improbable Story of Our Life in Musical Comedy.* New York: Simon & Schuster, 1953. Print.

Wolf, Rennold. "The P.T. Barnum of the Theatre." *Green Book* June 1914: 933–946. Print.

Ziegfeld, Florenz. "How I Pick Beauties." *Theatre Magazine* Sept. 1919: 158–160. Print.

_____. "What Becomes of the Ziegfeld Follies Girls?" *Pictorial Review* May 1925: 12–13. Print.

Ziegfeld Follies. Dir. Lemuel Ayers, Roy del Ruth, et al. Perf. William Powell, Judy Garland, Lucille Ball. MGM, 1945. Film.

Ziegfeld Follies of the Air. Dir. Florenz Ziegfeld. Perf. Eddie Dowling. CBS, 1932, 1936. Radio.

Ziegfeld Girl. Dir. Robert Z. Leonard, Busby Berkeley. Perf. James Stewart, Judy Garland, Hedy Lamarr. MGM, 1941. Film.

Ziegfeld, Richard, and Paulette Ziegfeld. *The Ziegfeld Touch: The Life and Times of Florenz Ziegfeld, Jr.* New York: Harry N. Abrams Publishers, 1993. Print.

Ziegfeld: The Man and His Women. Dir. Buzz Kulik. Perf. Paul Shenar, Samantha Eggar. Columbia Pictures Television, 1978. TV Film.

Adapting Dachau: Intertextuality and Martin Scorsese's *Shutter Island*

WALTER C. METZ

In a remarkable cultural formulation, Dennis Lehane's best-selling novel, *Shutter Island* (2003), concerns Teddy Daniels, a federal marshal who may or may not have invented his experience of liberating the Dachau concentration camp at the end of World War II as an intricate psychological defense for murdering his wife after she drowns his children in an act of insanity. In his 2010 film adaptation of the novel, Martin Scorsese continues his career-long exploration of the relationship between violence and a specifically American masculinity. Particularly in his recent use of Leonardo DiCaprio, whom he casts as Teddy, Scorsese grapples with the larger historical issues pertaining to violent American masculinity. For example, in *Gangs of New York* (2002), Scorsese explores the relationship between governmental corruption, racism, and the Civil War in 19th century New York City.

Scorsese's turn to the Holocaust in *Shutter Island* continues this project. Offering an extremely different valence on "the greatest generation" than hagiographers such as Tom Brokaw,[1] Scorsese interrogates the American World War II veteran as a tormented soul, unable to accept the psychological help he needs because of the American male's belief that to ask for assistance is to display weakness. In 1998, journalist Brokaw celebrated the World War II generation's ability to overcome all obstacles by getting down to the hard work of winning the war and then building the largest and most successful economy in the history of human civilization (Brokaw). Lehane's novel and Scorsese's film express the counterargument to Brokaw: the same fixated work ethic that won the war also resulted in a myth of indestructible masculinity. Given that the cultural subtext of this torment is a conflation of private familial trauma overwriting the public memory of the Holocaust, *Shutter Island* offers a remarkable site for investigating popular Hollywood cinema's exploration of such issues of American masculinity and historical trauma.

Indeed, pursuant to this book's focus, Scorsese adapts not only a popular American thriller, but also relies on the adaptation of history to weave together an intertextual grid of film referents to accomplish his thematic project, the investigation of male violence. Scorsese develops visually the plot of Lehane's novel such that the film's images resonate with significant cinematic explorations of masculinity and historical trauma. As Teddy Daniels (Leonardo DiCaprio) tries to climb the lighthouse tower at the end of the film, to discover what he believes to be evidence of Nazi experimentation within the very boundaries of the United States, he instead discovers his psychiatrist Dr. Cawley (Ben Kingsley) attempting one last time to rescue him from his delusional state. Whereas Alfred Hitchcock's *Vertigo* (1958) features an arduous two-hour ordeal in which Scotty (James Stewart) must overcome psychological torment to finally summon the strength to climb the bell tower and solve the murder of Madeleine Elster (Kim Novak) by Gavin Elster (Tom Helmore), *Shutter Island*'s Teddy climbs the lighthouse tower without hesitation, only to discover that his internal world is a fiction. Scorsese thus positions *Shutter Island* in intertextual dialogue with *Vertigo*, relying on Hitchcock's pre-existing depiction of shattered American masculinity as the inspiration for revealing Teddy's distorted perception of "reality." In this way, Scorsese engineers a dual reinvention of history, activating both World War II as an historical event, and Hitchcock's cinematic reconstruction of 1950s America.

More directly pertinent to *Shutter Island*'s status as a film about the Holocaust, Scorsese also weaves an intertextual thread connecting to Robert Weine's *The Cabinet of Dr. Caligari* (1919), the hallmark case study of Siegfried Kracauer's seminal work *From Caligari to Hitler* (1947), a post–World War II sociological study of the relationship between destroyed masculinity and the political destabilization of Germany, which resulted in the rise of Nazism and the barbarity of the Holocaust (Kracauer). *Shutter Island* is an intertextual adaptation of *The Cabinet of Dr. Caligari*; in both films, the doctor whom we believe is a brutal killer, narrated as such to us by someone we now learn is a madman himself, turns out to be a psychiatrist trying to help the narrator overcome his psychosis.

The fact that Teddy's psychosis uses a narrative about Dachau to mask the murder of children in 1950s America is the subject of this essay. Relying on filmic imagery of the liberation of a concentration camp, *Shutter Island* brings into focus the use of the Holocaust as a trauma narrative central to 21st century American self-fashioning. What is the significance of *Shutter Island* calling into question the veracity of its images of the liberation of the camps? Scorsese's film is no *Schindler's List* (Steven Spielberg, 1993), attempting a definitive portrait for American audiences of the barbarity of the camps. Instead, *Shutter Island* shares its narrative interest in the Holocaust with many recent films and television shows that use the stock images of the liberation of the camps to perform other cultural work. As Laurence Baron explains, the opening of *X-Men* (Bryan Singer, 2000) shows how the trauma of the camps produced a superhero (Baron 45). The liberation of a camp in *Band of Brothers* (HBO, 2001) shows how American soldiers were galvanized to fight against Nazi barbarity, even if after the fact. *Shutter Island* is the only film that questions the veracity of these stock images of the camps. While by no means a Holocaust denial narrative, it raises important questions about the uses to which Holocaust imagery is put in contemporary American culture, in the wake of Alain Resnais' lament (in his 1955 documentary *Night and Fog* (*Nuit et Brouillard*)) that the black-and-white documentary footage proving the existence of the camps as centers of mass death is incapable of answering our more pressing question: "Who is responsible?"

Scorsese's adaptation of the images from the liberation of the Nazi concentration camps is rooted in Dennis Lehane's novel. Teddy Daniels, who we think is a federal marshal at the beginning of the novel, but whom we learn is actually his wife Dolores' murderer (real name Andrew Laeddis), is first introduced to the reader via his doctor's journals, which are soon superseded by Lehane's third-person narration. The marshals are purportedly summoned to Shutter Island, a former Civil War POW camp off the coast of Boston, to investigate the disappearance of Rachel Solando, an inmate at Ashecliffe Hospital, an institution for the criminally insane. As part of their investigation, they speak with the chief of staff, Dr. Cawley. We learn that Teddy, a World War II veteran, helped liberate the Dachau concentration camp; Lehane simultaneously introduces Dr. Cawley, who "was thin to the point of emaciation. Not quite the swimming bones and cartilage Teddy had seen as Dachau, but definitely in need of several good meals" (37). Thus begins Lehane's fictional magic trick, using a common rhetorical strategy of the Holocaust as a floating signifier, which ranges from a symbol of victimization at the hands of the Germans (Dr. Cawley is here a concentration camp victim of the atrocities) to the embodiment of Nazi horrors (in his paranoia, Teddy comes to see Dr. Cawley as spearheading the importation of Nazi medical experimentation onto the shores of the United States, located in the island's mysterious lighthouse).

Indeed, the entire novel is dedicated to the dual fear (sometimes our real worry, and sometimes just Teddy's paranoiac visions) of the return of the repressed of World War II to 1950s American life. Two examples from the first chapter will suffice: first, Teddy's partner Chuck Aule (in reality, Andrew's doctor, Dr. Sheehan) relates the horrors of living in 1950s Seattle with his Japanese-American wife, who grew up in an internment camp; significantly, it is Chuck who now suffers discrimination at the hands of Pacific Northwest Americans for being married to a Japanese woman ("no one likes me being with her" [15]). Second, Chuck observes that the island's mental asylum is barbaric, a remnant of Victorian thinking, and that these primitive methods of treatment are soon to be a thing of the past. Stunningly, he links this transformation to the Allied rehabilitation of post-war Germany: "Incorporation, they'll say. Incorporation will be the order of the day. You are all welcomed into the fold. We will soothe you. Rebuild you. We are all General Marshalls. We are a new society, and there is no place for exclusion" (18). The slippage between General Marshall, and Chuck's feigned role as a U.S. Marshal is one of the linguistic joys of reading the novel.

Lehane reveals more of Teddy's connection to Dachau when Teddy and Chuck interview Dr. Cawley's associate, Dr. Jeremiah Naehring, a neurosurgeon. Having a drink in the doctors' living quarters, Cawley plays a recording of Mahler; Teddy immediately associates the music with the liberation of Dachau:

> Then a balm of strings and piano replaced the hisses. Something classical, Teddy knew that much. Prussian. Reminding him of cafés overseas and a record collection he'd seen in the office of a subcommandant at Dachau, the man listening to it when he'd shot himself in the mouth. He was still alive when Teddy and four GIs entered the room. Gurgling. Unable to reach the gun for a second shot because it had fallen to the floor. That soft music crawling around the room like spiders. Took him another twenty minutes to die, two of the GIs asking der Kommandant if it hurt as they ransacked the room [76].

Chuck, perhaps masking his true role as Teddy's doctor, asks if the music is Brahms, but Teddy knows it is Mahler. As the doctors perpetrating this show know, Teddy psychically links Dr. Naehring to the Nazi perpetrators at Dachau. During Teddy's interrogation of Dr. Naehring, he spits: "You see a death camp someday, Doctor, then get back to me with your feelings about God" (78). The real plot of *Shutter Island* concerns the doctors' use of performance to attempt a radical cure of Andrew Laeddis: the U.S. Marshal killed his wife Dolores after she went insane and drowned the couple's three children. He has repressed this fact, inventing the persona of Teddy Daniels in order to protect himself from the psychic pain of his actions. The doctors hope that by play acting within Teddy's constructed world, they can lead him to a cure and reality. Thus, Andrew's remembrance of the liberation of Dachau is a mere prop in the doctors' ploy to get Andrew to remember that he is not Teddy. However, as the reader does not know this until the end of this classical suspense novel, Dachau to both us and Teddy represents a warning about the Nazi experimentation on the mentally ill which might be continuing in postwar America. In this way, Lehane's adaptation of Dachau has it both ways: the Holocaust is both a warning about redeeming the American future of its potential Nazi past, and also a fantasy which needs to be unwritten if Andrew is to return to sanity. Did Andrew Laeddis liberate Dachau? We might think so, but we cannot be sure, as this is Teddy's narrative, not Andrew's. In short, the Holocaust in Lehane's novel is both a real historical event and a fantasy, finding a middle-ground theoretical position in between positivist history's dominant understanding of the straightforward facts of the Holocaust and the false, untenable position of those who deny that the event took place. In *Shutter Island*, there is more at stake than whether Dachau existed. The narrative is concerned with how we remember Dachau, and why.

As the novel progresses, the legacy of the Holocaust begins to spread across the island. When they are interviewing one of the patients, a rapist and murderer, Peter Breene, Chuck defends Rachel Solando (Teddy's invented doppelgänger for his wife, Dolores) for having drowned her three kids: "People have problems. Some are deeper than others. Sick, like you said. They need help" (111). Andrew's doctor, in disguise as Teddy's partner Chuck intervenes in Teddy's conversation with the madman. Peter responds with Nazi solutions: "They need gas. Gas the retards. Gas the killers. Killed her own kids? Gas the bitch" (111). Indeed, what Andrew comes to realize as his doctors successfully strip him of his "Teddy" defenses, is that he, not his doctor, is the Nazi. Unable to cope with Dolores' insanity at killing their three children, Andrew does in fact follow Hitler's prescription as voiced by Peter the killer: Andrew shoots his wife in the belly and then retreats into the safe persona of Teddy Daniels (an amalgam of his two murdered boys' names, Edward and Daniel).

As a filmmaker adapting Lehane's novel, Martin Scorsese activates these plot details, but situates them into an alternative intertextual grid. During the production of the film, Scorsese, well known for his status as a film buff, showed his crew two films, Jacques Tourneur's *Out of the Past* (1947) and Alfred Hitchcock's *Vertigo* (1958). The first film, on account of its interest in the past's relationship to the present as it affects a former gangster trying to escape his previous bad deeds, is an obvious template. The film noir techniques inspire Scorsese to shoot *Shutter Island* as a tension-filled, bleak psychological drama. Furthermore, the film is able to use the flashback structure of film noir to find a visual correlative to Lehane's shifting from Teddy living at the institution, to his remembrance of the liberation of Dachau. However, it is the second intertext that proves most intriguing. In the book Lehane invokes Hitchcock's *Shadow of a Doubt* (1943), significantly set on the World War II American home front. While Teddy is interrogating Rachel Solando, he tells her that she is as American as Betty Grable. When the purported inmate says she does not look like Betty Grable, Teddy responds: "Only in your obvious patriotism. No, you look more like Teresa Wright, ma'am. What was that one she did with Joseph Cotten, ten, twelve years ago?" (169). The actress Rachel responds: "*Shadow of a Doubt*. I've heard that" (169). In this way, Lehane shows how he partially reworks the Hitchcock film: Uncle Charlie's (Joseph Cotten)'s masquerading as a family man when he is really a serial killer is replicated in Teddy Daniels' belief that he is not the murderer of his wife, Dolores.

In the film Scorsese reworks Lehane's fiction into a template for exploring a different Hitchcock intertext, *Vertigo*. In the novel, Teddy storms the lighthouse, but nothing is made of its verticality; it is only in Scorsese's imaging of the verticality of the lighthouse that *Vertigo*'s central metaphors come into play. In the novel, when Teddy enters the lighthouse, the narrative is austere and efficient: "He heard a scraping sound above him and he went back out to the stairs and followed them up another flight and came to a heavy iron door [of Dr. Cawley's room], and he pressed the tip of the rifle barrel to it and felt it give a bit" (315). In the film Scorsese shoots Teddy's entrance with obvious visual references to *Vertigo*. The sequence begins with Teddy swimming secretively to the banks of rocks surrounding the lighthouse. Scorsese cuts between close-ups of Teddy swimming to a reaction shot, an extreme long shot from a low angle looking up at the barbed wire and guards protecting the lighthouse. Teddy climbs out of the water, steals a guard's rifle, and breaks through the chain-link fence. He enters the lighthouse and immediately looks up at a huge spiral staircase. This sequence replicates the two tower ascent sequences in *Vertigo*. In the first of these (when Scotty fails to reach the top of the tower, allowing Elster to get away), Scotty begins by looking up the outside of the tower in a low-angle extreme long shot. As Scotty ascends the spiral wooden staircase in pursuit of whom he believes to be Madeleine (but is really Judy Barton the actress [also played by Kim Novak]), he looks downward (and here, Hitchcock uses his famous technique of zooming and tracking simultaneously to simulate Scotty's illness). In *Shutter Island* Teddy runs up the metallic spiral staircase in search of his quarry. Scorsese cuts between close-ups of Teddy's running feet and medium shots of him searching the rooms in the lighthouse at various stories. Whereas Hitchcock offers point-of-view high angle shots of Scotty looking deliriously down the staircase, Scorsese replaces these with high-angle camera positions that identify Teddy as searcher. This difference is crucial thematically: Hitchcock's point-of-view technique allows us to experience Scotty being duped by Judy and Elster, whereas Scorsese's camerawork foreshadows the subsequent reveal by Dr. Cawley that Teddy Daniels is in fact Andrew Laeddis, and that essentially *Shutter Island* is a *Vertigo* in which the central character has duped himself.

Thematically, this sequence is crucial for understanding Scorsese's reworking of Lehane's novel. As Robert Corber suggests, *Vertigo* is a film about the allegorization of American history. Corber begins his analysis, "There Are Many Such Stories," with the oft-overlooked scene in which Scotty and Judy-as-Madeleine stand before a cross-section of an ancient Sequoia tree. The tree's rings are marked with a history of democracy, from the signing of the Magna Carta to the Declaration of Independence. Judy-as-Madeleine summarizes the most recent two hundred years of this history by pointing to the edge of the tree: "Here is where I was born, and here is where I died." Corber argues that the post-war American crisis embodied by the Beat poets of the 1950s is allegorized by Scotty's crisis of masculinity. He lives in North Beach, foundational location of the Beat revolution, and yet he does not look at all like a countercultural Beat rebel. Instead, his "man in the gray flannel suit" masculinity dating from the post–1945 era is in free fall, allegorizing the collapse of manhood in a masquerade of conventional 1950s Hollywood film style (Corber 154–83).

Hitchcock provides an inspiration for Martin Scorsese's allegorical method in his filmmaking. He is usually seen as a classical realist, one whose film style accentuates the gritty, violent nature of masculinity on the mean streets of New York City (from 1976's *Taxi Driver* to *Gangs of New York*). However, I believe it is Lehane's interest in oscillating between 1950s domestic male violence to the institutionalized violence of Nazism that resonates with Scorsese's origins as a filmmaker. To cite one example: during one of Teddy's reminiscences about his life with Dolores (played in the film by Michelle Williams) before the murder of the children, Lehane describes Teddy's repressed, buttoned-down masculinity, one of the reasons for the collapse of their marriage. One morning, Teddy is shaving, getting ready for work, while Dolores is trying to get him to acknowledge and discuss their sex life:

> "What word about my body won't cause you to make a fist? You can lick it and you can kiss it and you can fuck it. You can watch a baby come out of it. But you can't say it?" "Cunt," she said. The razor slid so far through Teddy's skin he suspected it hit jaw bone. The blood poured into the white clouds and water in the sink [...] He didn't know what she was becoming or what the world was becoming with its lesions of tiny, dirty wars and furious hatreds and spies in Washington, in Hollywood, gas masks in schoolhouses [...] And it was, somehow, all connected — his wife, this world, his drinking, the war he'd fought because he

honestly believed it would end all this [...] He hated how fucked up and obscene the world and everything in it had become [127–8].

Here Lehane employs an adaptive technique of history that slides between the personal traumas of Teddy's and Delores' marriage and the larger national crises, particularly the Cold War with the Soviet Union. I believe that this scene is particularly resonant in terms of Scorsese's early films; the most important intertext being *The Big Shave* (1967), made while he was still a student at New York University. This astonishing experimental shot links masculinity, the Vietnam War, and sanitary bathrooms; essentially a music video, it sets images to a jazzy, Big Band song by trumpeter Bunny Berigan. It begins with the camera on the floor, beneath a white porcelain toilet set onto gray tile with a white bath and shower in the background. Scorsese pans the bathroom, giving us close-ups of the toilet paper, the chrome handles of the toilet, the sink drain, and the like. A young man in a white t-shirt enters the bathroom to splash water on his face. He takes off his shirt and begins to shave. In medium shot, we see both his body and his reflection in the mirror. The man meticulously scrapes the hair and shaving cream off of his face. Scorsese cuts to close-ups of the man's motions to the beat of Benigan's song. Well over three minutes into the five-minute film, the man cuts himself innocuously on the cheek. However, each subsequent shot begins to reveal more and more blood, both streaming down his face, and dripping into the white porcelain drain. Seemingly unaware of this carnage, the man continues to carefully shave, removing the white shaving cream, but doing nothing about the streaming red blood all over his face. Scorsese's camera does not react to this change, focusing instead on the man's movements in brief close-ups. Four and a half minutes into the film, Scorsese cuts to a medium shot of the man driving the razor horizontally across his neck, severing his carotid artery. Blood now literally covers the man's body and the sink, now dripping onto his toes and the formerly pristine tiles. Scorsese cuts to a frontal medium shot as the man carefully shaves a few stray hairs on his neck, despite the fact that they are obliterated by the massive amounts of blood. Scorsese cuts to a close up of the man's white chest, with five streams of blood running vertically down the image. The final shot of the film proper shows the man delicately placing the razor on the edge of the sink. The image fades to orange and an end credits title card. Scorsese is listed as the filmmaker, as well as his four-man crew. However, the bottom of the title card offers the key to the film's meaning. Bunny Berigan's song from 1939 is listed, but so is "whiteness herman melville" and "VIET '67."

Scorsese announces that *The Big Shave* is in fact an adaptation of Herman Melville's *Moby Dick* (1851), a novel whose commitment to allegorizing whiteness is as important in the late 1960s as it was when it first appeared ("Scors-ese's Cinematic Sources"). Melville used a microcosm of the American expe-rience, the Pequod (holding rich and poor people, white people and people of color) to suggest that if we did not change our ways, our ship of state would be sunk by the Civil War. Sure enough, no one listened to Melville, and the country was devastated. Melville conflates whiteness and war in an allegorical ballet. Early in the novel, the narrator Ishmael wakes up in bed next to Quee-queg, a Pacific Islander. At first petrified that he will have his head shrunken, Ishmael immediately changes his mind, instead noticing Queequeg's beauty (Melville 43). The description of Ishmael in bed with his islander brother offers the most radical statement of the American 19th century, that Queequeg resembles George Washington, the white founding general of the nation's Revolutionary War period. Scorsese invokes Melville in *The Big Shave*: the hyper-violence of the pristine white bathroom turned into a bloody horror show comments on American involvement in the Vietnam War. Forty-three years later Scorsese reworks Melville by way of Lehane's novel, both at the level of the individual American (as in Teddy's relationship with Dolores), and the questioning of the national construction of male power in war (Teddy overwriting the liberation of Dachau with his personal melodrama).

Scorsese's intertextual reworking invites a new theoretical approach to historical filmmaking, in which the adaptation of history is of primary inter-textual significance. The fact that Scorsese's domestic scene in *The Big Shave* (rearticulated in Teddy's and Dolores' bathroom in the novel *Shutter Island*) are also re-workings of J.D. Salinger's *Franny and Zooey* (1961) indicates that the more one unravels the intertextual threads, the more it becomes clear that literature and film offer complex adaptations of historical material. In J. D. Salinger's *Zooey*, first published in *The New Yorker* in 1955, and reissued six years later, the traumatized Glass family members (allegorists of vision, after all) struggle with the legacy of vaudevillian parents having genius children who are reduced to radio quiz show spectacles, forever ruining their lives. Seymour Glass, the oldest child, returns from World War II only to kill himself in "A Good Day for Bananafish." Zooey, for his part, interrogated by his mother about the ill health of his younger sister, Franny, wakes up one morn-ing and enters the bathroom to sulk. His mother refuses to let him alone, instead entering the young man's private space to grill him about his sister. In a twenty-eight page literary tour de force, Salinger details how mother and child rip one another apart, as gruesome a shaving sequence as Scorsese's, with nary a drop of actual blood spilled. Zooey calls his mother, cruelly, "a fat old Druid" (111). Unlike the young man in *The Big Shave*, Zooey does not cut himself, rather taking out his aggression on the bathroom itself: "Zooey slammed his comb into the medicine cabinet, then impatiently flipped the cabinet door shut" (107). Zooey warns his mother not to submit Franny to the kind of psychoanalysis that resulted in Seymour's suicide:

> You just call in some analyst who's experienced in adjusting people to the joys of television, and *Life* magazine every Wednesday, and European travel, and the H-Bomb, and Presidential elections, and the front page of the *Times* [...] and God knows what else that's gloriously normal — you just do that, and I swear to you, in not more than a year Franny'll [...] be in a nut ward [107–108].

Salinger engages in an allegorical engagement between the large-scale issues of post-war American history and the specific issues of this dysfunctional family of performers. The fact that these strategies recall Melville and adumbrate Lehane and Scorsese indicate that we can only disinter the layers of American masculinity throughout history by analyzing intertextual webs of significance attached to banal locations such as bathrooms.

Should it really be that much of a surprise that Salinger intertextually haunts *Shutter Island*— both novel and film — as much as the ghosts of Melville's Civil War and the more recent history of Nazi experimentation? The revelation that the central character is insane is a central trope of literature encompassing such foundational texts of post-war American culture as *The Catcher in the Rye* (1950). While Salinger's hero is not doubled in the same way as Teddy Daniels/Andrew Laeddis, it is certainly the case that both Andrew and Holden voice their beliefs in failed masculinity from the confines of an insane asylum.

This type of narration points to one final filmic intertext — Robert Wiene's *The Cabinet of Dr. Caligari*, that film emanating from an earlier world war. Scorsese screened only American films—*Out of the Past* and *Vertigo*— for his crew; from a film scholar's point of view, it is clear that Lehane's *Shutter Island* is built on *Caligari*'s back: a narrator tells a story of a mad killer and we come to learn that the "killer" is the director of a mental institution housing the insane narrator. Both novel and film versions of *Shutter Island* replicate the infamous multiple release prints of *The Cabinet of Dr. Caligari*. In one version of the film, without the frame narration, the people track down Dr. Caligari (Werner Krauss), a mountebank responsible for controlling Cesare (Conrad Veidt), a monster responsible for several murders in a small town. In another, with the frame narration, we come to realize that the details about Dr. Caligari's behavior have been invented. Lehane's novel likewise ends with an analysis of Teddy's paranoiac imaginings of Nazism running rampant in 1950s America. The chapter ends with what appears to be a remarkable cure, as Teddy undergoes radical performance therapy: "I won't regress. My name is Andrew Laeddis. I murdered my wife, Dolores, in the spring of fifty-two" (366). However, in the last chapter, all of this progress is tragically undone:

Andrew's doctor, Lester Sheehan, is doomed to play the role of Chuck Aule, purportedly helping Teddy to expose Nazi atrocities, but in actuality being involved in a melancholic loop where the performance never cures the patient.

Scorsese's film fundamentally alters this ending. Over two hours into the film, Andrew is again cured by the performance therapy ("I murdered my wife in the spring of 52") but regresses: accordingly, Dr. Cawley orders Dr. Naehring (Max von Sydow) to perform a lobotomy. However, Andrew is in fact sane, but unwilling to live his life with the unendurable pain of knowing that his wife killed their children, and he killed her in return. The doctors are successful in curing Andrew of his psychological disease, but they cannot resolve his crisis of masculinity, at both national (the horrors of the concentration camps that Andrew discovers as a soldier) and personal levels. Scorsese solves the adaptational problem the same way Andrew solved the melodramatic problem: Andrew kills Dolores, and Scorsese and his screenwriters kill Andrew.

This confrontation of transhistorical violence is the central thematic tenet of Scorsese's cinema. In *Gangs of New York*, he suggests that New York City was established by means of tribal violence in the 19th century between Irish immigrant and local gangs. When the film (slated for a late 2001 release) was delayed for a year on account of 9/11, Scorsese was able to go back into the end of the film and re-edit it. It now ends with an historical panorama of shots of New York City, the last of which reveals the World Trade Center still standing. In this way, Scorsese links the tribal violence in the nineteenth century to the early twenty-first century conflict between two very different civilizations.

The transhistorical nature of both gang warfare and the consequences of Dachau in the cinema of Martin Scorsese requires further intertextual analysis. One of his great triumphs is his ability to use historical images to adapt the past; he melds adaptational sources as diverse as Edith Wharton's *The Age of Innocence* (1920) and Herbert Asbury's *The Gangs of New York: An Informal History of the Underworld* (1928) (Wharton, Asbery), in order to grapple with his cinematic vision of American male violence. In the case of *Shutter Island* and *The Cabinet of Dr. Caligari*, the 1919 film offers an allegorical key to understanding the novel's use of Dachau. In *From Caligari to Hitler: A Psychological History of the German Film* (1947), Siegfried Kracauer argued that interwar German cinema reveals the sickness of the national psyche. Kracauer was largely correct in his assertion: the devastation of the German soul after the defeat in World War I allowed for the rise of a fascist counternarrative which eventually led to the construction of the concentration camps (Kracauer). This essay has attempted to imagine a more nuanced, but nonetheless forceful historical adaptation of Kracauer's thesis with specific reference to *Shutter Island*. What sickness of contemporary American social life does Scorsese reveal to us? In its adaptation of the historical event of Dachau, haunting the American soldier played by Leonardo diCaprio, it reveals that a post–9/11 masculinity of vengeance is eating the American soul to death.

Notes

1. See Tristram Hunt, "One Last Time They Gather: The Greatest Generation," *The Observer* (London), 6 June 2004, for the use of this term coined by Brokaw.

Works Cited

Asbery, Herbert. *The Gangs of New York: An Informal History of the Underworld.* 1928. New York: Vintage, 2008. Print.
Band of Brothers. Dir. David Frankel, Mikael Salomon et al. Perf. Scott Grimes, Damian Lewis. HBO, 2001. TV Series.
Baron, Lawrence. *Projecting the Holocaust into the Present: The Changing Focus of Holocaust Feature Films Since 1990.* Lanham, MD: Rowman & Littlefield, 2006. Print.
The Big Shave. Dir. Martin Scorsese. Perf. Peter Bernuth. 1967. Film.
Brokaw, Tom. *The Greatest Generation.* New York: Random House, 2004. Print.
The Cabinet of Dr. Caligari. Dir. Robert Wiene. Perf. Hans Janowitz, Carl Meyer. Decla-Bioscop AG, 1919. Film.
Corber, Robert J. *In the Name of National Security: Hitchcock, Homophobia, and the Political Construction of Gender in Postwar America.* Durham: Duke University Press, 1996. Print.
Gangs of New York. Dir. Martin Scorsese. Perf. Leonardo DiCaprio, Cameron Diaz, Daniel Day-Lewis. Miramax, 2002. Film.
Hunt, Tristram. "One Last Time They Gather: the Greatest Generation." *The Observer* (London) 6 June 2004. Web. 14 Mar. 2012.
Kracauer, Siegfried. *From Caligari to Hitler: A Psychological History of the German Film.* Princeton: Princeton University Press, 2004 [1947]. Print.
Lehane. Dennis. *Shutter Island.* New York: HarperCollins, 2003. Print.
Melville, Herman. *Moby-Dick, or The Whale. The Writings of Herman Melville.* The Northewestern-Newberry Edition. Vol. 6. Evanston and Chicago: Northwestern University Press, 1988. Print.
Nuit et Brouillard (Night and Fog). Dir. Alain Resnais. Perf. Michel Bouquet, Reinhard Heydrich. Argos Films, 1955. Documentary Film.
Out of the Past. Dir. Jacques Tourneur. Perf. Robert Mitchum, Jane Greer, Kirk Douglas. RKO Radio Pictures, 1947. Film.
Salinger, J.D. *The Catcher in the Rye.* New York: Little, Brown, 1951. Print.
_____. *Franny and Zooey.* New York: Little, Brown, 1955. Print.
_____. "A Perfect Day for Bananafish." *Nine Stories.* Little, Brown, 1948. 3–26. Print.
Schindler's List. Dir. Steven Spielberg. Perf. Liam Neeson, Ralph Fiennes, Ben Kingsley. Universal Pictures/ Amblin Entertainment, 1993. Film.
"Scorsese's Cinematic Influences for *Shutter Island.*" *YouTube* 11 Mar. 2010. Web. 20 Nov. 2011.
Shadow of a Doubt. Dir. Alfred Hitchcock. Perf. Joseph Cotton, Teresa Wright. Skirball Productions/Universal, 1943. Film.

Shutter Island. Dir. Martin Scorsese. Perf. Leonardo DiCaprio, Emily Mortimer, Mark Ruffalo. Paramount Pictures, 2010. Film.

Vertigo. Dir. Alfred Hitchcock. Perf. James Stewart, Kim Novak. Paramount Pictures, 1958. Film.

Wharton, Edith. *The Age of Innocence.* 1920. New York: Barnes and Noble, 2004. Print.

X-Men. Dir. Bryan Singer. Perf. Patrick Stewart, Hugh Jackman, Ian McKellen. Twentieth Century–Fox, 2000. Film.

The GDR Founding Myth: Adapted History in Children's and Young Adults' Fiction of Post-War Germany and the GDR

ANNE KLAUS

According to Karsten Leutheuser, a German scholar of children's literature, it is generally agreed upon that children's and young adults' fiction mirrors the canon of values, norms and rules of the respective society from which it springs (19). It comes as no surprise that works for children and adolescents have therefore been frequently used as political instruments to indoctrinate ideologies. Studies like Reiner Wild's *Geschichte der Deutschen Kinder- und Jugendliteratur* (*The History of Children's and Young Persons' Literature in Germany*) (2002) or Karsten Leutheuser's *Freie Geführte und Verführte Jugend: Politisch Motivierte Jugendliteratur in Deutschland 1919–1989* (*Guided and Seduced Youth: Politically Motivated Teenage Literature in Germany 1919–1989*) (1995) have had a close look at the literature that was considered suitable for children and young adults during the Nazi regime (1939–1945), and have illustrated how the corpus of literature was subject to censorship according to the Nazi's idea of "purification," in which only Aryan authors should be promoted. With this in mind, this essay looks at how the idea of purification was deliberately used as a means of manipulating young readers during the Third Reich. It subsequently discusses how literary works for children and adolescents published after the Hitler regime adapt the issue of World War II, and how these postwar literary works examine the ways in which East, West and unified German societies come to terms with their pasts, and thereby examine what Bernard Lewis has claimed in *History — Remembered, Recovered, Invented* (1975): "Those who are in power control to a very large extent the presentation of the past and seek to make sure that it is presented in such a way as to buttress and legitimize their own authority" (53). This assertion certainly applies to East Germany's (GDR's) attempts to justify its foundation by forming a strong anti-fascist protection wall that found its expression in the veneration of communist resistance fighters as martyrs. The founding myth of the GDR became a secular state religion and laid the basis for the way in which World War II was reconstructed in GDR textbooks. By contrast in West Germany (DDR) and in the years after unification, there has often been a systematic attempt to minimize the horrors of the Third Reich, allowing Germans to hide behind the illusion that they themselves were the victims of Hitler's crimes and had no hand in the suffering inflicted on the Jews (Shavit 123–32). It is only in recent years that writers have come to terms with their collective pasts and produced new adaptations for the future.

Children's and Young Adults' Fiction in the Third Reich

In the language of Nazism, *Gleichschaltung* meant the complete ideological coordination of all political, social, and cultural activities. This, of course, also affected the field of literature that was designed to become part of the National Socialist machine under Hitler's dictatorship. Literary works were banned, censored, "adjusted" to Nazi mythology, or produced specifically for propagandist purposes. Under the proclamation of a nationwide "Action against the Un-German Spirit," books that were deemed "un–German" or "*entartet*" (degenerated) because of their communist or critical pro–Jewish standpoints were burned in symbolic acts.

As the Nazis were aware that books for children and adolescents play a fundamental role in the construction of identity, children's and young adults' fiction was adapted to reflect the values of the existing political system. School textbooks were reissued with carefully chosen illustrations to promote the 25-point Nazi Party program (Fray and Spar). Bernhard Rust, the Minister of Education, saw the main purpose of school textbooks as a means of "ideological education of young German people, so as to develop them into fit members of the national community [...] ready to serve and to sacrifice" (qtd. in Pine 42). Additionally, by means of distributing the school magazine for pupils called *Hilf mit* (*Contribute to Help*), topics such as heraldry, racial ideology, the Germanic history ('Germanic' designating the Teutonic and thus going beyond the boundaries of Germany, including for example Scandinavia), or bibliographies of important Nazi figures, such as Lochmüller's *Hans Schemm*, were further promoted (Wild 282).[1] Another example for young adults was Karl Aloys Schenzinger's *Der Hitlerjunge Quex* (*Quex of the Hitler Youth*) (1932), which reached a circulation of almost half a million copies and was regarded as a prototype of fiction for adolescents (Leutheuser 96). This propaganda book featuring the story of a boy named Heini Völker, was based on the life of Herbert "Quex" Norkus, a Hitler Youth member who was chased and killed by Communist youths in 1932 and was commemorated as a martyr, his grave turning into a Nazi shrine. Biographies of pilots and aviators such as Wolf Hirth, a German gliding pioneer and sailplane designer or Hans Grade, a German aviation pioneer, enticed young boys with their celebration of technological skill.

The glorification of Nazi figures and their deeds culminated in a comparison between themselves and Jesus Christ. Josef Viera's book on the Nazi activist Horst Wessel (author of the Nazi Party anthem and member of the Nazi's paramilitary organization [SA]) states that "What we Nazis do, mother, is like a mission of God" (qtd. in Wild 281). Even more bluntly, Schenzinger in his 1934 fiction *Der Herrgottsmacher Schülermarsch* (*The Lordmaker Schülermarsch*) compared Adolf Hitler to Jesus, and entitled the chapters of his book "Advent," "Passion" and "Ascension" (Wild 269).

Children's literature outside the classroom was fiercely controlled and channeled. According to the decrees of the *Wissenschaftsministerium* (*Ministry of Science*) issued in 1937 and 1939, the only topics that were permitted to be incorporated in children's literature were as follows:

- *Volksgut, Sagen, Märchen, Schwänke* (*folklore, legends, fairy tales, droll stories*)
- *Nordische Heldengestalten* (*Nordic heroic figures*)
- *Deutsche Kämpfe* (*German battles*)
- *Deutsche Größe in Opfern und Führern* (*German greatness: victims and leaders*)
- *Dem Gedächtnis des Weltkriegs* (*Memories of World War I*)
- *Unvergessene Kolonien- Deutsche in aller Welt* (*Unforgettable colonies — Germans all over the world*)
- *Natur und Heimat* (*Nature and homeland*)
- *Jugend marschiert ins neue Deutschland* (*Youth marching into new Germany*)
- *Fröhliche Jugend* (*Merry youth*)
- *Taten- und Abenteuerdrang* (*The desire for action and adventure*)
- *Fliegerbücher* (*Books on pilots and aviators*)
- *Die Welt der Arbeit* (*The world of work*)
- *Basteln und Werken* (*Handicrafts*)

The veneration for the German people as well as the romanticization of the German countryside is evident. However the bulk of children's literature was dedicated to teaching children and adolescents about the alleged evils of the Jewish race. A striking example of this literary smear campaign was *Der Giftpilz* (*The Poisonous Mushroom*), published by Julius Streicher in 1938. In this anti–Semitic book, seventeen short stories made use of the most primitive clichés, such as that Jews can be distinguished by their outward appearance, that they are criminals and that they lure kids away from their homes with sweets (Hiemer 1938). It not only taught children how to distinguish Jews from non–Jews but also warned them not to trust their Jewish classmates.[2] The texts were accompanied by Philipp Rupprecht's exaggerated illustrations, showing, for instance, an elderly Jew in a bowler hat towering intimidatingly over two small Aryan children.

Such propaganda adapted German history to such an extent that the Jews were held responsible for the entire "degeneration" of the local population. Readers were given advice to watch out for them: "Just as it is often hard to tell a toadstool from an edible mushroom, so too it is often very hard to recognize the Jew as a swindler and a criminal." They are depicted as racist: "In the Talmud it is written: 'Only the Jew is human. Gentile peoples are not called humans, but animals.' Since we Jews see Gentiles as animals, we call them only Goy." More significantly, they are a potential danger to children ("Here, kids, I have some candy for you. But you both have to come with me"), and unpatriotic ("The Jew cries, 'We don't care about Germany [....] The main thing is that things go well for us'") ("Der Gitfpilz"). There was only one thing to do in such situations; to ensure that Jews no longer had any influence in Nazi society. These constructions only emphasized the extremes to which the Third Reich would go to guarantee the "purity" of their race.

Children's and Young Adults' Fiction in Post–war West Germany (GDR)

Regardless of which secondary work on post-war German children's literature one consults, the authors seem to agree upon the fact that until far into the 1960s, literature for children and young adults in West Germany was unwilling to come to terms with the national past. Leutheuser refers to this phase as "*Der Verpasste Neuanfang*" (*The Lost Recommencement*) (Leutheuser 137). Dagmar Betz also identifies the wish of the West German population to return to some form of "normality," meaning a daily routine devoid of political disputes or analyses of World War II in retrospect. Betz demonstrates that the topics of children's literature in the Adenauer era (1949–1963) focused on the economic miracle than any form of analyzing World War II (176–210).

Wild blames West Germany for assuming the "business as usual" mentality (299), as if they had not been involved in World War II at all, and coins the term "*Verschwörung des Schweigens*" (conspiracy of silence) (299). This attitude seems difficult to understand, especially in view of the fact that the American Civil Affairs Division, responsible for the occupation of West Germany, explicitly stated that it would provide aid for "the writing of proposed juvenile texts." Most German authors, however, rejected this opportunity (Wild 300).

Very few books for children examined the National Socialist past, among them Erich Kästner's *Die Konferenz der Tiere* (*The Conference of Animals*) (1949) in which he gives a general warning against violence; or Herbert Kaufmann's *Der Teufel Tanzt im Ju-Ju-Busch* (*The Devil Dances in the Ju-Ju-Bush*) (1956), in which opportunities for communication between different races are imagined (Leutheuser 146). The extremely popular stories of the Swedish author Astrid Lindgren, who was committed to the rights of children and young people, merit particular attention in this context. Her stories feature unleashed and provocative children, such as in the *Pippi Longstockings* series (1945–1975), instead of presenting children forced into established systems.

Swastika graffiti and incidents like the trial of the so-called "architect of the Holocaust" Adolf Eichmann in Israel in 1962 — which led to anti–Semitic riots in West Germany — attracted attention throughout the world. It was generally agreed upon by the media covering the events that the German past could not be hidden any longer and that young people had to be enlightened on their country's dark history. Kästner vehemently demanded the removal of this big taboo topic and strongly recommended the book *Sternkinder* (*Star Children*— referring to the Jewish star) written by the Dutch author Clara Asscher-Pinkhof (1946) (Betz 22–3). In her book, the author narrates the moments in the life of suffering of Jewish children in the Netherlands, starting with their stigmatization, and the exclusion from schools and playgrounds, and leading to the depiction of their life in the ghettos and their deportation to the extermination camps (Asscher-Pinkhof). On the other hand, Asscher-Pinkhof generates concern but fails to discuss the question of who the perpetrators were. With her episodic portrayal of different Jews and their fate during World War II, her focus is on the victims rather than on the ones responsible.

Another advocate for the inclusion of World War II material was the author Hans Peter Richter (1925–93), who called for elucidation, and, with his deliberately factual style of narration, aimed to raise awareness among young people (Leutheuser 162). His most famous story for children and young adults is *Damals war es Friedrich* (*Then it was Frederick*) (1961) for which Richter was awarded the Mildred L. Batchelder Award of the American Library

Association in 1972 as the most outstanding of those books originally published in a language other than English. In his novel, Richter depicts two boys of Jewish and Christian heritage respectively during Hitler's rise to power. Although the story is told from the point of view of Friedrich's friend, the Jew Friedrich is the protagonist who has to face not only expulsion from school and public places like the swimming pool, or the movie theater, but also has to witness the murder of his mother by an anti–Jewish mob, and his father's expulsion and arrest for hiding a rabbi in their house. After Friedrich is refused entry into the air raid shelter by the Nazi landlord, he is killed by shrapnel (Richter).

The author, like Asscher-Pinkhof, refrains from giving his first-person narrator and his family any names. Due to their anonymity they can be seen as representatives for millions of people who also supported non-rebellion (Leutheuser 164). Obviously, this underlying critique is not agreed upon by all scholars: Zohar Shavit, who examined 345 books for children on the Third Reich and the Holocaust, accuses Richter and most of his fellow writers of the decade of failing to acknowledge German responsibility for the sufferings caused during the Holocaust and thus of creating "a wishful picture of the German past with which the German people can live comfortably, and which they can, without question, pass on to their children" (Shavit 130). Shavit continues: "The horror of the Third Reich is systematically screened and filtered, concealing the darker, most oppressive aspects of German history" (129). Many books for children and young adults portray German victimization: "The recurrent descriptions of countless German victims seem to suggest that Germany was in fact guiltless: an innocent nation suddenly confronted with a monstrous war that inflicted a terrible toll" (129).

While Shavit's judgment might be valid from the perspective of the early 2000s, we have to understand that Richter was writing at a time when West German writers were only just beginning to contemplate the implications of the past on the present. His work was brave — in terms of its point of view about the Holocaust — for that period. It took until the 1970s for German children's literature to emancipate itself and question received historical adaptations. According to Reiner Wild, sixty works appeared on the Holocaust between 1979 and 1989, focusing on the brutality of those enforcing it (361). The author Hajo Steinert has a more cynical view on the boom of Holocaust literature: like many of the big publishing houses for adult literature, those that possess a substantial adolescent readership deliberately orient themselves to the demands of their audiences. If the topic of the Holocaust sells well, then everyone wants to publish (qtd. in Betz 25).

However the new adaptations of the Holocaust in children's literature were not always received positively. In fact, they triggered a general discussion on whether the consequences of World War II could ever be completely understood. Betz speaks of an "*Undarstellbarkeitspostulat*" (a proposition suggesting the impossibility of coming to terms with the negative past in any form of aesthetic discourse) (35). She stresses the paradox of having the responsibility of depicting the murder of six million people in words on the one hand, and the impossibility of doing so on the other (35). Following Adorno's dictum "To write a poem after Auschwitz is barbaric" (Adorno), author Elie Wisel also believes in the impossibility of what she describes as the "aestheticization of the horror" (qtd. in Betz 36). This squeamishness might be part of a more general unwillingness either to write about the horrors of war, or to place the burden of guilt for that war on the German people.

Others remind us that to comment on these disastrous events is imperative as a way of preventing future tragedies. One of the most successful books to appear on the subject was Horst Burger's *Vier Fragen an Meinen Vater* (*Four Questions for My Father*), in which uncomfortable questions like "Why did you enter the Hitler Youth?" were raised by a teenager who is bewildered by his father's involvement in the war. The reader is encouraged to empathize with this teenager as he struggles to make sense of the past so as to determine his future course of action (Burger). Nonetheless, most published works during this period lack any acknowledgment of the collective guilt of the German people, despite President Richard Weizsäcker's famous speech on May 8, 1985, in which he accused any German who shut their eyes to Nazi atrocities as guilty (Weizsäcker-Rede). Eventually the Holocaust became an acceptable subject for historical adaptation: at first authors linguistically distanced themselves from the events of the Third Reich by describing it as "*Die Braune Vergangenheit*" (brown past — brown hinting at the colors of the Nazi party) or "The National-Socialist Reign of Terror." Later terminology tended to remain more neutral; a commonly used name is, for instance, *Shoah*, derived from the Hebrew word for destruction. This term has not only been used by German authors, but also by the Jewish people, as the word holocaust refers to the religious sacrifice of animals, and hence suggests that the Jews were somehow victims of a bloody ritual (Betz 43). By contrast, to adapt the Holocaust under the umbrella-term *Shoah* also encompasses other minorities like disabled people, homosexuals or gypsy groups such as Sinti and Roma.

Children and Young Adults' Fiction in East Germany (GDR)

Throughout the 40 years of its existence, the GDR made attempts to justify its creation by means of a strong anti-fascist ideology, culminating in the construction of the Berlin Wall in 1961, designed to protect its people from fascist elements in the west. Through this strategy the GDR implied that Nazism was a West German notion. By locating fascist tendencies in the west, while glorifying communist resistance fighters and honoring them as the originators of their state, the leaders established a feeling of innocence regarding the horrors of the Third Reich. The "founding myth" of the GDR, as the contemporary scholar Herfried Münkler describes it, became a secular state religion which completely erased the Nazi past and concentrated instead on adapting the myth of communist resistance fighters as martyrs (423). The sociologist Rainer Lepsius develops this idea further by claiming that the GDR adapted the Nazi past so as to make it a component part in a larger struggle between capitalism and socialism. The GDR celebrated itself as the winner of this struggle (qtd. in Münkler 435–6).

This uncritical adaptation of German history found its way into children's and young adults' fiction published by the two state-controlled GDR publishing houses—"*Der Kinderbuchverlag*" (*Children's Books Publisher*), and "*Verlag Neues Leben*" (*Publishing House "New Life"*). Their literary output was controlled vigorously by the "*Hauptverwaltung Verlage und Buchhandel*" (*Headquarters of Publishing Houses and Book Trade*). Writers who published with both companies were showered with financial inducements that could be withdrawn at the first sign of any challenge to the founding myth (Münkler 427). As Günter de Bruyn emphasizes, to write about World War II was only possible by consciously withholding certain information, such as the barbaric behavior of Soviet soldiers in the aftermath of the conflict (62). These methods illustrated what Benedict Anderson describes as the creation of an "imagined community" (114), based on consciously adapted traditions designed to create a "suitable historic past" (Hobsbawm 1).

Children's fiction in the GDR was meant to have a corrective and educational function by reinforcing the idea of class struggle. This led to the adaptation of popular fairy tales such as those written by the Brothers Grimm, where kings were replaced by characters from proletarian backgrounds (Wild 392). These stories followed a familiar scenario: thoroughly helpful and modest heroes from the proletarian working class were driven to spontaneous and intuitive acts of resistance, and consequently became role-models for young readers. Alternatively anti-fascist resistance was considered a suitable topic for adventure fiction, offering challenging quests usually culminating in happy endings (Wieckhorst 89–90). Sacrifice for others, empathy and solidarity were also popular, in tales constructed according to a basic black-and-white moral scheme. While GDR authors published more material on the Holocaust compared to their contemporaries in the West, they offered an equally one-sided adaptation of history, focusing exclusively on fascist atrocities and communist resistance to them. As Reiner Wild points out, it was only from the

1980s onwards that the literature of the GDR acknowledged the presence of other victims of the Nazis. Throughout that decade GDR literature underwent a radical transformation, although the party policy had not altered (Wieckhorst 104–105). Clean-cut anti-fascist warriors were superseded by more complex protagonists, while tentative doubts were raised as to the adaptation of the past and its relationship to state policy. The new mode of skepticism was echoed in peaceful mass demonstrations, eventually leading to the fall of the Berlin Wall on 9 November 1989.

While West Germany tried to come to terms with its horrific past, the East German state authorities readily adapted the events of World War II in line with its ruling ideology. By focusing on notions such as communist resistance, they helped to perpetuate the foundation myth which laid the blame for any mishaps on others, rather than admitting that their people had been in some way responsible for the atrocities during the War.

Conclusion

Voltaire once famously observed that "history consists of a series of accumulated imaginative inventions" (Voltaire). We have seen this process at work by analyzing how German history has been adapted in children's literature according to the prevailing ideological values of the period. In general, history has been written by the victors; as Bernard Lewis stresses, they "seek to make sure that it is presented in such a way as to buttress and legitimize their own authority" (Lewis 53). Politicians adapt myths to establish a connection between the current nation and a "suitable historic past" (Hobsbawm, 1), such as the stereotyping of the Jews as evil profiteers so as to marginalize them in the Nazi state. The tacit repression of Holocaust–related material in the post–World War II period offers another example of how history was deliberately adapted for ideological purposes. A third example is the selective presentation of communists as the only resistance fighters in the former GDR which was held up to foster the belief in the political system as the only upright one. Schopenhauer sharply comments: "Clio, the muse of history, is as thoroughly infected with lies as a street whore with syphilis" (qtd. in Himmelfarb 224). One must, however, distinguish between official state interventions in the portrayal of history, and "unwritten" rules emerging from societies themselves and not based on any state legislation. Such "unwritten laws of adaptation" are characteristic of the DDR.

All these forms of German "invented history" were designed to promote "social cohesion" (Hobsbawm 9) among members of the respective nations. I entirely concur with Eva Muhle, who writes that children's fiction plays a decisive role in this creative process, as they reach an audience in whom "an awareness of history begins to develop" (Thaler 4). Children and young adults are exposed to adapted depictions of past events—no matter whether prescribed by the state or upheld by members of their society. We might ask whether children's literature can emancipate itself, or whether it is doomed to be an organ of the *Zeitgeist*? Deborah Stevenson suggests a way out by recommending that authors examine the process of history-making, and thereby call into question the existence of a "knowable" history (Stevenson 23–24). She suggests that readers should be encouraged to believe that history is created through individual viewpoints, and that these viewpoints are not necessarily reconcilable (24). Maybe German children's literature will soon espouse the notion that there is no such thing as "universal history," but rather that historical adaptations are merely states of being. Roy P. Basler expresses this idea in a nutshell: "To know the truth of history is to realize its ultimate myth and its inevitable ambiguity" (Basler).

Notes

1. Hans Schemm (1891–1935), a Gauleiter in Nazi Germany and founder of the National Socialist Teachers Federation.

2. Extracts from the English translation of the book—published by the Friends of Europe in London in 1939—can be found at the *German Propaganda Archive*, maintained at Calvin College, Michigan, 26 Mar. 2006. Web. 20 Mar. 2012.

Works Cited

Adorno, Theodore W. "To Write a Poem After Auschwitz is Barbaric." 1969. *Evelyn Wilcock Website* 28 July 2003. Web. 20 Mar. 2012.

Anderson, Benedict. *Imagined Communities: Reflections on the Origin and Spread of Nationalism*. Rev. ed. London and New York: Verso, 2006. Print.

Asscher-Pinkhof, Clara. *Sternkinder (Star Children)*. 1946. Hamburg: Verlag Friedrich Oetinger GmbH, 1998. Print.

Basler, Roy P. "Quotes about History." *George Mason's University's History News Network* 6 Jan. 2005. Web. 1 Mar. 2012.

Betz, Dagmar. *Vergegenwärtigte Geschichte. Konstruktionen des Erinnerns an die Shoah in der zeitgenössischen Kinder- und Jugendliteratur (Envisioned Past. Constructions of Remembering the Shoah in Contemporary Fiction for Children and Young Adults)*. Hohengehren: Schneider Verlag, 2001. Print.

Bruyn, Günter de. *Vierzig Jahre. Ein Lebensbericht (Forty Years. Memoirs)*. Frankfurt am Main: Fischer, 1996. Print.

Burger, Horst. *Warum Warst du in der Hitler-Jugend? Vier Fragen an Meinen Vater (Why Were You in the Hitler Youth: Four Questions for My Father)*. 1976. Reinbek: Rowohlt Verlag GmbH, 1978. Print.

Fray, William C., and Lisa A. Spar. *The Avalon Project: Program of the National Socialist German Workers' Party*. 1997. Web. 7 Feb. 2012.

Hiemer, Ernst. *Der Giftpilz (The Poisonous Mushroom)*. Berlin: Julius Streicher, 1938. Print.

Himmelfarb, Gertrude. *The New History and the Old: Critical Essays and Reappraisals*. Cambridge: Harvard University Press, 1987. Print.

Hobsbawm, Eric, "Introduction: Inventing Traditions." *The Invention of Tradition*. Eds. Eric Hobsbawm and Terence Ranger. Cambridge: Cambridge University Press, 1983. 1–14. Print.

Kästner, Erich. *Der Konferanz der Tiere* (*The Conference of the Animals*). 1947. Berlin: Atrium-Verlag AG, 1998. Print.

Kaufman, Herbert. *Der Teufel Tanzt im Ju-Ju Busch* (*The Devil Dances in the Ju-Ju Bush*). 1954. Berlin: Obelisk-Verlag, 1977. Print.

Leutheuser, Karsten. *Freie geführte und verführte Jugend. Politisch motivierte Jugendliteratur in Deutschland 1919–1989* (*Guided and Seduced Youth: Politically Motivated Teenage Literature in Germany 1919–1989*). Paderborn: Igel Verlag, 1995. Print.

Lewis, Bernard, *History — Remembered, Recovered, Invented*. Princeton: Princeton University Press, 1975. Print.

Muhle, Eva. "History in Irish Historical Fiction for Children and Young Adults." Diss. University of Osnabrück, 2009. Print.

Münkler, Herfried. *Die Deutschen und ihre Mythen* (*The Germans and their Myths*). Berlin: Rowohlt, 2009. Print.

Pine, Lisa. *Education in Nazi Germany*. Oxford and New York: Berg, 2010. Print.

Richter, Hans Peter. *Damals war es Friedrich* (*Then It Was Friedrich*). 1961. München: Deutscher Taschenbuch Verlag GmbH, 1987. Print.

Shavit, Zohar. "On the Use of Books for Children in Creating the German National Myth." *The Presence of the Past in Children's Literature*. Ed. Ann Lawson Lucas. Westport, CT: Praeger, 2003. 123–132. Print.

Stevenson, Deborah. "Historical Friction: Shifting Ideas of Objective Reality in History and Fiction." *The Presence of the Past in Children's Literature*. Ed. Ann Lawson Lucas. Westport, CT: Praeger, 2003. 23–30. Print.

Thaler, Danielle. "Fiction Versus History: History's Ghosts." *The Presence of the Past in Children's Literature*. Ed. Ann Lawson Lucas. Westport, CT: Praeger, 2003. 3–11. Print.

Voltaire, "Voltaire Quotes." *Finest Quotes*. 2009. Web. 20 Mar. 2012.

Weizsäcker, Rede. "Speech." *Spiegel Online* 8 May 2005. Web. 14 Nov. 2011.

Wieckhorst, Karin. *Die Darstellung des „antifaschistischen Widerstandes" in der Kinder- und Jugendliteratur der SBZ/DDR* (*The Depiction of ‚Anti-Fascist Resistance' in Children's and Young Adults' Fiction of the GDR*). Frankfurt am Main: Peter Lang, 2000. Print.

Wild, Reiner. *Geschichte der deutschen Kinder- und Jugendliteratur* (*History of German Children's and Young Person's Literature*). 2nd ed. Stuttgart: J. B. Metzler, 2002. Print.

Kneehigh Theatre's Brief Encounter: "Live on Stage — Not the Film"

CLAUDIA GEORGI

Interrelations and cross-fertilizations between history and film have existed since the early days of film. The affinity between both is illustrated, for instance, by the ways in which film draws upon historical evidence for its material. When such historical films are further adapted into stage plays, I would argue that such transformations may be more successful when being purposely "creative," taking a free and cavalier approach to the notion of "truth" in order to create a piece of theater. When they are consciously "unfaithful" to the historical facts or their adaptation in film, they thereby prove the truth of Julie Sanders' assertion that "it is usually at the very point of infidelity that the most creative acts of adaptation and appropriation take place" (20). Inspired by this assumption, this essay will analyze the British Kneehigh Theatre Company's highly acclaimed production of *Brief Encounter* as an example of an adaptation that not only adapts David Lean's immortal film (1945), but also draws on Noël Coward's play *Still Life* (1936), as well as several of his poems and songs. The production does not provide a straight-forward representation of British history, but explores the possibility of multiple histories, thereby creating what Sanders describes as a "web of intertextuality that [...] resists the easy linear structures of straightforward readings" (159). Kneehigh Theatre's artistic director Emma Rice explains that, when adapting any text, she considers "how [she] can make this [each production] into a piece that is mine, not somebody else's" (qtd. in Radosavljević 93). She therefore uses her "emotional recall" and "cultural memory" (93) of the source texts as points of departure. Her production of *Brief Encounter* includes re-enacted film clips within the performance, a combination which, as Greg Giesekam observes, is often used to "lay bare the making of the performance" (249) and to render visible its theatricality, while also lifting the "normal cloak of invisibility that is cast over [the screen] in cinemas and on television" (252). For Emma Rice this strategy was inspired by the desire for "really honouring cinema and really honouring theatre" (qtd. in Radosavljević 93). As she explains: "That is why I wanted the cinema screen but I also wanted the front cloths" (93). Kneehigh Theatre's *Brief Encounter* enters into a dialogue with its historical sources and, rather than being merely derivative, asserts its own adaptation of history that consciously differs from the historical construction of the source texts. Rice is right when pointing out that "you can see the play, and then you can go and watch the film again and — nobody has touched it, nothing is altered, I have not touched anybody's work" (qtd. in Radosavljević 97). Yet, Kneehigh's adaptation creatively engages with the Coward play and the Lean film; while recalling the historical context in which both texts originated, it creates its own interpretation of the material.

Kneehigh Theatre's *Brief Encounter* and Its Hypotexts

In its 30 years of existence, the Cornwall–based Kneehigh Theatre Company not only produced stage adaptations of novels such as Jules Verne's *Journey to the Center of the Earth* (1864) and Angela Carter's *Nights at the Circus* (1984), both performed in 2006, but also repeatedly experimented with filmic sources. In addition to the adaptation of Michael Powell's and Emeric Pressburger's wartime fantasy *A Matter of Life and Death* (1946) for the Royal National Theatre in London in 2007, and the more recent adaptation of Jacques Demy's and Michel Legrand's 1964 musical film *The Umbrellas of Cherbourg* (2011), *Brief Encounter* was yet another adaptation of a film classic. Produced in association with David Pugh and Dafydd Rogers, *Brief Encounter* was first performed at the Birmingham Repertory Theatre and the West Yorkshire Playhouse, Leeds, in 2007 before opening at the Cinema Haymarket in London's West End in February 2008. After its successful run until November 2008, it toured England and America, and eventually closed at Studio 54 on Broadway in January 2011.[1]

The history of *Brief Encounter* dates back to the premiere of Noël Coward's play *Still Life* as part of his multi-play anthology *To-night at 8.30* (1936), directed by Coward and starring Gertrude Lawrence and Coward himself. As Sheridan Morley points out, many of the plays from *To-night at 8.30* proved to be fruitful sources for subsequent adaptations into movies or stage musicals, and most of them were revived for television in a 1992 series for BBC Television, with Joan Collins taking the leading roles (Morley xiv). *Still Life* ranked as Coward's own favorite among these plays, because he considered it "the most mature play of the entire sequence, well written, economical and well-constructed" (qtd. in Morley xiv); and he therefore decided to co-write the script for the film adaptation *Brief Encounter*, directed by David Lean and starring Celia Johnson and Trevor Howard. With its three Oscar nominations, this film surpassed the play in popularity, even though both works present an extra-marital affair between middle-class housewife Laura Jesson (Johnson) and married doctor Alec Harvey (Howard), set against the drab background of northern English suburbia in the mid-twentieth century. Whereas the play is entirely set "in the refreshment room of Milford Junction Station" (Coward, *Still Life* 336), the film includes scenes and settings that are merely implied or referred to in passing in the play, and develops them into fully-fledged elements of its fictional world. It incorporates several exterior shots of the train station and Laura's home at Ketchworth, and accompanies the lovers to the Palladium Cinema, to lunch at the Kardomah Restaurant, and to their secret rendezvous at the apartment belonging to Alec's friend Stephen. Moreover, the film expands the plot of the play by inventing supplementary elements such as Laura's fears and daydreams on the train home, her lying to her husband Fred (Cyril Raymond) about having spent the day with Mary Norton (Marjorie Mars) and her subsequent phone call to Mary. Whereas the play presents the love affair chronologically from the first encounter to the final parting of the two lovers, the sequence of events is circularly constructed in the film. After an establishing shot of the train station, the film begins with the lovers' final goodbye in the refreshment room at Milford Junction Station. The film then proceeds to reveal past events by means of flashbacks with voice-over monologues by Laura, which present the story entirely from her point of view, as she imagines confessing her affair to her husband Fred. Towards the end the first scene, the lovers' farewell is repeated, this time zooming in on Laura's face and fading out the conversation in order to demonstrate Laura's inner turmoil by means of her voiceover monologue. The film ends with Laura's return to her husband Fred, who notices her emotional distress, though not its cause, and soothingly puts his arms around her.

Produced over six decades later, Kneehigh's *Brief Encounter* is more than a transformation of Coward's play and Lean's film into a theatrical performance. Rather it freely adapts the historical context of the 1940s, drawing upon both texts as sources of inspiration. Just like the film, Kneehigh's production expands the sub-plot revolving around the working-class staff employed at Milford Junction Station, and exploits these sequences for comic relief as a contrast to the affair between Laura and Alec. Some of the scenes from *Still Life* are omitted in the film version yet retained in Kneehigh's stage production — for example, Myrtle's (Tamzin Griffin's) dissatisfaction with people eating on the platform (cf. *Still Life* 344); the reference to Alec (Tristan Sturrock) and Laura (Naomi Frederick) as "Romeo and Juliet" (*Still Life* 373); or Mildred's errand to the refreshment room to take Beryl (Amanda Lawrence) home to her dying mother (cf. *Still Life* 373ff.). More importantly, however, Laura's childhood memories of secret nocturnal dips in the ocean with her sister, which symbolize her desire to escape from her dull married life, do not appear in the film; in Kneehigh's production, however, the sounds and projections of waves on a screen are recurring motifs, and the production ends with a close-up of Laura's face superimposed on a projection showing her swimming in the ocean. These childhood memories and longings are not only a means of implicit characterisation, but also serve to allow for occasional glimpses of Laura's state of mind which are otherwise denied to the audience.

The stage production deliberately references the historical context evoked by Lean's film. It not only imitates the costumes worn by the film actors, but also more or less faithfully recreates many of the scenes that were added for the film. Like the film, the theater production expands the historical setting of the play at Milford Junction Station, restages the film's scenes between Laura, her husband and children at their poky suburban home, and presents the lovers having lunch at the Kardomah Restaurant, shows them at the cinema, and later enjoying a lavish meal at the Royal Hotel.

However, other additional scenes from the film are dropped in Kneehigh's production, which omits Laura's train rides home, her lying to Fred (Andy Williams), the lovers' excursions to the stone bridge in the countryside, and several shorter scenes set in Milford such as Laura's smoking at the war memorial. Laura's romantic daydreams of a life with Alec that includes dancing under chandeliers, attending the Paris opera, and standing on board an ocean liner are merely hinted at in Kneehigh's production. Whereas the film transforms the play's chronological order into a circular structure by beginning with Laura's and Alec's farewell, this initial scene is omitted in Kneehigh's production. Instead, the production creates its own circular structure by framing the story with a repeated exchange between Laura and her husband Fred, in which Fred wakes Laura from her daydreams and says: "You've been a long way, haven't you? Thank you for coming back to me." This alteration emphasizes the hopes for marital contentment rather than the misery of the lovers' failed romance. In between these scenes the audience travels back in time to the affair with Alec, which is revealed in the form of an internal analepsis. This creates an effect similar to the flashbacks in the film, where the romance between Laura and Alec is only presented in hindsight through Laura's memories.

The Juxtaposition of Stage and Screen

Despite the obvious dependence on the film, Kneehigh Theatre ensured that their production of *Brief Encounter* could not be mistaken for a historical recreation of the film. Their production was repeatedly advertised on the 2007–8 tour and the London run as "Noël Coward's *Brief Encounter*: Live on Stage — Not the Film" on publicity posters, in the playbill or in reviews. This marketing ploy made sure that the production could draw on the film's popularity and prestige, and would attract the film's fan audience, while at the same time avoiding direct competition. At the same time Kneehigh establishes an even more noticeable and meaningful link to its filmic progenitor by actually incorporating pre-recorded video snippets, that show the stage actors in historically accurate costumes re-enacting black-and-white sequences from the film. The production thus takes advantage of the singular nature of theater as an inherently composite medium that can incorporate or absorb any other medium without altering its mediality or "physical integrity" (Klaver 93). The projection of these mock film sequences onto a screen cut into vertical stripes allows for a seamless blending of live and mediatized action, as the onstage characters disappear between the slats of the screen and enter the world of the film where they reappear in pre-recorded interaction with the other filmed characters. When Fred is seen on the screen calling for Laura (who is still visible live on stage), Laura seems to walk straight into the film by disappearing between the slats and reappearing next to Fred on the screen. In a similar way, Alec's eventual departure is represented by the arrival of a filmed train on the screen, accompanied by sound-effects. Alec appears to get on the train through the door of the carriage by vanishing between the slats of the screen. The interaction between stage and screen is further sustained when Alec's pre-recorded image looks back at Laura who, still live on stage, waves at him departing on the train.

This movement from stage to screen is reversed in the scene presenting the lovers' boat trip, which begins with the boat slowly appearing in the top left corner of a projection of a lake on screen. After a close-up of Laura's face, a real boat is similarly pushed into view from upstage left, as if emerging from the film, and the action continues live on stage. Laura's childhood memories of swimming in the ocean are repeatedly invoked through a combination of live action and filmed material — although they are not based on actual sequences from the film but merely on a brief reference in Coward's play (cf. *Still Life* 347). While the screen displays water, waves and a swimming person as a backdrop, Laura is seen on stage as she undresses and begins to mime the act of swimming.

Kneehigh plays with the mediality of stage and screen, sometimes emphasizing their differences, sometimes attempting a convergence. Yet, as smooth as the transitions may be at times, they never permit the audience to confuse the live and mediatized performers. Occasionally the screen is reduced to a static or semi-static backdrop, serving as a prop to set the atmosphere for a particular scene or functioning as a substitute for stage scenery — as for example, when it provides a suitable backdrop of trains and platforms for the station, or shows airplanes to accompany the song "Goodbye, Dolly Gray,"[2] or displays the wallpaper for scenes set in Fred's and Laura's house. The screen also indicates the passing of time by showing successive pages of a tear-off calendar, accompanied by the ticking sound of a clock; and on other occasions it functions as a display-board onto which historical information on the play's time and location can be projected (such as "England, 1938" or "Southern Railway — S.R. — Milford Junction").

The stage production further highlights the mediality of film by adopting Lean's self-reflexive framing device of a film-within-the-film during the lovers' two visits to the Palladium Cinema. In Lean's film, these sequences are mostly presented with a focus on Laura and Alec sitting in the gallery among the rest of the audience, while the films and trailers they are watching are heard from off-screen. Only the trailer for the fictional film "Flames of Passion" is actually shown in a film-within-a-film. Kneehigh's production begins with Laura and Alec taking their seats in the front row of the auditorium among members of the audience to watch the opening credits on the screen announcing: "Kneehigh Theatre presents Noël Coward's *Brief Encounter*." By such means the production fuses Laura's and Alec's experiences with those of the theater audience, creating the impression that the ensuing performance on stage and screen will be watched alike by the real audience and the fictional lovers. A similar effect is created when the screen projects the legend "The End" before the final scene, in which all the characters sing the Noël Coward song "A Room with a View" on stage. The notion of the entire performance as a film screened in a cinema is sustained by the mock commercial break performed by the actors just before the interval ends, which depicts advertisements for Camp Coffee, soap, pipes and toupées. The production also shows an on-screen variety performance witnessed by Laura and Alec from the auditorium, including a rendition of the Coward poem "Put Out My Shooting Suit, Walters" set to music by Stu Barker, where the theater audience is encouraged to sing the lyrics projected onto the screen. Hence Kneehigh's production not only redefines the relationship between theater and film, but subverts the theatrical convention of the "fourth wall." This happens most effectively via the ushers — played by members of the cast — who witness the performance and guide the theater audience to their seats before the performance begins. A comparable effect is created by Myrtle serving cucumber sandwiches from her refreshment room to members of the audience during the intermission, or by the actors making repeated remarks to the spectators—as for example, when Myrtle tells them to "stop sniggering." In his review for the London *Daily Telegraph*, David Cheal remarks that "This is a Kneehigh trademark—not only is the "fourth wall" demolished, but the other three are swept aside too" (Cheal). By such means Kneehigh underline the constructed nature of their performance—and by extension, the constructed nature of the histories adapted for the stage. While past and present are deliberately collapsed, as we are transported back into the world of the 1940s, the production paradoxically shows the impossibility of re-living that past: what we see on the stage is a modern recreation of the past through sounds, images, costumes and other effects.

The production further emphasizes the constructedness of its past through deliberate techniques—for example, by having some of the actors doubling or even trebling roles without much change in costume. This theatricality is enhanced by the presence of stagehands and musicians on stage as well as by the use of puppetry, primitive props and deliberate stage-business, all of which have by now become trademarks of Kneehigh Theatre's performance style. The actors are continuously seen on stage as characters involved in the action, as musicians, dancers, entertainers, or stagehands responsible for props and sound effects. The setting is kept deliberately minimalist: Laura's piano simultaneously functions as the shop counter of the refreshment room, while a gantry serves as a railway bridge, a nursery for Laura's children and an apartment. Most of the scene-changes are quickly executed by the cast, and when the curtain is used, its folds are meticulously straightened by the ushers.

At other moments the production repeatedly stresses the impossibility of historical recreation: the arrival and departure of the steam-trains from Milford Junction is not only shown on the screen but parodied, as Alec runs to catch a toy train that is pulled across the stage. An imaginary vibration caused by the trains is indicated as the actors tremble and shake the furniture. The newspaper that is ominously blown across the subway to indicate the impending storm in the film is imitated on stage by an usher waving a stick with a newspaper attached to its end; later on the effect of rain is re-created by pouring water from a can into a bathtub. While such elements serve as nostalgic parodies of moments within the film which only aficionados can decode and make sense of, they simultaneously show how history (in this case, the history projected in Lean's film) will always be reconstructed in different ways in different historical periods. Kneehigh are not "parodying" the Lean film or the Coward play, but displaying a sophisticated understanding of the difficulties of representing the past. Emma Rice emphatically argues that none of her adaptations contain either pastiche or cynicism: "The absolute heart of everything I do is being honoured" (qtd. in Radosavljević 97). In Thomas Leitch's typology of adaptation, Kneehigh's *Brief Encounter* comes under his sixth category of "(meta)commentary or deconstruction," in which the target text highlights its status as an historical adaptation by combining and contrasting its own medium-specificity with that of its source texts. It "deconstruct[s] the mimetic illusion by examining the problems of arranging or staging preexisting material for the theater or the cinema" (112). Leitch's definition does not go far enough: what Kneehigh's production shows is that mimetic illusion — understood in this context as historical recreation — is generally impossible to achieve. Every reconceptualization of "pre-existing material" (i.e., works produced in the past) is going to be different, shaped by the conventions of the present.

The Adaptation of Cultural Context

Kneehigh's approach does not treat the play *Still Life* or the film *Brief Encounter* as isolated hypotexts, but considers their broader historical context as equally significant. As Linda Hutcheon observes: "[a]n adaptation, like the work it adapts, is always framed in a context — a time and a place, a society and a culture; it does not exist in a vacuum" (142). Director Rice not only retains the historical setting of Coward's and Lean's story but additionally tries to re-create an approximation of the experience of the 1930s and 1940s, when cinema-going was the principal mass entertainment for an audience not weaned on television, with little other forms of entertainment except the radio. By such means Kneehigh attempt to increase the contemporary British playgoer's emotional identification with their production by evoking the so-called "golden age" of British cinema. Kneehigh deliberately chose to perform at the Cinema Haymarket in the West End, one of London's oldest cinemas, that was originally built as the Carlton Theatre in 1927. With the coming of the talkies it was no longer used for live performances and has since then — with only brief intermittent closures — served as a cinema. The London premiere of *Brief Encounter* took place there in 1946. Since the cinema still displays some of the original period décor, it lent itself as an ideal venue for Kneehigh's production. One critic described the experience of the London performance as a "time-travelling experience," that "begins before the play starts, as the members of Kneehigh, dressed as ushers in the smartly buttoned attire of the era, casually entertain the audience in their seats with music and singing, breaking off occasionally to show someone to their seat or compliment a lady's dress" (Cheal). On its webpage, Kneehigh Theatre Company advertises its production as an event that "takes you back to a bygone age of romance and the silver screen from the moment the commissionaire opens the doors" (Kneehigh). This might be a good advertising ploy, but is actually slightly disingenuous: as explained earlier, the production simultaneously emphasizes the disjunction between past and present.

The Role of Music

As part of the evocation of the historical conditions of production of the *Brief Encounter* film, the use of music is worth noting. Whereas the background music is directly inspired by the film, the musical interludes incorporate songs from the period. Like Lean's film, the stage production uses an adapted version of Rachmaninoff's Piano Concerto No. 2 that accentuates moments of extreme passion and thereby functions as an extradiegetic soundtrack for the love scenes. Moreover, both the film and Kneehigh's stage production use this composition intradiegetically, as a constituent part of the story. Towards the beginning of the film, for instance, Laura turns on the radio to listen to Rachmaninoff's music before imagining confessing her affair to Fred. The music emanating from the radio is transformed into background music for the ensuing memories in flashbacks, with its volume increasing whenever the memories become intensely passionate — as, for example, when Laura brings to mind her first kiss with Alec at the train station. In the subsequent scene, however, this memory subsides when Fred wakes Laura from her dreams by asking her to turn down the volume of the radio, thus transferring the by now unbearably loud accompanying music back to an intradiegetic level. A similar effect is created in Kneehigh's stage production where Fred switches off the radio, thus curtailing Rachmaninoff's Concerto that served as an accompaniment for the preceding scene between the lovers. When Laura's memories of swimming in the ocean are projected onto the screen towards the end of the performance, she plays Rachmaninoff on the piano, linking the music to moments of intense emotion, and at the same time transferring it from this extradiegetic level of illustrative accompaniment to an intradiegetic level on which the music directly results from the action on stage.

Yet, as previously explained, Kneehigh also advertise the differences in the way they adapt the historical material, compared to the Coward play and the Lean film, by including several lyrics and songs that were originally composed by Noël Coward but appeared in neither of the two earlier texts. The love song "Any Little Fish," for instance, originally appeared in Cochran's 1931 *Revue* and is used by the cake-seller Stanley (Stuart McLoughlin) to woo Beryl. Coward's song "Alice Is at It Again" from the 1946 musical *Pacific 1860*, with its implied subtext of prostitution, is in turn enacted as a suggestive balloon dance by Beryl. "Go Slow, Johnny" from Coward's musical comedy *Sail Away* (1961) accompanies Laura's and Alec's confessions of love in the boat shed. Taken from Coward's musical show *This Year of Grace* (1928), the hit song "A Room with a View" is used twice within the production; it is first sung by Alec after the failed rendezvous with Laura at Stephen's apartment, and later establishes the final scene of the production where it is eventually sung by all characters.

Other songs in the production are modern adaptations, using Coward's words set to music by Stu Barker. These include "Put Out My Shooting Suit, Walters," which functions as a sing-along curtain raiser for the lovers' visit to the cinema. Coward's poem "Bora Bora," that describes a desert island's beautiful lagoon and beaches, is used as a musical accompaniment for Laura's memories of swimming in the ocean in Cornwall. Myrtle's song "I Am No Good at Love" is based on yet another of Coward's poems (Coward, *Lyrics* 26). Occasionally the production also transforms words derived from Lean's film into songs. "Like a Romantic Schoolgirl" is adapted from Laura's voice-over monologue in the film, which is spoken on her train ride home after her first kiss with Alec; in Kneehigh's stage production it is sung during the scene of the lovers' lunch at the Royal Hotel. Kneehigh's song "This Misery Can't Last," also comes from Lean's film as Laura takes the train home after her final date with Alec. In Kneehigh's production the song is sung at the point when Alec has eventually disappeared on the train. Kneehigh's production also includes two songs that, although not written by Coward himself, were featured in Frank Lloyd's 1933 film adaptation of Coward's Drury Lane stage pageant *Cavalcade* (1931): "Oh, You Beautiful Doll" is sung at the very beginning of the production, whereas "Goodbye, Dolly Gray" is performed by soldiers to signal an air-raid, while aeroplanes are projected on the screen. The cumulative effect of the songs is complex: on the one hand audiences are drawn into an historical approximation of a period where popular songs expressed the kind of emotions that ordinary people found difficult to voice in their everyday lives. On the other hand the spectators are made perpetually aware of the constructed nature of this adaptation, as they are reminded that a contemporary theater company is offering its own (highly entertaining) interpretation of a past era.

Other Adaptations of *Still Life* and *Brief Encounter*

Just how idiosyncratic Kneehigh's approach to adapting history is can be understood if we compare their production with other adaptations of the Coward play and the Lean film. *Still Life* was adapted and updated into the West End musical *Mr. and Mrs.* in 1968 that starred the late John Neville,

Honor Blackman and Hylda Baker and came off after only 44 performances (Cheal). Most adaptations of the film *Brief Encounter* have been equally ill-starred: the remake directed by Alan Bridges (1974) turned out to be a flop, despite the presence of Sophia Loren and Richard Burton in the cast. Cheal, for example, refers to it as a "pale shadow of its [1945] forebear" (Cheal). Nor could the modernized 1984 adaptation *Falling in Love* directed by Ulu Grosbard with Meryl Streep and Robert DeNiro in the leading roles live up to the success of Lean's film. The short film *Flames of Passion* (1989), produced by Richard Kwietniowski, provides a more interesting case; while the title refers to the sensational trailer of the same name that is seen by Laura and Alec at the cinema, Kwietniowski's film rewrites *Brief Encounter* into a homosexual context and thus supplies a "queer reading" in form of an update that nevertheless recreates the historical context of the film by imitating its cinematography (Street 193). More recently, *Brief Encounter* was adapted for the stage by Andrew Taylor in a production directed by Roger Redfarn that ran at the Lyric Theatre in London from September to December 2000. Starring the late Christopher Cazenove and Jenny Seagrove, this adaptation tried to recreate the historical atmosphere of the Lean film by "giv[ing] no new dimension [...] beyond the addition of stage colour" (Shenton) and even retained Laura's voice-over monologues that were simply played back from a tape. However it was largely derided for its unimaginative treatment of the film by critics. On October 30, 2009, BBC Radio 2 broadcast a live production of Maurice Horspool's 1947 radio adaptation of Coward's screenplay that had only once before been produced in 1963. Although interesting as a historical period-piece, with accents, sound-effects and mannerisms deliberately based on the kind of radio drama one might have listened to during the 1940s, the performances (with Nigel Havers in the Trevor Howard role and Jenny Seagrove repeating her role from the 2000 stage production) were considered wooden, "an exercise in retro styling and outdated mores," as Moira Petty claimed in her review for *The Stage and Television Today* (Petty). Petty's comment underlines the difficulties of adapting historical texts; just to imitate the styles, fashions and mores of a particular period will seldom work, simply because the readers,' listeners' and viewers' perceptions have changed. By comparison Kneehigh proved the value of their approach to *Brief Encounter* by looking at the past through the lens of the present.

Conclusion

Although the comparison between the three versions of *Brief Encounter* has illuminated many correspondences and parallels, Kneehigh's stage production consciously advertises itself as being historically similar to and yet radically different from the earlier texts. It should be approached as a palimpsest combining different strategies of adaptation such as "selection" and "amplification" (Stam 68). When occasionally Kneehigh's production adheres more to Lean's film than to Coward's play, it can also be seen as an adaptation of an adaptation, a "secondary" imitation (Leitch 120) of an intermediary hypotext in which the Coward play appears as already filtered through the Lean film. Kneehigh adapts the historical context of its hypotexts, specifically the film, by trying to approximate the experience of cinema-going in the 1930s and 1940s. It not only serves as a "celebration" or "homage" to its source texts (Leitch 96) but pays tribute to a whole era, even while advertising its fundamental difference from the texts produced in that era. Without doubt, Kneehigh's production benefits from the popularity and commercial success of its film source by drawing on what Leitch has referred to as "the marketing aura" (260). Yet, the stage adaptation develops its own view of history by reinventing its hypotexts. Despite the use of the film title, the audience is left in no doubt that this is the "live" experience — "not the film." Kneehigh's *Brief Encounter* demonstrates that historical adaptation is not a straightforward transformation of characters, plot and style from one medium, genre or period into another, but rather an "intertextual dialogism" that provides a "multilaminated" experience (Hutcheon 21). In this sense, the production evokes the spirit associated with the story's creator Noël Coward who as writer, actor, composer and director over a period of nearly five decades was brilliant at reinventing his own histories and could himself be considered a truly "multilaminated" personality.

Notes

1. This essay is based on a performance of Brief Encounter seen at Cinema Haymarket in London on February 20, 2008.
2. Although here used as a World War II song, "Goodbye Dolly Gray," written by Will D. Cobb and Paul Barnes, was first heard as long ago as 1901.

Works Cited

Brief Encounter. Dir. David Lean. Perf. Trevor Howard, Celia Johnson, Stanley Holloway. Rank, 1945. Film.
_____. Dir. Alan Bridges. Perf. Richard Burton, Sophia Loren. Hallmark Hall of Fame, 1974. TV Film.
_____. Dir. Maurice Horspool. Perf. Nigel Havers, Jenny Seagrove. BBC Radio 2. 30 Oct. 2009. Radio.
_____. Dir. Emma Rice. Kneehigh Theatre Company. Cinema Haymarket, London. 20 Feb. 2008. Theatre Performance.
Cavalcade. Dir. Frank Lloyd. Perf. Diana Wynyard, Clive Brook, Una O'Connor. Fox Film Corporation, 1933. Film.

Cheal, David. "*Brief Encounter*: 'I Want People to Laugh and Cry. That's Our Job.'" *The Daily Telegraph* 9 Feb. 2008. Web. 8 Dec. 2010.

Coward, Noël. *The Lyrics of Noël Coward*. London: William Heinemann, 1965. Print.

_____. *Still Life*. 1936. *Plays Three — Design for Living, Cavalcade, Conversation Piece, Hands Across the Sea, Still Life, and Fumed Oak*. London: Methuen Drama, 1994. 335–381. Print.

Falling in Love. Dir. Ulu Grosbard. Perf. Robert De Niro, Meryl Streep, Harvey Keitel. Paramount Pictures, 1984. Film.

Flames of Passion. Dir. Richard Kwietniowski, 1989. Film.

Giesekam, Greg. *Staging the Screen. The Use of Film and Video in Theatre*. Basingstoke and New York: Palgrave Macmillan, 2007. Print.

Hutcheon, Linda. *A Theory of Adaptation*. New York and London: Routledge, 2006. Print.

Klaver, Elizabeth. *Performing Television: Contemporary Drama and the Media Culture*. Bowling Green: Bowling Green State University Popular Press, 2000. Print.

Kneehigh Theatre. "Kneehigh Theatre Presents Noël Coward's *Brief Encounter*." Kneehigh Theatre. Web. 19 Dec. 2010.

Leitch, Thomas. *Film Adaptation and Its Discontents: From "Gone with the Wind" to "The Passion of the Christ."* Baltimore: Johns Hopkins University Press, 2007. Print.

A Matter of Life and Death. Dir. Michael Powell, Emeric Pressburger. Perf. David Niven, Kim Hunter. The Archers, 1946. Film.

Morley, Sheridan. Introduction. *Noël Coward Plays: Three*. London: Methuen Drama, 1994. vii–xv. Print.

Petty, Moira. "Radio Review — Drama." *The Stage and Television Today* 2 Nov. 2009. Web. 19 Jun. 2011.

Radosavljević, Duška. "Emma Rice in Interview with Duška Radosavljević." *Journal of Adaptation in Film and Performance* 3.1 (2010): 89–98. Print.

Sanders, Julie. *Adaptation and Appropriation*. London and New York: Routledge, 2006. Print.

Shenton, Mark. "Brief Encounter." *Whatsonstage Review* 12 Sept. 2000. Web. 18 Dec. 2010.

Stam, Robert. "Beyond Fidelity: The Dialogics of Adaptation." *Film Adaptation*. Ed. James Naremore. New Brunswick, NJ: Rutgers Univesrity Press, 2000. 54–76. Print.

Street, Sarah. *British National Cinema*. London and New York: Routledge, 1997. Print.

The Umbrellas of Cherbourg (Les Parapluies de Cherbourg). Dir. Jacques Demy. Perf. Catherine Deneuve, Nino Castelnuovo. Parc Film, 1964. Film.

The Worst of Youth:
Mario Martone's
Noi Credevamo *as a*
Contested Historical Adaptation

MARCO GROSOLI

"Try again. Fail again. Fail better." — Samuel Beckett, *Worstward Ho.*

In 2011, Italy turned 150 years old. Predictably, along with official cele-brations, the local cinema seized this opportunity to revisit *Risorgimento*, the huge and complicated series of internal fights and wars that led to the nation's unification in 1861. Orthodox historiography has often removed the element of conflict from this affair; by contrast, the director Mario Martone adapts a novel by Anna Banti, *Noi Credevamo* (*We Believed*) (1967), which particularly emphasizes the discontinuous and fragmented nature of the events taking place over a century beforehand. Conflict not only influences the content of Martone's film, but also form, as the director both adapts and extends an his-toric milestone of Italian cinema that likewise deals with the subject of unifi-cation — Luchino Visconti's melodrama *Senso* (*Sentiment*) (1954).[1] This essay will look at the book and film of *Noi Credevamo*, to show how both deal with the historical events of 1861; and subsequently examine how *Senso* epitomizes melodrama as a classically Italian genre. It will finish by looking at the ways in which Martone adapts this genre as a way of commenting on Italy both in the past and present. He shows how the country is seemingly stuck in an eter-nal distrust of progress, yet takes a stand against this cynical, reactionary fatalism that he believes is characteristic of Italian melodrama.

Banti's book is the imaginary autobiography of Domenico Lopresti, a pro–Italy conspirator born in 1813, who remembers (and recounts) his whole life in one long flashback shortly before his death. He is particularly concerned with his involvement in the struggle for the liberation of his country, as well as the harsh 12 years he served as a prisoner in various jails belonging to the Bourbon family. The book ends with him as a free but elderly person reflecting on the consequences of the revolution: class conflict remains, while the regional differences between north and south have not been removed. The south remains essentially backward, while the élite based in northern cities such as Turin (the new capital city) are ruthlessly exploiting the rest of the country. As Antonio Gramsci famously observed, *Risorgimento* was a "failed revolution": the utopian dream of the emancipation of Italian people suppressed by another oppressive monarchy (qtd. in Clark).

Lopresti's first-person retrospective narration is devastatingly bitter and cynical; the voice of someone who looks for coherence in his life, but only finds a mass of scattered ruins. Martone's film version discards the subjective element, while increasing the number of main characters. Domenico (played by Edoardo Natoli as a young man and by Salvatore Lo Cascio as a grown up later in the film) shares the narrative with Angelo Cammarota (Andrea Bosca, Valerio Binasco) and Salvatore Tambasco (Luigi Pisani). These three men are patriots from Cilento (a region next to the city of Salerno, in the south) striving to do anything they can to further the cause of unification. The narrative is divided into four sections: the first begins in Cilento with the brutal repression following the 1828 riots against the Bourbons—the royal house of French/Spanish descent that had been ruling the South of Italy for over one hundred years. The rebellion spurs the three friends to continue the fight, so they join the *Giovane Italia*—the secret society dedicated to Italian unification. However subsequent events serve to test their morale: when Salvatore announces his intention to withdraw, Angelo accuses him of being a traitor and a spy, and stabs him to death.

The second section shows Domenico being detained in Montefusco prison for three years (1852–1855), emphasizing not only the harsh conditions, but showing how class differences (rich vs. poor) are replicated in jail. The third section, set in London between 1856 and 1858, shows Angelo being implicated in a plot to kill the Emperor Napoleon III. The plan is discovered and all are guillotined. The final section has Domenico realizing that nothing has really changed, in spite of the uprising: the old injustices linger on, while the rebels have been brutally annihilated.

The film's sprawling structure owes a lot to melodrama — that specifically Italian genre that summed up the conflicts of that time. What all Italian patriots had in common was the belief in the fact that virtue had to stand up against oppression — the basic kernel of melodramatic narration. Martone includes several conventions characteristic of the genre: non-classical narrative mechanics including outrageous coincidences, implausible situations, convoluted plotting, *deus ex machina* resolutions, and episodic strings of action that "stuff too many events together to be able to be kept in line by a cause-and-effect chain of narrative progression" (Singer 46).

To understand Martone's technique of adapting history in more detail, we should consider it in relation to *Senso* (1954), the classic adaptation of the *Risorgimento* conflict in melodramatic form. Visconti's film had a tremendous impact on Italian cultural life in general, and on film criticism in particular. One of its most important advocates was Guido Aristarco of the Marxist film journal *Cinema Nuovo* (*New Cinema*). In his article "È realismo," he saw the film as a good example of cinematic realism, a movement following the inevitably transitory phase known as "Neorealism." Using a definition formulated by Hungarian philosopher György Lukács, based on the belief that a text becomes "realistic" by a means of a unification between "universal" and "particular" elements, Aristarco praised *Senso* for having created a coherent system of connections between the narrative and the historical context in which it was placed (Aristarco).[2] Aristarco defined "Neorealism" as something that had sprung out of the ruins of Italian cinema a few years before, whose purpose was to document the harsh post–1945 reality of the country. For him, "cinematic" realism could only be one that laid bare (notably through narrative) the inherent, deep structures and relationships of a given social and historical context.

Itself an adaptation from an 1883 short story by Camillo Boito, *Senso* is set in 1866 Venice, shortly before its annexation to the kingdom of Italy. The main character is Countess Serpieri (Alida Valli), a noblewoman torn between Ussoni, a patriotically-engaged relative of hers (Massimo Girotti), and Mahler (Farley Granger), a young Austrian officer. She turns away from politics, as she gives Mahler the money that Ussoni wanted her to deliver to the Italian patriots (non-aristocratic volunteers) involved in *Risorgimento*. Serpieri does not remain faithful to Mahler either; she cannot comfort him when he gets severely defeated by History along with his country (Austria, the decaying invaders). Rather than becoming involved in the conflict, she stands apart, choosing the path of self-interest instead. All she cares about is the preservation of her aristocratic status: she cannot leave the past and face a more egalitarian future. Through this plot-structure Visconti wanted to emphasize how history repeats itself: in the years following World War II Italy was equally indolent, as if they were reluctant to embrace historical change. This kind of connection between past and present is precisely what Lukács thinks about historical novels—for example those of Walter Scott:

[Scott] is a patriot, he is proud of the development of his people. This is vital for the creation of a real historical novel — i.e., one which brings the past close to us and allows us to experience its real and true being. Without a felt relationship to the present, a portrayal of history is impossible. But this relationship, in the case of the really great historical art, does not consist in alluding to contemporary events, a practice which Pushkin cruelly ridiculed in the work of Scott's incompetent imitators, but in bringing the past to life as the prehistory of the present, in giving poetic life to those historical, social and human forces which, in the course of a long evolution, have made our present-day life what it is and as we experience it [53].

In the first version of *Senso*, Visconti included a scene — eventually cut from the release print — in which Ussoni is shown as completely unprepared for change. He is told by his superiors that the rebels have to withdraw and be replaced by the regular army — just like the 1943 partisans, who liberated Italy from Nazism and Fascism but were excluded from the decision-making process after the war had ended. The existing hegemony takes advantage of the spontaneous and relatively non-organized status of the fighters, and frustrates any expectation for change by positing the necessity for order (which they, of course, represent) in opposition to a disorder which was, nonetheless, at the very heart of any new regime.

In spite of Aristarco's claims, *Senso* is in truth a straightforward historical melodrama that avoids any analysis of the existing socio-political situation, either in the past or the present. There is only Serpieri's drama; the only background is the *mise-en-scène* which functions rather like a set in a theatrical play. As an example, we might consider the scene when Mahler visits Serpieri in Villa Aldeno. The camera focuses on the relationship between Valli and Granger, while the rest of the world (at war) outside is only incidentally referenced through dialogue and off-screen noise — just as it would be onstage. This impression has been reinforced by Visconti's use of symbolism — for example the obsessively-employed mirror and veils. When Mahler and Serpieri encounter one another for the first time, Visconti's camera frames them in a mirror, suggesting that the love affair is fake, a play between two images. The image is one of extreme narcissism; the personal overwhelms the political, and ultimately prevents any kind of historical change. Visconti adapts history to the melodramatic genre to depict the slow death of a declining class (and world) based on excessive individualism. Personalization and anthropomorphism (the attributes of a feudal and pre-capitalistic world) are presented as impossible to get rid of. It might be argued that melodrama has an inherent emancipatory potential, in that it is essentially a way to personalize social, political, economic and gender issues. Yet there is also a risk inherent in this process, as individuals value personal well-being rather than working for change. *Senso* demonstrates this process at work: by personalizing the revolution, the Piedmont aristocracy actively neutralize it — something that was also characteristic of the early 1950s, when the local unofficial groups that fought against fascism were brutally marginalized by the new establishment.

Melodrama represents both a striving for progress (the virtue that shines against its oppressors) and the incapability to confront the issues that struggle involves. It is this conflict that distinguishes melodrama from tragedy: the grandeur of tragic characters emerges from the fact that they can confront any horrors in their lives. As Claire Aziza observes, Serpieri and Mahler cannot do this: they are enslaved to the roles allotted to them in a feudal society (134). *Senso* adapts nineteenth century history to emphasize the fact that everyone is trapped by their social roles; there is no possible way for people from different backgrounds to work together for the betterment of their country. The film suggests that Italy will never attain modernity; it is stuck in melodrama's vicious circle, the epistemological tool for the individuation of conflicts that melodrama essentially is (Brooks 24–55).

Martone's *Noi Credevamo* has clearly been inspired by *Senso*: as seen, for instance, in a sequence taking place in a Parisian theater, where a play by Victor Hugo is interrupted by a furious audience. This serves as a visual metaphor for the process of stagnation characteristic of the Visconti film. But Martone offers a way through: Domenico (the main character) and his friends begin to shout "Laissez–les jouer!" ("Let them play!") The audience quietens and the show continues. Martone adapts history to show the melodramatic curse being broken, a curse explicitly referenced in a monologue in which Cristina Belgiojoso (Francesca Inaudi) — a noblewoman from Milan in exile in Paris because of her patriotic sympathies — asserts that the patriots are doomed to call illusion the truth, and truth the illusion, forever missing that point where the two poles coincide, and hence inspire affirmative action. Martone uses a melodramatic style to emphasize this sense of inertia.

The echoes of *Senso* are very direct in the film's first act, which suggests that revolts mostly fail because common people are not ready to embrace the struggle for emancipation. The melodramatic ambience is reinforced both by an overly theatrical acting style, and a constant and symbolic use of objects: for example, in a sequence that begins with Angelo knocking at Domenico's door; Domenico opens it, and Angelo tells him "please give me a clean shirt." Domenico goes and fetches it, then he looks at the blood-stained shirt Angelo is wearing and consequently realizes Angelo has been involved in a murder, so he lets the clean shirt fall on the floor with contempt and walks back horrified. Angelo picks up the shirt and runs away. While no less theatrical and melodramatic in tone, the remaining three parts of the film deconstruct the inertia lurking behind melodrama, and show how its capacity for indecisiveness overwhelms any attempts at change, whether personal, social or political. The second section contains plenty of action, but most of it takes place off-screen: instead we see characters talking within claustrophobic ambiences. What is mostly relevant in terms of the plot does not happen in front of the camera: the latter focuses on the imprisoned characters who merely hear rumors concerning major events that take place "out there," in the "real world" outside jail. The focus is on character and place: very little happens. The third section focuses on Angelo and his attempts to become a terrorist. It is soon very clear that behind this intention lies an unsolved conflict: he cannot come to terms with Salvatore's murder. Like Hamlet, he looks for confirmation that the moral issues surrounding this act are as black-or-white as he would like them to be, but such proof is nowhere to be found. He goes to visit Antonio Gallenga (Luca Barbareschi), a former comrade of his who attempted to kill the King of Piedmont, to ask him if Salvatore really was a traitor — and since he receives no answer, Angelo overacts pathetically. He desperately looks for a rigid, stern opposition between "good" and "bad" that would justify murdering his friend; what he finds, however, is that circumstances are more complex than what he would like them to be. Until such time as he embraces these complexities, he can never determine a positive course of action for the future. Through this aspect of the film Martone adapts the prevailing strain of Italian history — which favors inertia — to show its shortcomings.

In the film's fourth and last part, the goal has been reached, unification has been achieved (it is 1862 here, one year after unification), but Domenico finds himself and those around him stuck in an infernal repetition: oppression, misery, brutal violence and corpses on the streets are widespread just like under the Bourbons thirty years before. When Domenico joins a group of patriots waiting for Garibaldi, he recalls his younger days, when he was full of enthusiasm — but to his cost he witnesses his new, less aged and less experienced comrades committing the same acts of violence that he did. An epic, teleological narration would end with the final, triumphal unification of the nation. *Noi Credevamo* ends instead with a return to historical stagnation.

The film adapts history to suggest that Italy is burdened by similar intellectual impasses. This message is reinforced in structural terms: the action is largely static, with the emphasis placed on visual details rather than plot-development. Martone's camera pans the grimy streets, the dry bushes by the sea, the wild vegetation and the scrubs in Cilento and Calabria. Stagnation amidst landscape is more significant than action; space is more important than time (annihilated by the return of the same).

However Martone is not content to leave viewers with this sense of nothing having changed; he wants to inspire them to action. He achieves this through another act of historical adaptation. Francesco Crispi was a patriot who, after having been elected in the Parliament (in 1861), provoked, as the years went by, an impressive escalation of corruption and authoritarianism. Played by Luca Zingaretti in Martone's film, he appears a couple of times in the background, as well as in the final scene, where Domenico visits the empty Parliament and sees him (but only as a ghostly vision) claiming that Italy must be united at all costs. "Monarchy unites us, republic divides us." At that point, Domenico pretends to be shooting at him. The enemy of Italian progress is clearly delineated: it is anyone who pretends to advocate change while being concerned to reinforce the forces of authoritarianism. Crispi was a monarchist while claiming to be a revolutionary. The implication is clear: for real change to occur, individuals must be prepared to maintain their beliefs at all costs, and not rely on others to do the work for them. The lack of self-determination is precisely what has condemned Italy to perpetual stagnation (as evidenced, for example, in the popularity of the melodramatic form). Martone here uses the past to advocate a future course of action; to go beyond received ideas and strike out for oneself.

In the conclusion of his volume on melodrama, Peter Brooks affirms that the bipolar, Manichean management of conflicts (i.e., reducing them to issues of good vs. evil) so typical of modern politics has everything to do with melodrama (203–5). In *Noi credevamo*, on the other hand, Martone repudiates this binary opposition to show that conflict is everywhere: it cannot be polarized. The only way to escape conflict is to trust in oneself (in thematic terms), and to adopt a dramatic form that favors individual resolution rather than abstract ideas—i.e., good vs. evil. This can be summed up axiomatically: "one can only defuse conflict thanks to a conflict of a different kind." Anthropomorphic conflict can be defeated only by showing that conflict is everywhere. This latter proposition is foreign to melodrama.

Martone emphasizes the importance of this notion through a deliberately "foggy" type of dramaturgy, that frustrates one's melodramatic expectations of clarity. One representative sequence is the battle in northern Italy organized by Angelo and his comrades in the first act, where almost nothing but fog is shown. At first, the scene is entirely enveloped by fog. Then, Angelo's silhouette becomes visible, followed by a few shots where some totally unrelated images are juxtaposed without any mutual connection: Angelo wandering, the firing of guns, corpses lying on the ground, soldiers walking, a horse trotting on the background. This sequence sums up Martone's adaptation of the *Risorgimento* conflict: rather than being a melodrama, it was a war where the warring factions could not be clearly defined. The only way to plot a course through this labyrinth of conflicts was to rely on individual judgment.

If one were to pin down Martone's style in *Noi Credevamo*, it could be defined as arbitrary—each sequence follows another in an apparently disjointed manner. The result is a peculiarly shapeless film. Yet the form is also a function of content: Martone wants to suggest the "shapelessness" of Italian history, so he repudiates the idea of "unity at all costs," and thereby repudiates the melodramatic form. This represents a complete volte-face from the structure employed in *Senso*. To suggest an alternative to the kind of inertia that has bedeviled Italian history, he chooses a quintessentially Italian dramatic form and subverts it through a deliberate complication of the linear plot-line and simplified moral schema that are so characteristic of the genre. By doing so he transforms his film into a manifesto of hope: the individuation of possible sites for struggle does not always and necessarily point at an insurmountable situation, but also at a (hard but actual) possibility for change.

Notes

1. The film was first released in the United States as *The Wanton Contessa* (inspired by the Joseph L. Mankiewicz film released in the same year—1954—*The Barefoot Contessa*).
2. For his celebration of realism in Visconti's works in general, see Guido Aristarco, "Esperienza Culturale ed Esperienza Originale in Luchino Visconti" (Cultural and Original Experiences in Luchino Visconti), Introduction to the screenplay of *Rocco e i suoi Fratelli*, ed. G. Aristarco and G. Carancini (Bologna: Cappelli, 1960), 3–28.

Works Cited

Aristarco, Guido. "È realismo." *Cinema Nuovo* 55 (March 1955): 226–8. Print.
_____. "Experienza Culturale ed Esperienza Originale in Luchino Visconti" (Cultural and Original Experiences in Luchino Visconti). Introduction. *Rocco e i Suoi Fratelli* (*Rocco and His Brothers*). Eds. Aristarco and Gaetano Carancini. Bologna: Cappelli, 1960. 3–28. Print.
Aziza, Claire. "Mélodrame expérimental." *Théorème Visconti: Classicisme et Subversion.* Ed. Michèle Lagny. Paris: Publications de la Sorbonne Nouvelle, 1990. 121–136. Print.
Banti, Anna. *Noi Credevamo.* Milano: Mondadori, 1967. Print.
Beckett, Samuel. *Worstward Ho.* Ed. Colin Greenlaw. *The Samuel Beckett On-line Resources and Links Page* 14 Mar. 2007. Web. 18 Mar. 2012.
Brooks, Peter. *The Melodramatic Imagination: Balzac, Henry James, Melodrama and the Mode of Excess.* New Haven: Yale Univesity Press, 1976. Print.
Clark, Martin. *Antonio Gramsci and the Revolution that Failed.* New Haven: Yale University Press, 1977. Print.
Lukács, György. *The Historical Novel.* Lincoln: University of Nebraska Press, 1983. Print.
Noi Credevamo (*We Believed*). Dir. Mario Martone. Perf. Luigi Lo Cascio, Valerio Binasco, Toni Servillo. Palomar/ Les Films d'Ici/ RAI Cinema 2010. Film.
Senso (*Sentiment*). Dir. Luchino Visconti. Perf. Farley Granger, Alida Valli. Lux Film, 1954. Film.
Singer, Ben. *Melodrama and Modernity: Early Sensational Cinema and Its Contexts.* New York: Columbia University Press, 2001. Print.

Cinematic Reinventions of the 1825 Decembrist Uprising in Post-Revolutionary Soviet Russia

DUNJA DOGO

Decembrism and Political Memory

Various scholars of Soviet history have shown how the interpretation of the past was of crucial importance to the Bolsheviks, since the legitimacy of the dictatorship born of the October Revolution depended upon it. Immediately after seizing power, they began a campaign to reinvent the country's history, a practice which at the end of the nineteenth century had often accompanied the formation of the modern nation-state (Ferretti 451–54). Constituting themselves as the sole custodians of the laws of historical development, the Bolsheviks adapted Russian history in such a way as to identify as its culmination their own rise to power. However, not having a past to which they could anchor themselves deeply, they took steps to invent one by assimilating the various nineteenth century Russian socialist currents that otherwise had no direct contact with Bolshevism — including the revolutionaries of the Decembrist uprising — a revolt conducted by Russian officers against the Tsar between December 1825 and January 1826. Initially this operation of inventing a tradition — to invoke E. J. Hobsbawm and Terence O. Ranger's 1992 book of the same name–was performed in political conditions that guaranteed historians, philosophers and filmmakers a certain freedom of expression. As a result, certain well-known figures, who had rebelled against the monarchy in the years leading up to the Russian Revolution (Sofia Perovskaja, Sergej Nečaev, Vera Figner, Dmitrij Karakozov, Stepan Chalturin, together with their followers) appear in epic films that were produced between 1918 and 1932 (Ginzburg 436–41).

It is within this context that the Decembrist movement was considered not simply as an historical event (from the Party's point of view), but also as an object-lesson in insurrection against a tyrannous regime, something to cherish as part of Russia's revolutionary past (O'Meara 3–14). One factor that favored the revival of interest in Decembrism was, without doubt, the emergence of numerous primary source materials from the national archives that came about as a result of the Soviet government's control of NARKOMPROS (People's Commissariat of Enlightenment) from 1917 onwards (Salomoni 3–10). This reorganizing and centralizing process yielded a rich hoard of papers, private and official, connected with the Decembrist story, amounting to half a million documents (Gitermann 62–74; Mazour 75, 155, 181–184, 294).

The emerging Soviet cinema took advantage of this renewal of interest in revolutionary history (both Russian and European): as a matter of fact, in the second half of the 1920s almost one third of the films produced by local film studios dealt with historical-revolutionary subjects (Kenez 206–19; Lebedev 487–564). Through an analysis of two films, *Dekabristy* (*The Decembrists*, directed by Aleksandr Ivanovskij, (1927)) and *S.V.D.* (aka *Sojuz Velikogo Dela*) (*The Union for the Great Cause*), directed by Leonid Trauberg and Grigorij Kozincev (also 1927), this essay will discuss how Soviet directors created an imagined Decembrism in the collective memory of the filmgoers of the newly established state. Up to the 1920s Russian historiography agreed on the thesis that almost all the men involved in the revolt of 1825 were aristocratic, high-ranking soldiers who joined secret societies and Masonic lodges that were beginning to emerge in the Russian Empire between 1810 and 1820. Soviet filmmakers elaborated on this story by suggesting that the soldiers had encountered Enlightenment thought, as well as the leading lights of the English and German Romantic movements. This kind of broadly humanist education inspired them to seek a radical change of government in their own country, which in the early nineteenth century was dominated by a despotic autocracy that would neither cede power, nor abolish serfdom, but rather reduced the domestic economy to a condition of total backwardness (Nekipelov 76).

The Adaptation of History in *Dekabristy*

Dekabristy focuses on the officers' experiences as they initiated their rebellion against Tsar Nicholaj I. In the film the historical account of the 1825 campaign is interwoven with a romantic subplot involving the handsome officer Lieutenant Ivan Annenkov, for which screenplay writer P. E. Ščëgolev used Puškin's poem *Polina Gebl'* (Ščëgolev and Tolstoj 505–42) as well as relying on archival material. Ščëgolev had long been preoccupied with the Decembrist movement, having established direct contact with the descendants of the officers, such as Varvara Von Annenkova. In 1906 Ščëgolev published one of the very first accounts of the campaign, which he believed was inspired by populist concerns; rather than upholding aristocratic values, the soldiers believed in "going to the people" (Emeljanov 86–92). In *Dekabristy*, he retold the Decembrist story from a contemporary perspective, designed to make audiences understand the significance of the events a century earlier. Ščëgolev placed considerable importance on the officers' cultural background, in order to show the continuity between various European revolutions, beginning with the 1789 French Revolution (Ščëgolev IRLI RAN 627–3–62). The Decembrists are characterized as men of action, rather than mere idealists who simply talked about revolt (Nevelev 56).

By doing this, Ščëgolev departed from the orthodox interpretation of 1920s Russian historians—for example Michail Pokrovskij, who maintained in *Russkaja Istorija v Samom Sžatom Očerke* (*A Concise History of Russia*) (1920), that the Decembrists were no more than an élite circle of high-ranking Tsarists without any real influence over the vast majority of the population. Pokrovskij suggested that the reason for the rebellion's failure was chiefly due to the indecision of the officers' Commander-in-Chief, Prince Trubeckoj, who did not realize how to make the soldiers join forces with the crowd. By contrast Ščëgolev placed individual episodes in sequential order, forming links in a chain that led inevitably to the December 14 uprising. This structure represented the revolt as a courageous act of justice in "an age of abuse of peasants and soldiers held in a state of servitude," as the title-card announces at the beginning of the film.

The director of *Dekabristy* Aleksandr Ivanovskij engaged a cast of professional actors—many with a background in the theater—who bore a striking resemblance to the real personalities in history (Ivanovskij "Dekabristy," 4). Šiško played the aristocrat Ryleev, aspiring poet and assessor of the St. Petersburg criminal court from January 1821; the stage actors G. Mičurin and E. Borochin acted the roles of Prince Trubeckoj and Nikolaj I. Ryleev, contrasting starkly with the bellicose Kachovskij—played by P. Volkonskij—the soldier of strong radical convictions, moved by a profound love of his country. In contrast to the other Decembrists, Kachovskij emphasizes that to liquidate the Tsar would be tantamount to "signing a death warrant," even though it would signal the liberation of Russia. He is the rebel *par excellence*; one who observes a particular code of honor, thinks like a man of the Enlightenment, and understands the people whom he claims to represent.

In adapting the Decembrist revolution for 1920s' audiences, Ščëgolev and

Ivanovskij suggest that the main person responsible for the failure of "the day of protest" was the ineffectual Commander-in-Chief Prince Trubeckoj, portrayed in the cinematic narrative as "the deluded liberal" (Emeljanov 78–79). All the major historical characters of the revolution appear — with two exceptions, as we shall see. The film suggests that the crowd allies with the officers to pose a genuine threat to Tsarist General Miloradovič,[1] who considers them capable of "razing the city to the ground in less than half an hour," as stated in an intertitle. However Ščëgolev makes clear that the crowd play only a peripheral role in the rebellion, compared to the Decembrists who, after having refused to swear allegiance to the new Tsar, broke ranks and faced the Tsar's troops on their own. They appear as the heroes of the hour, whose brave action in the face of adversity provides an object lesson for Soviet audiences a century later. There is a clear parallel between the Decembrist uprising and the Bolshevik Revolution in one sequence just before the end. After the suppression of the revolt, Ryleev is examined by Nicholas I: as the Tsar extorts a confession from him, Ryleev predicts that "there be the Revolution in Russia, there will be!"

Despite such patriotic sentiments, *Dekabristy* received harsh criticism from a substantial portion of the Party press. In newspapers such as *Pravda* the reviewer castigated the film for placing too much emphasis on individual action (Gusman 6). Ščëgolev was believed to have disdained the orthodox adaptation of the Decembrist story; he had not sketched in the social context which served as the background to the movement, concentrating instead on a few protagonists, while minimizing the role of the peasants whom, it was believed, fulfilled an active role during the campaign. The cinematic representation of *Dekabristy* was more concerned with character and incident, rather than the representation of the collective story of the movement, in order to convey a captivating image of the Decembrist uprising.

The Adaptation of History in *S.V.D.*

S.V.D. was planned as a "romantic melodrama against the background of history," according to its creators, Grigorij Kozincev and Leonid Trauberg, in a 1927 interview (Trauberg 42). The film was almost totally lost on March 30 of that year, as a result of an arson attack that severely damaged the Sovkino studio. With considerable difficulty, Kozincev and Trauberg made a second version of the film corresponding to the production script; the final result was released at the end of August 1927 and proved a great success with the public both in the metropolis and in the provinces (Glagoleva 224).

The historical background of *S.V.D.* concerns the armed uprising that broke out in the southern part of the Russian Empire (now the Ukraine) between December 29, 1825 and January 3, 1826, the final stage of the Decembrist movement. Historians commonly agree that the officer in command was Sergei Murav'ev Apostol who, with the support of the Society of United Slavs, was inspired to initiate the revolution and led the uprising together with Bestužev-Rjumin; despite their initial enthusiasm, the rebellion was brutally suppressed by government forces on January 3, 1826. The film's representation of these events begins in mid–December 1825, as the officers prepare to fight the Tsar's army. According to Soviet historians such as Michail Pokrovskij — one of the founders of the Society of Marxist Historians — these men were not revolutionaries *per se*, but rather a group of affluent guards who adopted a reformist position in an attempt to defend their own aristocratic interests. This representation did not square with the Soviet desire to represent the Decembrist campaign as being led by simple, valorous heroes. Consequently Kozincev and Trauberg invited Julian Oksman, another well-known Soviet historian, to write the screenplay; he advocated that it was certain radical characters of the South, and not the liberals of the North, who formed the cornerstone of the Ukrainian campaign.

When *S.V.D.* was released, new research had appeared, drawing on contemporary archives as well as serials and historical novels. In 1928 A. Slonimskij's novel *Černigovcy* (*The Inhabitants of Černigov*) focusing specifically on the officers' experiences, was widely circulated and met with a generous reaction from the Soviet press. Oksman drew on Slonimskij's insights in the screenplay for *S.V.D.* He omitted some historical characters such as the head of the revolt (Murav'ev-Apostol and Bestužev-Rjumin), and created new fictional characters instead (Lotman and Civ'jan 52–78). Co-screenwriter Jurij Tynjanov recalled in 1929 that they wanted to distort historical events in an attempt to "emphasize the braggadocio of the Decembrists [...] we examined every aspect rigorously, down to the smallest detail [...] in an attempt to render effectively through the medium of film the progressive alteration of the Decembrists' state of mind" (Tynjanov 104). Consequently the historical events in the screenplay were transformed into a melodrama focusing on the shifting passions of the protagonists.

There are three narrative strands: the romantic attachment between Višnevskaja, Medoks and Suchanov (Sof'ja Magarill, Sergej Gerasimov, and Pëtr Sobolevskij); the personal story of Suchanov; and an adventure story involving General Višnevskij (played by Oleg Žakov). The scene involving the death of Suchanov was changed so as to render it more acceptable to different countries in the European market (Civ'jan 327–30). *S.V.D.* focuses less on the story of the regiment and more on the stories of individuals; by such means Kozincev and Trauberg produced an imaginative historical adaptation, involving new characters who, although based on historical fact, nonetheless embodied different political viewpoints—a feature that was noticed by many of those reviewing the film for the popular press (Perov 26).

The main protagonists of the film were the streetwise Medoks, the revolutionary Suchanov (who in historical reality was known as Suchinov), the easygoing liberal high officer Višnevskij and his wife, who became Suchanov's lover. Invented characters, such as Medoks and Suchanov corresponded to the prototypes that Oksman identified among the "masons" and the "radicals," to which the free-thinkers of the South (active in 1825) belonged (*Večernaja Moskva* 1). However such characters were given a firm historical background: in a short promotional article appearing on the film's release, the imagined secret society from which the acronym of the title derived (S.V.D. or "the Union for the Great Cause") was described as if it had really existed as the nucleus of the "southern group of Decembrists" (Kozincev 26). Kozincev and Trauberg constructed a gripping story about an episode of the rebellion that became part of Soviet mythology. Suchanov, the figure they placed at the center of the narrative, gave voice to the various spirits of the Decembrist movement.

Behind the historical intrigue of *S.V.D.* there is also the intrigue that brings together Suchanov and Medoks. In a gambling den in St. Petersburg, Medoks fools Suchanov into believing that he (Medoks) is actually an ally, and shows Suchanov a ring engraved with the initials S.V.D. Medoks explains that the three letters correspond to the monogram "Sojuz velikogo dela," the secret password of a group of rebels he claims to represent, but which in reality does not exist at all. As Suchanov leads the revolt, Medoks reports him to the Tsarist authorities; Suchanov has no option other than to flee, and subsequently organize the escape of his Decembrist companions from prison. In the meantime Medoks informs Tsarist troops about the plot; as a result the rebels are ambushed. Suchanov is mortally wounded and dies on the bank of the river in front of the prison.

In *S.V.D.* the heroes are distinguished according to a code that divides them into two groups: one comprises a number of officers led by the moderate Major-General Višnevskij, while the other consists of pro–Republican soldiers. Višnevskij was based on the General of the Second Army A. P. Juševskij; he plays the secondary role of the prudent officer opposing Suchanov, who encourages self-sacrifice for the sake of the Russian people. While the general demands that the prison break should take place "without further shedding of blood," Suchanov urges his fellow-officers to fight tooth and nail with pistols. Suchanov is the rebel *par excellence*, who disagrees with the decisions of his superior officers, and allies himself with ordinary soldiers. He is on the side of the people and ready to sacrifice himself in their interests; in return they "cheer him and excitedly surround him" when he calls them to arms, as an intertitle explains. In the original draft of the screenplay, Suchanov commits suicide, shooting himself through the heart, but this was considered an inglorious means of death.

Oksman based Suchanov on two historical sources: the memoirs of Ivan Gorbačevskij, member of the Society of the United Slavs and a second lieutenant in the artillery that revolted; and the biography of the historical character Suchinov written by the Soviet historian Milica Nečkina. Nečkina recounted Suchinov's heroic life after having been condemned to hard labor: his pilgrimage on foot at the head of a group of political prisoners, his attempts to organize a local revolt, his trial, and his suicide at dawn on the eve of his execution. According to the stories told by Gorbačevskij and Nečkina, Suchinov was a person of humble origins who led a life of adventure, and distinguished himself during the Napoleonic War of 1812. As a Warrant Officer of the charismatic Decembrist leader Murav'ev-Apostol — who does not appear in the film — Suchinov led the rearguard action after the ill-fated attempt at insurrection in December 1825. When the regiment was annihilated with machine guns, Suchinov escaped and wandered throughout the southwestern extremities of the Empire until the Decembrists surrendered to the Tsarist police in Kišinev (Nečkina 258–79).

In the film Suchanov encounters various dangers, but does not commit suicide. In an early stage of production of *S.V.D.* the directors considered the idea of Suchanov dying by his own hand, but dispensed with it, as this would have required him to proclaim the significance of his gesture to the Tsarist gendarmes while on the point of committing it: "You don't have to hang me, my dears!" (Kozincev 42). The characters of the two leaders Suchanov and Višnevskij are clearly defined in the film. They conduct a heated discussion concerning the Decembrist strategy: the one urges the pursuit of liberty while the other would like to negotiate a truce with the Tsar. Suchanov personifies the tragic hero *par excellence*: he reasserts his philosophy of the struggle to his fellow Decembrists: "They have caught us in a trap. If indeed we are destined to die, we will die weapon in hand!" This prophecy is fulfilled at the end of the sequence, as Suchanov finds himself face to face with the Tsarist police. He is slain by a member of the firing squad who lowers his rifle as a sign of truce (Kozincev 34).

At the end of *S.V.D.* an analogy is proposed between the death of Suchanov and that of a Christian martyr. He does not fall immediately but walks towards the camera without turning, his steps hesitant, with a rapt expression as if in a state of ecstasy. Then he goes to die in a pleasant hollow on the bank of the river. His face, filmed in close-up, has distinct visual echoes of images in medieval sacred art, where the martyr is shown at the moment of deposition: his eyes are closed and his chest is exposed. Surrounding his head there are brambles and shrubs that are not clearly distinguishable, but the impression they give is of a crown of thorns, giving the scene a strong Christian connotation.

Conclusion

Whilst *Dekabristy* celebrated the deeds of those at the head of the Decembrist Rising, *S.V.D.* adapted historical events into melodrama celebrating the first glorious anti–Tsarist exploits. This was a clever strategy: the melodrama genre had been popular for more than two centuries, and could readily achieve great success with Russian audiences. The characters were represented as exceptional individuals strenuously fighting for the entire people in a despotic society. They personified the driving forces of history which helped to inspire the Revolution.

Both *S.V.D.* and *Dekabristy* continued to enjoy widespread distribution and popularity in the late 1920s, despite negative publicity by a substantial portion of the Party press. In these two dramas, the history of the revolutionary movement was adapted into a kind of great historical novel, according to a Manichaean vision distinguishing good (the positive heroes who suffered death and exile — Pestel, Murav'ev Apostol, Ryleev, Kachovskij, Bestužev-Rjumin, Suchanov) from evil (those who supported the Tsar — Trubeckoj, Medoks). Both films participated in the process of molding a political memory of the Russian past that bore specific significance for the present. By 1920 a Commission had been established for the gathering, processing and realizing of materials concerning the story of the October Revolution and the Communist Party. By the end of that decade this task had been delegated to the Ideological Department of the Central Committee. While both films were independently produced, they nonetheless contributed to the Committee's task of adapting the past for ideological purposes. They underlined the significance of the Decembrist story according to official doctrine in the years immediately prior to the Stalinist purges of the early 1930s. They were inspired by many other cultural productions dedicated to the Decembrists, and in particular to the radical political beliefs inside the Černigovskij regiment. In 1923, for instance, an exhibition was held at the Museum of Revolution in Petrograd (now St. Petersburg), in which a place of honor was reserved for the Decembrists who had upheld the community ideal, despite persecution and prison (Ščëgolev *Muzej*, 4–7).

Notes

1. Unfortunately the actor playing this role is not credited in any published source.

Works Cited*

Civ'jan, Jurij. "The Wise and the Wicked Game: Re-editing and Soviet Film Culture of the 1920s." *Film History* 8 (1996) : 327–30. Print.

Dekabristy (*The Decembrists*). Dir. Aleksandr Ivanovsky. Perf. Vladimir Maksimov, Yevgeni Boronikhin, Varvara Annenkova. Leningradkino, 1927. Film.

Emeljanov, Jurij. *P.E. Ščëgolev — Istorik Russkogo Revoljucionnogo Dviženija (P.E. Ščëgolev: Historian of the Russian Revolutionary Movement)*. Moscow: Nauka, 1990. Print.

Ferretti, Maria. "Storia e memoria" (History and Memory). *Dizionario del Comunismo (Dictionary of Communism)*. Eds. Silvio Pons and Robert Service. Vol. 2. Torino: Einaudi, 2007. 451–4. Print.

Ginzburg, Semën. *Kinematografija Dorevoljucionnoj Rossii (The Cinematography of Pre-Revolutionary Russia)*. Moscow: Agraf, 2007. Print.

Gitermann, Valentin. *Storia della Russia, Volume Secondo: Dall'Invasione Napoleonica all-Ottobre del 1917 (History of Russia. Volume Two: Since the Invasion of Napoleon in October 1917)*. Firenze: La Nuova Italia, 1963. Print.

Glagoleva, Natalja, ed., et al. *Sovetskie Chudožestvennye Fil'my. Annotirovannyi Katalog (Annotated Catalog of Soviet Feature Films)*. Moscow: Iskusstvo, 1961–79. Print.

Gusman, Boris. "Dekabristy." *Pravda* 1 Mar. 1927 : 6. Print.

Hobsbawm, E. J., and Terence O. Ranger. *The Invention of Tradition*. Cambridge: Cambridge University Press, 1992. Print.

Ivanovskij, Aleksandr. "Dekabristy." *Sovetskij Ekran* 30 Mar. 1926: 4. Print.

Kenez, Peter. *The Birth of the Propaganda State*. Cambridge: Cambridge University Press, 1986. Print.

Kozincev, G. M. Archival Collection in TsGALI (Central State Archive of Literature and Art: Archival Collection, St. Petersburg). Serial no. 622–1–26. Print.

Lebedev, Nikolaj. *Očerk istorii kino SSSR. I. Nemoe Kino (The Outline of the History of the Cinema of the USSR Vol. 1: Silent Cinema)*. Moscow: Goskinoizdat, 1947. Trans. *Il cinema Muto Sovietico*. Torino: Einaudi, 1962. Print.

Lotman, Jurij, and Jurij Civ'jan. "SVD: Žanr Melodramy i Istorija" (SVD: History and the Melodramatic Genre). *Pervye Tynjanovskie čtenija. Tynjanovskij sbornik (The Tynjanov Collection: First Readings)*. Ed. M.O Čudakova. Riga: Zinatnie, 1984. 54–78. Print.

Mazour, Anatole G. *The First Russian Revolution, 1825: The Decembrist Movement, its Origins, Development, and Significance*. Stanford: Stanford University Press, 1961. Print.

Nečkina V., Milica, "Zagovor Zerentujskom Rudnik" (The Conspiracy in the Zerentuiskij Mine). *Krasnyj archiv* 13 (1925) : 258–79. Print.

Nekipelov, A.D., et al. *Novaja Rossijskaja Enciklopedija (New Russian Encyclopedia)*. Moscow: Dardan-Drejer Izdatel'stvo Enciklopedia, 2008. Print.

Nevelev, G.A. "P.E. Ščëgolev kak Istorik Dekabristkogo Dviženija" (P. E. Ščëgolev as a Historian of the Decembrist Movement). *Vestnik Leningradskogo Universiteta*, 20. 4 (1966): 6. Print.

O'Meara, Patrick. *K.F. Ryleev. A Political Biography of the Decembrist Poet*. Princeton: Princeton University Press, 1984. Print.

Perov, N. "Skol'ko Vybrošeno Deneg" (So Much Money Wasted). *Rabočaja Gazeta* 26 Aug. 1927 : 26. Print.

Pokrovskij, Michail N. *Russkaja Istorija v Samom Sžatom Očerke. Ot Drevnějših Vremen do Konca XIX Stoletija (A Concise Outline of Russian History from the Earliest Times*

*Unless otherwise stated, all translations in the Works Cited are by the author.

to the end of the Nineteenth Century). Moscow: Gosudarstvennoe Izdatel'stvo, 1920. Print.

Salomoni, Antonella. "Révolution Russe et les Archives. Un Savoir Historique d'État: les Archives Soviétiques." *Annales: Histoire, Science Sociales*, Jan.—Feb. 1995. Vol. 1: 3–10. Print.

Ščëgolev, Pavel, and Aleksej Tolstoj. "Polina Gebl.'" *Polnoe Sobranie Sočinenii* (*Complete Works*). Ed. Aleksej Tolstoj. Moscow-Leningrad: Izdatel'tsvo Chudožestvennoj Literature, 1949. Vol. 11: 505–42. Print.

_____. *Muzej revoljucij I* (*Museum of the Revolution I*). Petrograd: Izdatel'tsvo Chudožestvennoj Literature, 1923. Print.

_____. Archival Collection in IRLI-RAN (Institute of Russian Literature, St. Petersburg), Russian Academy of Sciences. Serial No. 627–3–52. Print.

Slonimskij, Aleksandr. *Černigovcy* (*Inhabitants of Černigov*). Moscow: Gosudarstvennoe Izdatel'stvo, 1928. Print.

S. V. D. Sojuz Velikogo Dela (*The Battle for the Great Cause*). Dir. Leonid Trauberg and Grigorij Kozincev. Perf. Emil Gal, Sergei Gerasimov, Konstantin Khokhlov. Sovkino, 1927. Film.

"S. V. D." *Večernaja Moskva* 9 (1927): 1. Print.

Trauberg, Leonid. "Iz Besedy s Režissërami G. Kozincevym i L. Traubergym" (A Conversation with the Directors G. Kocinsev and L. Trauberg). *Kino* 10 (1927). *TsGALI* 1–26: 42. Print.

Tynjanov, Jurij. "Feks." *Sovetskij Ekran* 2 Apr. 1929. Trans. Giusi Rapisarda. *Cinema e Avanguardia in Unione Soveitica* (Cinema and the Avant-garde in the Soviet Union). Roma: Officina Edizioni, 1975: 104. Print.

"The Physicists Have Known Sin": Hollywood's Depictions of the Manhattan Project, 1945–1995

A. Bowdoin Van Riper

It is now commonplace to say that July 16, 1945 — the day that the first atomic explosion split the night sky over a desolate patch of New Mexico desert — marked a watershed in the history of the United States and the world. Pronouncements that "this changes everything" have been cheapened by overuse, but here they are not only justified but necessary. The introduction of nuclear weapons into the world really did change everything: war, diplomacy, economics, society, culture, and — less obviously, but no less profoundly — science (Boyer; Winkler).

The story of the Manhattan Project — the three-year, multi-billion-dollar program to build the first atomic bombs — has been told scores of times in print. The stories of its principal scientists, brought from every corner of the United States and a dozen foreign countries to a remote New Mexico town called Los Alamos, are chronicled in novels (Smith), biographies (Bird; Lanouette), and histories (Rhodes) — but only rarely on screen. Over the first fifty years since Hiroshima, they were the focus of three Hollywood films and played supporting roles in three others. The first, *The Beginning or the End*, was completed in 1946 and released in 1947; the last, a miniseries titled *Hiroshima*, was aired on the Showtime cable network in 1995. In between came *Above and Beyond* in 1952; the made-for-television film *Enola Gay* in 1980; and *Fat Man and Little Boy* (along with the made-for-television production *Day One*) in 1989. Historical events are fixed, but our understanding of them is fluid. All six films depict the military-industrial-scientific *ménage-a-trois* that the Manhattan Project helped to create, but each adapts its retelling of those events—its judgment of the scientists' involvement in that then-nascent relationship—to reflect the times in which it was made. The release dates of the six films map, with uncanny precision, onto the peaks and valleys of the nuclear age. *The Beginning or the End* was released during America's postwar atomic monopoly, while *Above and Beyond* and *Enola Gay* appeared during the first and second peaks of Cold War tensions. *Day One* and *Fat Man and Little Boy* were conceived as the Soviet empire was weakening, and reached audiences in the year that it began to collapse. *Hiroshima* appeared after the collapse of the Soviet Union itself, amid the brief Indian summer of optimism and nostalgia that followed. Each film thus depicts the same historical events, the same characters, the same conflicts, and the same outcomes, but each adapts the protean story of the Manhattan Project to reflect—and shed light on—its own era's understanding of what the dawn of the atomic age meant. To watch the films in sequence is to see, in their serial adaptations of a single story, a time-lapsed history of America's evolving attitudes toward a nuclear-armed world.

Our adaptations of past events, whether into historical narrative or history-based drama, are origin myths for the present that we inhabit. They are designed to tell what was, but also to help us make sense of what is: to lend meaning to the world we see around us. As that world changes—showing us familiar elements from unfamiliar perspectives, rendering significant what once seemed inconsequential—the adaptations we create to explain its origins change as well. We look at the same historical events, and—with the passage of time—see different things. This essay explores the ways in which six film-makers, working at very five different moments in postwar American history, looked back at Los Alamos in 1944–1945 and saw six very different things.

The Manhattan Project and "Big Science"

The Manhattan Project deepened physicists' understanding of the interior of the atom and the forces that governed it. It drew them deeper into a world of tiny particles that moved at unimaginable speeds and behaved in incomprehensible ways and further widened the already yawning chasm between the world that physicists studied and the world of everyday experience. It also changed the way scientists worked, hastening the advent of "big science"—science done in big laboratories, using big machines attended by big staffs, and supported by big budgets underwritten by corporations or governments—as a dominant mode of research (Hughes). The era of the lone experimenter, the one-room laboratory, and the privately funded expedition was already in its twilight by the time the Manhattan Project began in earnest in 1942 (Nye 225–227). The world's centers of cutting-edge physics research — the Universities of Göttingen, Cambridge, and Chicago, the University of California at Berkeley, and the Massachusetts Institute of Technology among them — owed their reputations not only to brilliant individuals but to the research infrastructure that supported them. Research programs built around specialized instruments and purpose-built facilities were, by the mid–1940s, rapidly becoming the norm. Nuclear physicists were neither the inventors nor the sole beneficiaries of what Alvin Weinberg later dubbed "big science," but the Manhattan Project made them its most visible (and most visibly successful) practitioners. Massive particle accelerators—"atom smashers" to the popular press—became symbols of cutting-edge science in the immediate postwar era, as laboratory benches covered with elaborate glassware had been in the 1920s and 1930s (Gallison 1–17).

Big Science demanded big funding, and by the 1940s work at the cutting edge required infusions of cash on a scale that only corporations and national governments could provide. Dependence on expensive, purpose-built instruments, large teams, and specialized facilities made scientists dependent, in turn, on those funding sources, binding them to what retiring President Dwight D. Eisenhower would, in 1960, call the "military-industrial complex" (Eisenhower). In exchange for access to funds, facilities, and equipment, scientists accepted limits on what data they could share, and what colleagues they could share it with. They learned to function in a world where research was valued in direct proportion to its practical military and commercial applications, and where decisions about the value — or even the ethics— of such applications were firmly removed from their hands (Hughes 97–104). The rise of Big Science laid the groundwork for technologies that reshaped the postwar world: lasers, microelectronics, nuclear power plants, general-purpose computers, communication satellites, and rockets capable of reaching other worlds. It also made scientists complicit in the development of weapons that could, and in 1945 did, unleash destruction on a hitherto unimaginable scale.

The scientists of the Manhattan Project were the first to accept, with eyes open, the bargain implicit in the rise of Big Science. They did so in order to help solve what J. Robert Oppenheimer called the "technically sweet problem" of building an atomic bomb (Thorpe 223), but also because — as late as the early spring of 1945, when the first bombs were nearing completion — their vision of the bomb's purpose (defeating Hitler) to match that of the United States government. After Hiroshima, the scientists of the Manhattan Project also became the first to confront the side-effects of the bargain they had made:

a bitter combination of political impotence — dozens of them had entreated the Truman administration not to use the weapons against civilian populations without warning, and been rebuffed — and moral responsibility (Badash 48–54; Lifton and Mitchell 65–74). "In some sort of crude sense, which no vulgarity, no humor, no overstatement can quite extinguish," Oppenheimer wrote shortly after the end of the war, "the physicists have known sin; and this is a knowledge which they cannot lose" (Oppenheimer 11).

Uncertain Futures: *The Beginning or the End* (1947)

The United States was, in 1947, the world's only nuclear power, and a nuclear arms race was an abstract concept rather than a fact of geopolitical life. The harrowing descriptions of author John Hersey's *Hiroshima* was just beginning to be extrapolated into depictions of global nuclear war, and the surreal vocabulary strategists would one day use to describe it — "counterforce," "decapitation strike," "launch on warning," "massive retaliation," and "mutual assured destruction" — had yet to be invented.[1] The Baruch Plan, under which the United Nations would have taken control of all U.S. nuclear arms and enforced other powers' pledges not to build any, was still under active discussion and still seemed like it might represent the future. Presenting it to the United Nations on behalf of the United States, financier and diplomat Bernard Baruch declared:

> We are here to make a choice between the quick and the dead. That is our business. Behind the black portent of the new atomic age lies a hope which, seized upon with faith, can work our salvation. If we fail, then we have damned every man to be the slave of fear. Let us not deceive ourselves; we must elect world peace or world destruction [Baruch].

The promise of a Soviet bomb (achieved in 1949) caused the Baruch Plan to founder and made the arms race a reality, but in 1947 it was still possible for President Harry Truman to think about nuclear power in terms of its impact on humans in general, rather than on particular tribes of humans or the relations between them (Truman 91–96). It was also still possible to frame impact in the way that Baruch did, as a choice between opposites: elevation or damnation, Golden Age or Armageddon (Badash 68–79; Winkler 57–68; Powaski 29–45).

The Beginning or the End, released in 1947, comprehensively rewrites history in the process of adapting it as drama — concocting fictitious Japanese resistance over Hiroshima, imposing unanimity on deeply divided advisors, and giving wartime leaders the benefit of postwar hindsight — in order to endorse the Truman administration's position that the atomic bombing of Japan was righteous and justified (Broderick "Buck," 142–151). Simultaneously, however, it reflects the same postwar anxieties that lay behind the Baruch Plan (Reingold; Evans 23–41; Perrine 48–50; Shapiro 62–70; Hoberman 23–32). The film is framed as a message to the people of 2446: a brief prologue (purportedly a segment from an MGM newsreel) shows a cylindrical time capsule, containing a copy of the film as well as other records of the beginnings of the atomic era, being buried in a specially prepared vault in California. The title of the film and the act of creating the time capsule are, the newsreel's narrator intones, reflections of "the fear of people today that a future atomic war may destroy all humanity." The time capsule — and, by implication, the film — serve as "an enduring record" for future generations. "Come what may," the narrator concludes, "ours will be no lost race." The film proper begins with J. Robert Oppenheimer personally directing a message to the film's purported target audience: "you people of the twenty-fifth century." His lifetime, he explains, saw great technological progress, but also "87 million men and women" killed or wounded in two world wars, and now "the people of our era have unleashed the power that might — for all we know will — destroy human life on this Earth." Pausing for emphasis, Oppenheimer concludes: "We know the beginning. Only you of tomorrow, if there is a tomorrow, can know the end."

The film is steeped in the unselfconscious internationalism that flourished in the brief postwar moment that produced the Baruch Plan. The time capsule is buried under the watchful eyes of scientists, government officials, and senior military officers from the United States, the United Kingdom, and Canada ("the three nations that played the largest roles in unlocking the secrets of the atom," as the narrator of the newsreel points out), as well as the three whose call for international stewardship of nuclear arms led to the Baruch Plan. The newsreel narrator and Oppenheimer, who narrates the film itself, consistently use language that views humanity as a unified whole ("people today" and "people of our era") acknowledging neither national nor ideological boundaries. When the newsreel proclaims that "ours will be no lost race," it implies the entire human race; when Oppenheimer says "we," the clear meaning is not "we Americans" but "we human beings"; and when Matt Cochran (Tom Drake) — the young physicist who is the film's nominal hero — uses "we" and "us" he generally means not his colleagues or his countrymen but the world's population.

The scientific community functions, in *The Beginning or the End*, as a model of collective action. When Cochran remarks to Albert Einstein (Ludwig Stössel) that it is "all based on his theory," the great man firmly corrects him by reciting the names and nationalities of those who contributed: Marie Curie, a Pole; Ernest Rutherford, an Englishman; Enrico Fermi, an Italian; Otto Hahn, a German, and a half-dozen more.[2] A few moments later, the pattern is repeated when Oppenheimer, in voiceover narration, reels off a list of nuclear scientists hard at work in American universities before Pearl Harbor: Compton at Chicago, Lawrence at California, Urey at Columbia (John Hamilton), and (again) a half-dozen more.[3] Later still, the name-and-affiliation pattern is repeated a third time, as participants in a high-level planning meeting at the Pentagon announce themselves to the receptionist. The scientists, already familiar to the viewer from earlier scenes, declare themselves simply: "Chisholm, England [Richard Haydn] ... Wyatt, England [Hurd Hatfield] ... Bush, Office of Scientific Research and Development."[4] The representatives of industry are more explicit in their self-identification: "Teller, Chrysler Corporation ... Rafferty, Union Carbide ... P. C. Keith, Telex Corporation ... Willing, General Electric ... Carpenter, Dupont Company." The roll-call of names echo that in the "St. Crispin's Day" speech from Shakespeare's *Henry V* — Bedford and Exeter, Salisbury and Gloucester — evoking the image of a "band of brothers" united in a great cause.

The scientist-characters of *The Beginning or the End* depart, conspicuously, from their clearest cinematic antecedents. The historical scientists depicted in films such as *The Story of Louis Pasteur* (1936), *Dr. Ehrlich's Magic Bullet* (1940), and *Madame Curie* (1943) are lone heroes who struggle, supported by one or two loyal friends, against the closed-minded representatives of the scientific and political establishment (Frayling 133–164; Van Riper 67–74, 86–90, 135–141, 163–172). The "band of brothers" in wartime films such as *Destination Tokyo* (1942), *Air Force* (1943), and *Sahara* (1943) begin as conspicuously, symbolically diverse individuals who learn to work as a team for the Allied cause (Basinger 46–108). The heroes of *Captains of the Clouds* (1942) and *The Fighting Seabees* (1944), all specialist experts whose knowledge and skills are vital to the war effort, must similarly learn to submit to authority in order to make a contribution (Basinger 271–273). Cochran and the rest of the scientists in *Beginning* enter the story as a cohesive and disciplined team fully committed to cooperation with military and civilian leaders. While interpersonal conflict, among the scientists as individuals, and between the scientists and other groups (military officers or politicians), was all-pervasive in the real Manhattan Project, it is non-existent in the film adaptation.

Consistent with this, the individual scientists barely register as individuals. They have famous names — Enrico Fermi, Leo Szilard, Edward Teller — but they are faceless, muted, and interchangeable both with one another; Fermi is shorn of his sense of humor, Szilard of his moral qualms, and Teller of his ferocious intensity.[5] Einstein is gentle, grandfatherly, and oddly untroubled as — agreeing to alert Roosevelt to the possibility of an atomic bomb — he makes what he would later describe as the greatest mistake of his life. Vannevar Bush — the brilliant, iron-willed engineer who served as Roosevelt's de facto science advisor and as the administrative mastermind of the project (Zachary)—has the soft-spoken, pipe-smoking manner of a country doctor. Oppenheimer—intense, mercurial, and charismatic—is played as a short, mild-mannered, bespectacled nonentity by character actor Hume Cronyn, who specialized in such characters. Even Groves, the director of the Project—known for his force-of-nature personality—is portrayed by Brian Donlevy as merely brisk and efficient.[6] Like the industrialists who meet with them at the Pentagon, they are defined by their willingness to abandon individual motivations like profit, ambition, and curiosity in selfless pursuit of a greater goal.

The Beginning or the End ends with a scene that calls on humankind to exhibit a similar, collective spirit as it confronts the nascent Nuclear Age. Days after Hiroshima, Cochran's wife Ann (Beverly Tyler) sits at the Lincoln Memorial, reading his final letter from the Pacific. Though dying of radiation poisoning when he wrote it—the symbolic first victim of the Bomb—Matt is relentlessly upbeat. "In the past," he reassures her, "man has sought useless war, hunger and pain. He has often been stubborn and vile. Yet stubbornly he has stumbled out of the chaos, lifted his eyes, and gone on to make a better world." Now, presented with the secret of atomic energy, "men will learn to use this new knowledge well. They won't fail. For this is the timeless moment that gives us all a chance to prove that human beings are made in the image and likeness of God."

Scientists as Cold Warriors: *Above and Beyond* (1952) and *Enola Gay* (1980)

Cochran's closing speech, lofty and idealistic in 1947, would have seemed impossibly naive by 1952. Only five years separate *The Beginning or the End* from *Above and Beyond*—Hollywood's next film about the Manhattan Project—but the two films belong to different worlds. The announcement of the Truman Doctrine in 1947, the Soviet blockade of West Berlin (1948), the perceived "loss" of China to communism (1949), and the outbreak of the Korean War (1950) set the ideological stage for a four-decade Cold War. The rapid expansion of the American nuclear arsenal—from 6 bombs at the end of 1945 to over 1000 by the end of 1952—made sustained nuclear bombardment a realistic possibility: one that was considered (and rejected) both in 1948 and 1950. The Soviet Union's acquisition of its own atomic bombs—the first tested in 1949, and 50 stockpiled by the end of 1952—made nuclear war a theoretical possibility, and a nuclear arms race a virtual certainty (Winkler 61–83; Powaski 35–49). The hopes for a peaceful future embodied in the Baruch Plan and expressed in *The Beginning or the End* had crumbled by 1952. In its place stood the unsettling realization that nuclear weapons had increased war's potential for destruction without (necessarily) decreasing its likelihood.

Over the course of the Cold War, the growing sophistication of the super-powers' nuclear arsenals dampened some fears, but intensified others. Direct conflict grew less likely, but each new crisis or proxy war — Korea, Taiwan, Hungary, Berlin, Cuba, Vietnam, Syria, Iran, Afghanistan — raised the possibility that limited, conventional war could lead to global thermonuclear war (Newhouse; Bundy). Novels and films dramatized other possible triggers for war: a rogue commander in *Dr. Strangelove* (1964), equipment breakdown in *Fail-Safe* (1964), overreliance on computers in *War Games* (1983), miscommunication in *The Bedford Incident* (1965), or simply "the world going mad" in *On The Beach* (1959). A parallel thread in Cold War popular culture — from Ray Bradbury's short story "There Will Come Soft Rains" (1950) and Philip Wylie's novel *Tomorrow!* (1954) in the 1950s through the made-for-television films *The Day After* and *Testament* (both 1983)— depicted the likely consequences of nuclear war: massive casualties, social collapse, deformity and disease ... even extinction (Brians; Broderick, *Nuclear Films*).

Cold War popular culture also offered a countervailing narrative, however: one in which nuclear weapons enhance, rather than undermine, national security. The political leaders in this narrative are unfailingly judicious, the senior military officers invariably rational, and the men who control the weapons utterly competent (Call 100–131). *Above and Beyond* (1952) and its made-for-television remake *Enola Gay* (1980) focus on the third group, telling the story of the elite unit of B-29 bomber crews formed, and trained, to deliver the first atomic bombs. Colonel Paul Tibbets, who commanded the unit and led the attack on Hiroshima, is the central character in both films: a consummate professional who wrestles with his conscience (just long enough to establish that he has one) before the mission, but — once in the air —coolly and precisely does the job assigned to him.[7] The men who serve under Tibbets (collectively, the 509th Composite Group) display the same professionalism. Like him — and, the audience is invited to assume, like the men who fly the nuclear-armed bombers of 1952 and 1984 — they appear incapable of error or misjudgment. The nuclear weapons in their hands are ready for instant use if world events (as analyzed by judicious, rational leaders) require it, but safely under control until that moment comes (Evans 47–53; Hoberman 218–221; Perrine 50–55).

Broadly speaking, the scientists in both *Above and Beyond* and *Enola Gay* are, like the aircrew, servants of the state. They do not make policy, or even advise those who make it (as Einstein, Oppenheimer, and Bush do in *The Beginning or the End*), but only carry it out. In practice, however, these films treat the scientists as servants not just of the state but, specifically and directly, of the airmen. The scientists of the Manhattan Project act, in both films, as squires and armorers to the knights of the 509th Composite Group. One representative scene in *Above and Beyond* shows a group of scientists briefing Tibbets (Robert Taylor) on why the bomb must be exploded at a specific altitude. Aided by an elaborately detailed blackboard drawing of an airburst nuclear explosion over a city (chilling, in retrospect, but handled matter-of-factly), they show how the carefully calculated optimum altitude will maximize the size of the fireball and damage to the city. One of the film's few comic moments comes when Tibbets' wife (Eleanor Parker), to whom the nuclear physicists assigned to Wendover Air Force Base have been passed off as "sanitary engineers" working on the base sewer system, asks one of them to fix her kitchen sink. Based on an actual incident, the moment loses much of its comic impact because, in the context of the film, the befuddled scientist suffers no ego-deflating loss of status—merely a temporary shift from one technician-servant role to another. That his white outer garment is a tradesman's coverall, not a lab coat, underscores his place in the hierarchy.

Both *Above and Beyond* and *Enola Gay* regard scientists as useful, even valuable, so long as they know their place. Both films, however, include scenes in which they cease to be faithful servants: obstructing, rather than aiding, the military and (by extension) the nation. In *Above and Beyond*, their motivations are technical: concerned that the trigger mechanism for the Hiroshima bomb will not work properly, they ask that the bombing be delayed four months to allow for further tests. In *Enola Gay*, their concerns are ethical: troubled by the idea of using the bomb, without warning, against a civilian target, they call for a public demonstration in an isolated area that would (again) delay the actual attack for four months. Tibbets, in each case, slaps them down.[8] A delay of four months would, he sternly declares, lead to the unnecessary loss of thousands of American lives, and the bomb must therefore be used as soon as possible. The two scenes—each of which distorts the historical record to make its point—play on familiar stereotypes of scientists as dithering fussbudgets, obsessed with perfection and ethical niceties but blind to the complexities of the real world. Having established Tibbets' uncomplicated decisiveness and willingness to follow (just) orders as heroic, both *Above and Beyond* and *Enola Gay* portray the scientists' caution as misguided at best, and treasonous at worst.

Nuclear weapons were brand new in 1945, and the shape of the world they would create was still uncertain. *The Beginning or the End*, produced only a year later, captured that uncertainty and sense of infinite possibility; *Above and Beyond* did not and, perhaps, could not follow suit. The filmmakers knew too much, and the realities of the Cold War were too overwhelming, too all-pervasive, to set aside. *Above and Beyond* (and, by extension, *Enola*

Gay) are adaptations of the Manhattan Project story in which nuclear weapons, the alliance of science and industry that produced them, and the military infrastructure that stands ready to use them are taken for granted as facts of contemporary life. How the bomb came into being is irrelevant; what matters is how it can be used (or misused).

The Long Look Backward: *Day One* and *Fat Man and Little Boy* (1989)

The made-for-television film *Day One* and the theatrical film *Fat Man and Little Boy* were released in March and October, respectively, of the watershed year 1989. The Soviet empire was crumbling (the Berlin Wall would fall in mid–November), the Soviet Union itself was swaying, and Presidents Ronald Reagan and George H. W. Bush had — despite well-established credentials as Cold Warriors—committed the United States to its first significant nuclear arms reduction program. The Cold War was, if not yet past, showing encouraging signs of dying.

The two films adapt the same historical material as *The Beginning or the End* by portraying how science, industry, and the military came together to create the atomic bomb and usher in the nuclear age. Their perspective is shaped, however, by the forty years of Cold War history between them and the events they depict. *Beginning* asks: "What will come of this?" *Day One* and *Fat Man and Day One*, made as the Cold War was ending (though the filmmakers could not have been sure of that), ask: "How did we get here?" All three films contain essentially the same characters, but 1989 protagonists are subtly aware of what the future holds, in a way that the characters in *The Beginning or the End* are not. General Groves (Brian Dennehy), at one point in early in *Day One*, tells a roomful of physicists that if he is going to build a bomb factory, he needs to know whether to expect an output of 3 or 30 or 300 bombs a month. No one is shocked at the idea of such a factory (or at the implied assertion that nuclear weapons will become commonplace). Late in *Fat Man and Little Boy*, on the eve of the first bomb test, Dr. Richard Schoenfield (John C. McGinley), a (fictitious) friend of Oppenheimer (Dwight Schultz), confronts him with what he has done:

> "I've seen Oak Ridge, all right? And that place wasn't built to make one or two bombs, it was built to make thousands of 'em. Thousands. And pretty soon everybody's gonna have a bomb — they will — and what'll they do with 'em? Sit around and wait until they go off? And then we'll have one world full of [people], dying from the inside out. Is that what you're looking for? Cause *that's* the future you've made for us!"

Both films answer their question ("How did we get here?") by analyzing the partnership between American scientists and the military, as expressed through the relationship between Oppenheimer and Groves [Paul Newman]. *Fat Man and Little Boy* sees the relationship as inherently unequal, and paints Oppenheimer as a politically naïve innocent who gradually falls under the spell of the single-minded, manipulative Groves (Taylor 367–394; Perrine 60–65; Shapiro 70–72). Kitty Oppenheimer, played by Bonnie Bedelia as a worldly woman willing to speak truth to power, sardonically tells the general that they're "trying to seduce the same man." He bristles, but in the context of the film she is clearly right. Groves is a handsome and commanding figure, but also a master manipulator. He alternately flatters, bullies, and threatens Oppenheimer, sharing or withholding vital information about the course of the war so as to ensure that Oppenheimer remains committed to the project. At one point he forces Oppenheimer to break off his relationship with another would-be seducer: his long-time mistress Jean Tatlock (Natasha Richardson) who, because she is a communist, might compromise his ability to "perform." It is clear to the audience — but not to Oppenheimer — that Groves is using him to win the war and to advance his own career (which will be ruined if the bomb project fails to produce results). Like the duped, doomed protagonist of a film noir crime drama, Oppenheimer overestimates himself and underestimates his erstwhile partners, learning the truth too late. The closing titles reveal that, in 1954, Oppenheimer was stripped of his security clearance for opposing the hydrogen bomb. Ever the *ingénue*, he ends the film seduced and abandoned.

Day One, in contrast, portrays both Oppenheimer and Groves as consenting adults who enter into the relationship with their eyes more or less open (Perrine 55–60). Brian Dennehy's Groves is a more sympathetic figure than Paul Newman in *Fat Man*: used to precise answers, orderly job sites, and schedules that are accorded the status of holy writ, he finds most physicists vague, disorganized, and profoundly frustrating to deal with. (One of the film's small pleasures is that it adroitly captures the cultural differences between theoretical and experimental physicists.) He is initially drawn to Oppenheimer (David Strathairn) because he sees him as a kindred spirit — a man who gives precise answers rather than vague estimates, and who possesses the steely determination to urge the physicists onward in the same way that Groves drives construction crews. His relationship with Oppenheimer in *Day One* is not a seduction but a whirlwind courtship. Oppenheimer relishes the prospect of heading the largest scientific enterprise in history, and savors the "technically sweet" challenge of designing a working atomic bomb. He enters the relationship with his eyes open, knowing that Groves— and only Groves—can offer him such opportunities.

The Oppenheimer of *Day One*, however, is always fully aware of where his bargain with Groves will lead. Indeed, he proves to be Groves' equal as an operator and manipulator. When he and Groves go to Washington, late in the film, to discuss targeting options for the bomb with military and civilian leaders such as Secretary of State George Marshall (Hal Holbrook), Secretary of War Henry Stimson (Barnard Hughes) among others, they operate in an unacknowledged partnership, working together to steer the consensus toward using the bomb as quickly as possible and without warning, on a target that will give the clearest possible impression of its destructive power. Groves (despite his lack of combat experience) insists that the Japanese must be "shocked" and "crushed" into surrender. Oppenheimer (abandoning his usual crisp precision) is vague about why the bomb should not be demonstrated to Japanese observers in an uninhabited area would be, concluding that "I just don't favor that idea." Their sidelong glances at each other, however, suggest that each understands their real, shared motive: to have "their" bomb enter the public eye in the most spectacular and memorable fashion imaginable.

Oppenheimer is opposed, in both films, by fellow Manhattan Project scientists who reject his uncritical alliance of the military. These scientists are not, however, the disconnected ivory-tower intellectuals of *Above and Beyond* and *Enola Gay*, whose dithering endangers "American boys" fighting in the Pacific. They have deep, ethical reservations about what nuclear weapons could do to the postwar world, and express them forcefully and at length, in language calculated to resonate with viewers who (like the filmmakers) understand the destructive potential of nuclear weapons. "We are not in the army," Leo Szilard (Michael Tucker) tells a roomful of his colleagues after the targeting meeting in *Day One*, rejecting Oppenheimer's right to speak for them in striking a bargain with the military. "We are the men who conceived this bomb, and built it. And before God, and the world, we have the duty to see that it is used wisely. We will be held responsible." He invites them to sign a petition to President Truman (Richard Dysart), "stating that we are sacrificing everything good and moral that we believe in if we drop this bomb on people" (Lifton and Mitchell 65–74).

Szilard and others also speak for the film's modern audiences in passing judgment on Oppenheimer and Groves, suspecting what we already know. Schoenfield, railing at Oppenheimer in *Fat Man and Little Boy* after the death of a young physicist from radiation poisoning, yells at his departing boss through the window of an army staff car: "Hey, Oppenheimer! Oppenheimer! You oughta stop playing God, 'cause you're no good at it, and the position's taken!" Watching the first, successful bomb test from a bunker in the New Mexico desert in *Day One*, physicist Ken Bainbridge (Michael J. Reynolds) is more succinct, deflating Oppenheimer's awestruck reference to the Bahagavad Gita — "I am become Death, shatterer of worlds"— with a more prosaic judgment: "Yeah ... now we're all sons-of-bitches."

The Tides of History: *Hiroshima* (1995)

Hiroshima (1995) was, like *Day One*, produced for television — originally airing as a miniseries on the Showtime cable network. The Showtime miniseries was a curious hybrid: produced jointly by American and Japanese filmmakers, it combined episodes that adapted history into drama with "talking head" interviews interviews of Pacific War veterans from both sides, filmed against a simple black backdrop. Made to commemorate the fiftieth anniversary of the bombings, and the end of the war, it is the only one of the six films considered here explicitly designed to educate — as well as entertain — audiences. *Hiroshima*'s commemorative, overtly educational adaptation of the historical material gave it a strong backward-looking flavor; it was a look past, rather than at, the Cold War.

Only six years separated *Hiroshima* from *Day One* and *Fat Man and Little Boy*, but those years were as significant as the seven that divided *The Beginning or the End* from *Above and Beyond*. The Soviet Union had fallen, and Russia — which had inherited most of the Soviet nuclear arsenal and acquired the rest from Belarus, Ukraine and Kazakhstan by treaty — was cooperative and, seemingly, on the road to democracy (Cirincione et al., 365–382). Presidents Clinton and Yeltsin had ordered the technically trivial but symbolically major step of ordering the superpowers' nuclear missiles "detargeted" from one another; the nuclear ambitions of Iran and North Korea appeared manageable; and nuclear terrorism was still (at least in the public's view) the stuff of thrillers like Tom Clancy's novel *The Sum of All Fears* (1991) and John Woo's film *Broken Arrow* (1996). The Gulf War — despite involving multiple nuclear-armed states— had ended without going nuclear, and subsequent military operations in Somalia, Iraq and Bosnia had the character of police actions rather than full-scale combat (Atkinson 91–93; Halberstam). The Cold War and its threat of imminent nuclear attack had abated by 1995, and the United States was at the zenith of the geopolitical Indian summer that ended on the morning of September 11, 2001.

Hiroshima is thus, by virtue of both its timing and its commemorative intent, the only film about the Manhattan Project that is more concerned with the events of 1945 than with the world they brought into being. Alternating back and forth between Oak Ridge, Los Alamos, Okinawa, Washington, Tokyo, London, and the B–29 base on the Pacific island of Tinian, it documents the last months of the war — the political, military, social, and cultural context within which the first atomic bombs were used — in minute detail.

Its evident goal is to show the events, decisions, and assumptions that led both sides to make the choices they did: not to judge, but to explain.

When examining the work of the Manhattan Project scientists, *Hiroshima* implicitly rejects the positions taken by the earlier films. It suggests that they were neither visionaries out to reshape the world (as in *The Beginning or the End*) nor ivory-tower intellectuals hopelessly disconnected from it (as in *Above and Beyond* and *Enola Gay*); while Oppenheimer's actions were shaped neither by fatal naïveté (as in *Fat Man and Little Boy*) nor by vaulting ambition (as in *Day One*). *Hiroshima* portrays the scientists—and, for that matter, the politicians and generals with whom they worked—as capable-but-fallible individuals, who were obliged by the pressures of war to make momentous decisions under great pressure on the basis of limited and imperfect knowledge, and who sometimes misjudged.

The potential for misjudgment is compounded by the fact that, although the politicians and military officers in *Hiroshima* understand each other—and each other's frames of reference—well, neither truly understands (or is understood by) the scientists. Well-intentioned misjudgment and mutual incomprehension blend, with tragic effect, in a scene (unique to Hiroshima) in which Leo Szilard (Saul Rubinek) and two fellow scientists meet with Secretary-of-State-designate James Byrnes (Ken Jenkins) at his home.[9] "But we didn't know that," the courtly, southern-accented Byrnes says, responding to Szilard's frustration that the Manhattan Project was begun to counter a German atomic bomb project that, in retrospect, never came close to success. "We did what we had to do," he continues. "It's too late now." Szilard cuts him off with a frustrated wave. It is not too late, he argues, to save the world from a ruinous, potentially catastrophic nuclear arms race, so long as the United States does not use—does not even test—an atomic bomb. Byrnes, incredulous at the suggestion, delivers a lecture on the political reasons why such a course is impossible: the American people must be shown that the $2 billion spent on the Manhattan Project produced results, and Stalin must be shown the power of the bomb. If the bomb is used, Szilard retorts, then Byrnes and those who pushed for it will have "betrayed the only secret that is worth keeping. And what is the secret? The secret is *that it can be done.*" Soviet Russia is "desolated, almost exhausted by the war," and Stalin will not waste his country's few remaining resources on atomic weapons "unless he knows that it can be done. And then, when he knows that—God help them—he *will do it.*"

A similar gulf of understanding is apparent in an earlier meeting between Oppenheimer (Jeffrey DeMunn) and Groves (Richard D. Masur) in the forest outside Los Alamos. Both agree that, once complete, the bomb should be used as soon as possible, but from there their views diverge. Groves sees the bomb in uncomplicated, here-and-now terms as a tool to end the war and an instrument of revenge for Japanese atrocities. Oppenheimer sees it as a means to end the current war and perhaps to end all wars, but also as a "Faustian bargain" that places immense destructive power in the hands of deeply flawed individuals. "How much faith," he asks Groves rhetorically, "do you have in the human race?" The general, impatient with such philosophical meanderings, responds: "I will finish this bomb, doctor. We've come this far; there's no going back." Oppenheimer, looking past him and into the distance, takes a long drag from his cigarette before answering: "I agree: There is no going back. But isn't that the definition of Hell?"

The scientists in Hiroshima are, in a sense, tragic figures: smart enough to discern the future taking shape before them, but also realizing that—despite their best efforts—they can only alter its details, not its outlines. *Hiroshima* does not, however, play out as a tragedy. It knows—as its 1995 audience knew—that the story had a happy ending for all but those who died from the effects of the bomb. It knows that Japan rose again, that the Soviet Union fell, and that the bombs dropped on Hiroshima and Nagasaki were the last used in anger. It knows, above all, that the nuclear arms race that began in 1945—although every bit as perilous as Oppenheimer and Szilard feared it would be, it ended with civilization still intact. Armed with that knowledge, *Hiroshima* adapts the events of 1945 with a sense of distance that the other Manhattan Project films lack. Even the sepia-tinted cinematography of the dramatized scenes seems to say: "These were things that happened a long time ago. They belong to the past, not the present."

Conclusion: The Open Ledger

Nuclear weapons, of course, do not belong to the past. They persist, despite the best efforts of well-intentioned individuals and organizations to control them, and the "nuclear club"—comprised of nine members at the time of writing—is far more likely to expand than shrink. Terrorist attacks with stolen nuclear warheads or stolen radioactive materials have yet to take place, but in the first decade of the twenty-first century they have been reclassified from novelists' and filmmakers' fantasies to serious threats to national security. The alliance between science and the military established at Oak Ridge and Los Alamos—though less noticed and less demonized, today, than the alliance between science and industry—remains as strong and, at least in some fields, as vital to Big Science as it was in the 1940s. The Manhattan Project remains the iconic scientific enterprise of the twentieth century, overshadowing even the exploration of the solar system and the sequencing of the human genome. It continues to fascinate us in because, for better or worse, we continue to live in the world that it made.

The Manhattan Project's image in popular culture has been repeatedly adapted to fit the social and political landscape of successive eras. A symbol of the transformative and redemptive power of science in the uncertain years immediately following World War II, it became (during the "long, twilight struggle" of the Cold War) a model of how scientists—properly managed by a firm, preferably military, hand—could contribute to national defense. As the Cold War waned and the superpowers counted its cost, the Manhattan Project was readapted as a cautionary tale, while Oppenheimer became a tragic figure whose professional ambition trumped his ethical judgment. The Cold War safely past, the decisions to build and use the bomb became — on the occasion of its fiftieth anniversary — an object lesson in the complexity of recovering, much less fully understanding, the contexts within which such decisions were made. Each of those eras had its Manhattan Project film(s), and *Hiroshima* is unlikely to be the last. The films will continue because, for better or worse, nuclear weapons will remain a fixture of our world, and our need to make sense of them, and the changes their existence has wrought, will persist.

Hollywood's six (to date) Manhattan Project films are reflections of that need. They purport to depict history — to pull back the veils drawn over past events by time and secrecy, and show audiences what really happened in the New Mexico desert in 1944 and 1945 — but in fact they do something more subtle and complex. The films, even *The Beginning or the End* and *Hiroshima* with their quasi-documentary trappings, do not simply chronicle historical events; rather they adapt them to serve other purposes—for example, reframing them as drama, and also as explanation. In doing so, they fulfill two of history's principal functions: telling memorable stories about the past events that created our present, and imputing significance to those events that —for its audiences— allows past and present to illuminate each other.

Notes

1. Journalist and author John Hersey wrote a four-part article on Hiroshima for *The New Yorker* that recounted the effects of the atomic bombing through the eyes of six survivors with whom he conducted extensive interviews. It was intended for serial publication in four successive issues of the magazine, but the editors chose to run it as the entire contents of the August 31, 1946, issue. Widely discussed at the time of its magazine publication, *Hiroshima* was quickly issues as a book: first by the Book of the Month Club, which distributed it free to thousands of members, and then by trade publisher Alfred A. Knopf.

2. Marie Sklodowska Curie (1867–1934) discovered the radioactive elements radium and polonium and formulated a general theory of radioactivity. The achievements of New Zealand–born Ernest Rutherford (1871–1937), sometimes described as the "father of nuclear physics," include the discovery of the atomic nucleus, the concept of radioactive half-life, and the first splitting of the

atom, among many others. Otto Hahn (1879–1968), along with Lise Meitner (1878–1968) and Fritz Strassman (1902–1980), discovered nuclear fission in 1938.

3. Arthur Holly Compton (1892–1962), played by Moroni Olsen in the film, did pioneering work on X–rays and other forms of nuclear radiation, and invented the "cloud chamber" technique for studying subatomic particles. Nuclear physicist Ernest Orlando Lawrence (1901–1958), played by James Bush in the film, invented the cyclotron: a massive device (popularly known as an "atom smasher") with which scientists could produce collisions between atomic nuclei and fast-moving subatomic particles, sometimes producing entirely new elements. Harold C. Urey (1893–1981), who does not appear in the film, pioneered techniques for isolating heavy isotopes of hydrogen (which led to the discovery of deuterium) and for separating isotopes of uranium. All three won Nobel Prizes: Compton in 1927, Urey in 1934, and Lawrence in 1939.

4. Chisholm is played by Richard Haydn and Wyatt by Hurd Hatfield. Vannevar Bush (1890–1974), played in the film by Jonathan Hale, was an engineer who served as President Franklin D. Roosevelt's principal science advisor and director of the wartime Office of Special Projects. His 1947 *Atlantic Monthly* magazine article "As We May Think," described a desktop information-storage and retrieval device (the "Memex") that anticipated many of the features of the personal computer.

5. Enrico Fermi (1901–1954) and Leo Szilard (1898–1964), refugee physicists from Italy and Hungary respectively, conceived the idea of using uranium fuel rods separated by blocks of pure carbon to create a sustained nuclear chain reaction. They patented their design for a nuclear reactor in 1936, and oversaw construction of the world's first experimental reactor at the University of Chicago in 1942. Szilard's countryman Edward Teller (1908–2003), also a close friend of Fermi's, was instrumental in developing nuclear chain-reactions into the basis for a usable bomb, and in developing — after World War II — the fusion-based "super" or hydrogen bomb. In the film, Fermi is played by Joseph Calleia and Szilard by John Gallaudet; the actor playing Teller is uncredited and not listed in standard reference sources.

6. Kenneth D. Nichols, who worked under Groves on the Manhattan Project, described him thus: "First, General Groves is the biggest S.O.B. I have ever worked for. He is most demanding. He is most critical. He is always a driver, never a praiser. He is abrasive and sarcastic. He disregards all normal organizational channels. He is extremely intelligent. He has the guts to make difficult, timely decisions. He is the most egotistical man I know. He knows he is right and so sticks by his decision. He abounds with energy and expects everyone to work as hard or even harder than he does" (Nichols 108).

7. Scenes of Tibbets wrestling with his conscience were added at the behest of the United States Air Force, which feared that film showing Tibbetts untroubled by the mission (though he had repeatedly and unequivocally declared this to be the case) would allow Soviet propagandists to depict American pilots as ruthless killers unmoved even by the deaths of hundreds of thousands (Hoberman 220–221).

8. In *Enola Gay*, Tibbets is played by Patrick Duffy.

9. Byrnes also appears in *Day One*, where (in a small irony) he is portrayed by Hume Cronyn: the same actor who, forty-two years earlier, had played Oppenheimer in *The Beginning or the End*.

Works Cited

Above and Beyond. Dir. Melvin Frank, Norman Panama. Perf. Robert Taylor, Eleanor Parker. MGM, 1952. Film.

Air Force. Dir. Howard Hawks. Perf. John Garfield, Gig Young. Warner Bros., 1943. Film.

Atkinson, Rick. *Crusade: The Untold Story of the Persian Gulf War.* Boston: Houghton Mifflin, 1993. Print.

Badash, Lawrence. *Scientists and the Development of Nuclear Weapons: From Fission to the Limited Test Ban Treaty, 1945–1963.* Atlantic Highlands, NJ: Humanities Press, 1995. Print.

Baruch, Bernard. "The Baruch Plan." *The Atomic Archive.* Web. 12 Mar. 2012.

Basinger, Jeanine. *The World War II Combat Film: Anatomy of a Genre.* Middletown, CT: Wesleyan University Press, 2003. Print.

The Bedford Incident. Dir. James B. Harris. Perf. Richard Widmark, Sidney Poitier. Columbia Pictures, 1965. Film.
The Beginning or the End. Dir. Norman Taurog. Perf. Brian Donlevy, Robert Walker, Tom Drake. MGM, 1947. Film.
Bird, Kai. *American Prometheus: The Triumph and Tragedy of J. Robert Oppenheimer.* New York: Knopf, 2005. Print.
Boyer, Paul R. *By The Bomb's Early Light: American Thought and Culture at the Dawn of the Atomic Age, 1945–1950.* New York: Pantheon, 1985. Print.
Brians, Paul. *Nuclear Holocausts: Atomic War in Fiction, 1895–1984.* Kent, OH: Kent State Univesrity Press, 1987. Print.
Broderick, Mick. "'The Buck Stops Here': Hiroshima Revisionism in the Truman Years." *Filling The Hole in the Nuclear Future: Art and Popular Culture Respond to the Bomb.* Ed. Robert Jacobs. Lanham, MD: Lexington Books, 2010. 135–148. Print.
_____. *Nuclear Films: A Filmography and Critical Analysis of International Feature-Length Films Dealing with Aliens, Terrorism, and Holocaust.* Jefferson, NC: McFarland, 1992. Print.
Broken Arrow. Dir. John Woo. Perf. John Travolta, Christian Slater. Twentieth Century–Fox, 1996. Film.
Bundy, McGeorge. *Danger and Survival: Choices About the Bomb in the First Fifty Years.* New York: Random House, 1988. Print.
Captains of the Clouds. Dir. Michael Curtiz. Perf. James Cagney, Dennis Morgan. Warner Bros. 1942. Film.
Cirincione, Joseph, Jon B. Wulfstahl, and Miriam Rajkumar. *Deadly Arsenals: Tracking Weapons of Mass Destruction,* 2d ed. Washington, DC: Carnegie Endowment for International Peace, 2005. Print.
The Day After. Dir. Nicholas Meyer. Perf. Jason Robards, JoBeth Williams. ABC Circle Films, 1983. TV Film.
Day One. Dir. Joseph Sargent. Perf. Brian Dennehy, David Strathairn, Michael Tucker. Spelling Entertainment, 1989. TV Film.
Destination Tokyo. Dir. Delmer Davies. Perf. Cary Grant, John Garfield, Alan Hale. Warner Bros., 1943. Film.
Dr. Ehrlich's Magic Bullet. Dir. William Dieterle. Perf. Edward G. Robinson, Ruth Gordon, Otto Kruger. Warner Bros., 1940. Film.
Dr. Strangelove. Dir. Stanley Kubrick. Perf. Peter Sellers, George C. Scott. Columbia Pictures, 1964. Film.
Eisenhower, Dwight D. "Military-Industrial Complex Speech." 1961. *The Avalon Project.* Web. 17 Mar. 2012.
Enola Gay. Dir. David Lowell Rich. Perf. Billy Crystal, Kim Darby, Patrick Duffy. Viacom Productions, 1980. TV Film.
Evans, Joyce A. *Celluloid Mushroom Clouds: Hollywood and the Atomic Bomb.* Boulder, CO: Westview Press, 1998. Print.
Fail Safe. Dir. Stephen Frears. Perf. Walter Cronkite, Richard Dreyfuss. Maysville Pictures/ Warner Bros. Television, 2000. TV Film.
Fat Man and Little Boy. Dir. Roland Joffé. Perf. Paul Newman, Dwight Schultz, Bonnie Bedelia. Paramount Pictures, 1989. Film.
The Fighting Seabees. Dir. Edward Ludwig. Perf. John Wayne, Susan Hayward, Dennis O'Keefe. Republic Pictures, 1944. Film.
Frayling, Christopher. *Mad, Bad, and Dangerous? The Scientist in the Cinema.* London: Reaktion Books, 2005. Print.
Galison, Peter. "The Many Faces of Big Science." *Big Science: The Growth of Large Scale Research.* Eds. Peter Galison and Bruce Hevly. Stanford: Stanford University Press, 1992. 1–17. Print.

Halberstam, David. *War in a Time of Peace: Bush, Clinton, and the Generals.* New York: Scribners, 2001. Print.

Hersey, John. *Hiroshima.* New York: Alfred A. Knopf, 1946. Print.

Hiroshima. Dir. Koreyoshi Kurahara, Roger Spottiswoode. Perf. Lynne Adams, Wesley Addy, Allen Altman. 1995. TV Film.

Hoberman, J. *An Army of Phantoms: American Movies and the Making of the Cold War.* New York: New Press, 2011. Print.

Hughes, Jeff. *The Manhattan Project: Big Science and the Atomic Bomb.* New York: Columbia University Press, 2003. Print.

Lanouette, William, and Bella Silard. *Genius in the Shadows: A Biography of Leo Szilard, the Man Behind the Bomb.* New York: Scribners, 1992. Print.

Lifton, Robert Jay, and Greg Mitchell. *Hiroshima in America: A Half-Century of Denial.* New York: Avon, 1986. Print.

Madame Curie. Dir. Mervyn LeRoy. Perf. Greer Garson, Walter Pidgeon. MGM, 1943. Film.

"The Manhattan Project: Making the Atomic Bomb." *The Atomic Archive.* Web. 12 Mar. 2012.

Newhouse, John. *War and Peace in the Nuclear Age.* New York: Knopf, 1989. Print.

Nichols, Kenneth D. *The Road to Trinity.* New York: William Morrow, 1987. Print.

Nye, Mary Jo. *Before Big Science: The Pursuit of Modern Chemistry and Physics, 1800–1940.* Cambridge: Harvard University Press, 1999. Print.

On the Beach. Dir. Stanley Kramer. Perf. Gregory Peck, Ava Gardner, Fred Astaire. Stanley Kramer Productions, 1959. Film.

Oppenheimer, J. Robert. *Physics in the Contemporary World* [The Arthur D. Little Memorial Lecture]. Portland, ME: Anthoensen Press, 1947. Print.

Perrine, Toni A. *Film and the Nuclear Age: Representing Cultural Anxiety.* London and New York: Routledge, 1998. Print.

Powaski, Ronald. *Marching to Armageddon: The United States and the Nuclear Arms Race, 1939 to the Present.* New York: Oxford University Press, 1987. Print.

Reingold, Nathan. "Metro-Goldwyn-Mayer Meets the Atomic Bomb." *Expository Science: Forms and Functions of Popularization.* Eds. Terry Shinn and Richard Whitley. Dordrecht: D. Reidel, 1985. 229–245. Print.

Rhodes, Richard. *The Making of the Atomic Bomb.* New York: Simon & Schuster, 1986. Print.

Sahara. Dir. Zoltan Korda. Perf. Humphrey Bogart, Bruce Bennett, J. Carrol Naish. Columbia Pictures, 1943. Film.

Shapiro, Jerome Franklin. *Atomic Bomb Cinema: The Apocalyptic Imagination on Film.* Abingdon, UK: Psychology Press, 2002. Print.

Smith, Martin Cruz. *Stallion Gate.* New York: Random House, 1986. Print.

The Story of Louis Pasteur. Dir. William Dieterle. Perf. Paul Muni, Josephine Hutchinson. First National Productions, 1936. Film.

The Sum of All Fears. Dir. Phil Alden Robinson. Perf. Ben Affleck, Morgan Freeman, James Cromwell. Paramount Pictures, 2002. Film.

Taylor, Brian C. "*Fat Man and Little Boy*: The Cinematic Representation of Interests in the Nuclear Weapons Organization." *Critical Studies in Mass Communication* 10.4 (1993): 367–394. Print.

Testament. Dir. Lynne Littman. Perf. Jane Alexander, William Devane. Paramount Pictures, 1983. Film.

Thorpe, Charles. *Oppenheimer: The Tragic Intellect.* Chicago: University of Chicago Press, 2006. Print.

Truman, Harry S. "The Baruch Plan" [Memo from Harry S. Truman to Bernard Baruch,

May 7, 1946]. *The American Atom: A Documentary History of Nuclear Policies from the Discovery of Fission to the Present,* 2d ed. Eds. Phillip Louis Cantleon, Richard G. Hewlett, and Robert Chadwell Williams. Philadelphia: University of Pennsylvania Press, 1991. Print.

Van Riper, A. Bowdoin. *A Biographical Encyclopedia of Scientists and Inventors in American Film and Television.* Lanham, MD: Scarecrow Press, 2011. Print.

War Games. Dir. John Badham. Perf. Matthew Broderick, Ally Sheedy, John Wood. MGM, 1983. Film.

Weinberg, Alvin M. *Reflections on Big Science.* Cambridge: MA: MIT Press, 1967. Print.

Winkler, Alan M. *Life Under a Cloud: America and the Atom.* Urbana: University of Illinois Press, 2003. Print.

Zachary, G. Paschal. "Vannevar Bush Backs the Bomb." *Bulletin of the Atomic Scientists,* Dec. 1992: 24–31. Print.

Adapting History
and the History of Adaptation

CLARE FOSTER

Many classicists have welcomed the resurgence of ancient history films in the shape of, say, *Gladiator* (2000) or *300* (2007) as a good thing for their discipline, and evidence of a renewed popular interest in the ancient past.[1] In this, they have often taken an explicitly casual attitude towards the inaccuracy of such films in relation to the actuality which is the matter of their own expertise: as if any history is better than no history at all. But this apparent resistance to correct in the very constituencies who might be expected to find offence deserves further scrutiny. There are many factors at play, not least of which is the status of Classics as a discrete subject in education, which has seen its numbers drop dramatically in the past three decades (Lister 1; Forrest 143–154).[2] Ideas of "the truth" in works of fiction, or of the relationship between scholarly expertise and popular culture, are so difficult to distinguish that it is arguably entirely inappropriate to invoke high, or intellectual standards in the context of a work of popular entertainment whose primary aim is to make money. Yet these intellectual standards are allegedly important to the filmmakers. In the "making of" extra feature on the DVD release of *Troy* (2004), Nigel Phelps, production designer, said of the set: "It was important to Wolfgang [Petersen] that it was as authentic as possible," and an anonymous "classicist" from British Columbia is filmed saying it was "amazing" to walk through the set, "just like Troy 6 unfolding in front of her eyes" ("From Ruins to Reality"). Or as Zack Snyder said of the film *300* (2007): "the events are 90% accurate. It's just in the visualization that it's crazy. A lot of people are like 'you're debauching history!' I'm like 'have you read it?' I've shown this movie to world-class historians who've said it's amazing. They can't believe it's as accurate as it is" (Snyder). And while ancient historians, seeing *300* as merely popular fashion or commercial opportunism, rather than assuming the discourse of implicitly authoritative public statement, might understandably treat it colloquially, even collusively, as a kind of "knowing" self-reflexive joke, for those living outside western Europe or the United States this film is not a light matter. Nor is it trivial for historians who study the use of film as an ideological tool, such as Martin Ruehl who works on Nazi cinema (Ruehl and Machtans).[3] This essay suggests that the way a film like *300* "uses" history (and the fact this is not contested more), reveals interesting "truths" about its own originating historical context — contemporary western culture.

To be fair to classicists, the films' and filmmakers' claims to accuracy are, of course, both serious and not, as they themselves admit. In the same "making of'" DVD Phelps contradicts himself, saying that the set was precisely "where we really threw accuracy out of the window — 'cos the biggest statue there [in the supposedly 'real' Troy] was only ten feet tall [...] it was quite a bit smaller, the buildings were smaller — less majestic for the movie [...] to get the big landscapes, the big epic sweeps [we had to make it bigger]." Phelps expresses pride in the forty-foot walls and their pyrotechnic destruction: "[It was] the biggest use of propane [to make a burning city sequence] since *Gone With the Wind*." ("From Ruins to Reality"). In the same interview that Snyder claimed *300* was "90% accurate," he defended the charge that the film had offended members of other cultures by saying: "If anyone is offended by it, I'm deeply sorry because that's not the intention of the movie at all. To me, it's a work of fantasy: it's not intended *to depict any culture in a realistic way*. That's just not what the movie is"(Snyder) (italics mine). He emphasizes the extent to which the film strove to remain faithful to an entirely different source, the cult comic book by Frank Miller, whose ideological mission is an ongoing public matter of patriotic pride (Miller *300*, Moody). Miller defends the film *300* on the grounds that it was meant to be political, comparing America's need to respond to Al Qaeda with the need to respond to Hitler and the Japanese bombing of Pearl Harbor (Miller, "Talk"). As Edith Hall has pointed out, the decision to greenlight *300* was indirectly encouraged by the Bush administration, understandably keen to boost patriotism and a sense of national identity after 9/11 (Hall). After Hollywood leaders met with White House officials to discuss how they could help in the "War on Terror," MPAA President Jack Valenti issued a statement in which he said not only could films influence domestic opinion, but "the American entertainment industry has a unique capacity to reach audiences *worldwide* with *important messages*" (qtd. in Hall) (italics mine). Insofar as "history" *per se*, however professionally or not engaged in, might be seen as associated with skeptical, subject-positioned, self-conscious inquiry, this is a pretty clear indication that it is not a preoccupation or concern of a film like *300*. Nor is it likely that a culture that celebrates such a comic, videogame, and film would place a high value on the political power of knowledge, critical thinking, and curiosity. There are anomalies here worth exploring.

The reference to *Gone with the Wind* as a "source" to which the film *Troy* was also consciously referring is good example of the principal point of Maria Wyke's book on ancient Rome in film, *Projecting the Past* (1997): that the cinematic "history" being represented in these films is far more important than any notional actual past (Wyke). Even if those "really very small houses" (Phelps' phrase) were a city in some meaningful sense (although there is no evidence to suggest that such a city was ever more than a fiction in the first place), that belief would have no impact on the demands of the generic expectations at play. The film *Troy* is indeed a telling window onto a historical period: the nineteenth century, from which its cinematic antecedents—films like *Cabiria* (1914), *The Last Days of Pompeii* (1935, 1959), and *Cleopatra* (1934, 1963) themselves derive, drawing on spectacular theatre, and spectacularly successful historical novels. In the United States ownership of Lew Wallace's book *Ben-Hur* (1880), for example, was topped only by the Bible by 1900, and it remained the best-selling book ever until the mid–1930s, when Margaret Mitchell's *Gone with the Wind* exceeded it. Twenty million people saw the stage show of Ben Hur between 1899 and 1920 (Lifson 1).

Interestingly, these ancient historical novels appeared on the scene as part of a fierce negotiation of precisely the kinds of terminological "cans of worms" we now appear to be keen to avoid opening: the meaning of the incorporation of literal elements of "the truth" in a work of fiction; and the role of authoritative expertise in works of mass appeal. Simon Goldhill has recently argued that these novels, which themselves explicitly "discuss [the way scholarship and imagination should interact] to produce a true picture of the past" (Goldhill 159), appear at this time partly because the impact of scientific thought had caused an "aggressive realignment [...] of the relation of the past to the present as the prime explanatory model of things" (164–5). Geology and archaeology, in particular, were undoing previous knowledge, and undermining the veracity of the Bible (much archaeology was embarked on responsively, in order to prove its historicity). According to Goldhill, a pro–Christian desire to counter Edward Gibbon's searing critique of Christianity in *The Decline and Fall of the Roman Empire* (1772–9), was a key reason ancient-Rome set historical novels emerged, beginning with Bulwer-Lytton's *The Last Days of Pompeii* (1834); these works of fiction about "the truth" were a Christian reaction — especially in their embedding of "miracles"— against the enlightenment rationalism Gibbon and his ilk represented (Goldhill 166–

169). Their agenda in mixing one kind of truth — the literal, scientific, objective — with another — the Truth of Christ (another phrase which appears in this period is "true in spirit") was explicit. It made the idea of the "authentic" inherently a site of contest.

The romantic *Waverley* novels of Sir Walter Scott, appearing from 1814 onwards, have also been credited with launching the "historical novel" genre, and the idea of "authenticity" as a disputed value, but for a different reason. According to Barbara Bell, these works are not involved with the era's defining crisis of faith and doubt, but nevertheless seminally associated with the emergence of "authenticity" as a concept. Their sequential publication was closely involved with the commercial promotion of touring adapted stage productions of the books, which Scott himself attempted to police in association with his publishers (Bell). Bell's latest research suggests that the public dialogue between the theatrical audiences (who were largely the fans of Scott's books) and promoters of these shows, and between author and publishers, helped give rise to the idea of Scott's "authentic" text, and of Scotland's "authentic" historical past (there were arguments over the inaccurate use of tartans, for example) as recognizable, "original," and contestable "objects" which were sacred, and authoritative precisely in their "originality." We might choose to see in these stage productions of popular literature the emergence of what we today call adaptation, in the sense that as a term, it denotes a relationship to a recognized or declared source-text.

Space does not permit either a historical or theoretical survey of "adaptation," but it is worth briefly making some observations about how it is currently perceived in practice. In a recent (albeit highly unscientific) poll of fifty British undergraduates who were asked to write their definition on notecards during a lecture, their responses were predictable: "something which has been made from something else"; "a rework of an original text for a live or recorded production"; "the creative process of using a primary source material that in some way inspires a secondary material"; and "changing an original concept and putting your own unique spin on it."[4] In other words, the source text was not only present, but its recognition was itself the point.

Adaptation, as a label of choice, is a rhetorical term: a declaration that relationship to a stated source is a key part of a work's meaning.[5] For closeness of correspondence does not in itself conjure, or define it: we do not typically call Shakespeare's *Comedy of Errors* an adaptation of Plautus's *Brothers Menaechmi*, for example, although the most characteristic elements of the ancient comedy — its plot, tone and spirit — and chunks of verbatim text are lifted from the Latin. Conversely, it was so important to Darius Merjui, when he could not get the rights to J. D. Salinger's *Franny and Zooey* (1955), that he described his film *Pari* (1995) as an adaptation of Salinger, even though the correspondences between the two texts are highly theoretical and by no means obvious. Vocabulary like "reworking," "based on" and "inspired by" are available as alternatives: if the term adaptation is used, the role of the source text in active, co-present relation to the new work is signaled as important.

But with sources which are *repeatedly* adapted—canonical texts, or historical genres—there develops an implicit assumption that the reason for making an adaptation has to do with a (communally recognized) inherent quality, interest, or value of the source. In response precisely to being repeatedly reproduced or adapted, there evolves an assumption that the original is valuable *qua* original—in its very originality or integrity. It is differentiated from adapted versions of it, which are thus positioned as secondary, sequential, or inferior (and multiple: another aspect of the construct of the "original" is its supposed singularity, or uniqueness). As John Berger argued about oil painting in *Ways of Seeing*, the concept of originality is itself created by reproduction (Berger 19–33). In other words, not only is there a co-presence of texts in relationship, but there is also the assumption of obligation to the source. It is a self-sustaining circle, where the value of the "original" is increased and confirmed precisely by its repeated adaptation. We could call this a process of "classicalization"[6]: as Charles Martindale says, "a classic [is] a text whose "iterability" is a function of its capacity [...] for continued re-appropriation by readers" (52). But once these associations attach to the term, adaptation, as popularly understood, becomes essentially a paradox. If referencing a collectively *recognizable* "original," adaptation invokes the assumptions of translation ("as close to the original as possible") while at the same time functioning as the term to denote its effective absence. Adaptations sell themselves on the basis of relation to originals whose value they cannot, by definition as copies, effectively equal. It is the idea of an attempt at such a paradoxical goal which prompts the term into existence—as opposed to translation, where the source-text clearly takes priority.

Not only is this paradox very similar to the paradox of claiming a work of fiction is as "truthful" as possible, but both arguably have their origins in the early nineteenth century, when the advent of mass reproduction, mass literacy, and the beginnings of a consumer culture, helped give rise to precisely this concept of the original text, or past. When Bulwer-Lytton was inventing the historical novel in the 1830s, Pompeii and Herculaneum were being (supposedly scientifically) excavated: the "past" as a matter of fact, of actual objects, was taking shape. Over a decade earlier, Lord Elgin had struggled to sell his marbles to the British government (for what was then a government-financed and very "British" Museum): they turned him down in 1811, and five years later it still took months of parliamentary debate before the government was finally persuaded of the merits of the "originals," as opposed to plaster casting, which had already become common practice in the major museums of Europe (Settis 69–71). Originality was a romantic notion, but not a value in and of itself. This would change with the acceptance of scientific method as a new universal standard, or arbiter of value; a focus on the biography of the artist or author, and with it, new ideas of the integrity of the text or artwork; and the corresponding advent of major copyright legislation in 1833 and 1842 and the emergence of the modern art market.[7] All these developments combined to make the very idea of a "true" or original "text" or historical past a key site of contest; and the value of originality not only a cherished, but a highly visible cultural assumption.

Indeed, so embedded is this assumption of the cherished original today ('the film is never as good as the book') that it is hard it to believe it was not always so. But ancient literature itself arguably suggests a highly collegiate concept of competition between equal texts, in a kind of celebration of intertextuality itself: with sequence, but without any sense of "reverse" moral loading.[8] During historical periods when there is a fundamental association of art with illusionism, it is easier to imagine how relationships between works, even between works in different media, such as painting, sculpture, literature, or theatre, can be seen as sibling aspects of a totalized notion of "art," in which they all participate in parallel gestures. For the Greeks and Romans, this "game" with the real, and "games" between recognizable works and their sources, was fundamental to their notion of culture itself (Beard and Henderson 105). Ironically, it was these classical cultures which became, during the nineteenth century, positioned as the symbolic origins of an emergent European identity: Greek and Roman texts and objects were read as "original authorities," and as part of a chronologically progressive view of history.[9] But before such a notion of history, and before mass copying, there was no inherently unequal relationship between one text as source, and another as its adaptation. Similarly in nonwestern cultures there is far less emphasis placed on notions of authenticity and originality, as Judy Wakabayashi explains with explicit reference to South and Southeast Asia:

> [C]apitalist notions of ownership of the text and copyright — deriving partly from the fixedness and authoritativeness imparted by printing, are linked to [...] reverence for the written word, and a highly developed sense that [it] expresses the thoughts of individuals [...] this differs from traditional notions in South and South-East Asia where public/private boundaries are less delineated, multiple retellings make authorship (often anonymous) of little interest, and there is "creative disrespect" [...] concepts of originality, authorship, and the translator's subservience to the author, along with closer adherence to the original [...] are western imports [27].

An example of this difference is the recent treatment by the massive film and television industries in India of the Mahabarata cycle of myths. Superficially, the plethora of films, both live action and animated, which have come out in the last two decades about this pantheon of divine characters, would appear to have many similarities to the Greek myth-inspired retellings which have come out of Hollywood. Both references, in works of popular culture for the 21st century, supposed cultural origins. But the difference is that the Indian films explicitly show the gods, and their supernatural activities: there is no claim to history, no investment in actual fact. By contrast the 2004 film *Troy*— a city and a story which is famous in more literate circles precisely for its "fictionality"— styles itself as history, and removes the essential frame of the gods, who direct events in a way which makes us empathize with the ignorant humans. With no gods to make sense of the plot, Priam (Peter O'Toole) is given the absurd expository line, to explain why he and the Trojans will not simply "give Helen back" to save their city: "I suppose fighting for love is as good a cause as any other."

In this gesture towards history we might see that films like *Troy* and other ancient history films are channeling a Victorian debate about authenticity, as much as the subjects and titles of the Victorian popular books and plays they explicitly reference. Tension between popular and élite, familiar and foreign, entertainment and science, fiction and truth: these nineteenth century issues were absorbed into the new technology as much as nineteenth century stories. Zack Snyder's declarations of accuracy, accompanied by their immediate contradiction, are Victorian gestures, and speak to a long-established desire for, yet simultaneous distrust of, expertise in American political culture.

It is no accident that film studies is where Anglophone academic discussion of adaptation begins, as the advent of film, as a quintessentially popular medium, had the effect of vividly highlighting these already established debates. In other words, the paradox of adaptation is not only similar to, but part of paradoxical claims that accuracy is both important and not, or that their adaptation of history is partially "true." The paradoxes are part of each other, not only in terms of the hagiography of a notional original, but in terms of an implicit address to multiple — and often contradictory — audiences. For if we accept that adaptation connotes the simultaneous co-presence of two texts (in unequal relationship), then these also imply the simultaneous co-presence of two audiences (in implicitly unequal relationship): those who recognize something of the source text being alluded to; and those who have no knowledge of it. It is not that the latter audience is less important — on the contrary, no one would question that the new work, especially in the context of the film business, must stand in its own right, without requiring direct knowledge of the source to be appreciated. In this respect adaptations not only foreground their ability to be polysemically interpreted, but stand for the very polysemy of interpretation itself. Adaptation can be seen as a meeting point for audiences. It is, in many ways, about audiences: it is certainly about the present audience, the "us" consuming the new work in relation to all the "other" audiences we might imagine. What we do or do not recognize, or can or cannot relate to, enacts who "we" are. In this sense, not only does the success of a film like *300* not necessarily reveal an increase in popular interest in ancient history, but it may arguably indicate the opposite. But who would willingly point this out? Certainly not the film industry, which always stands to gain by inclusivity, as well as by sustaining the idea of the "history" brand.

For it is not Christian faith which is now at stake in harnessing the power of the "truth"—however piecemeal, decontextualized, or theoretically unsubstantiated—but dollars. The dollar value of being able to appeal simultaneously to two contradictory audiences helps explain many of the anomalies in recent tent-pole releases, which claim to be "based on" either literature or history (which because of their high production costs, most ancient history films are). Opening weekend theatrical grosses are important, which are dependent on pre-selling the concept to what is principally a demographic of boys aged 12–25 who play computer games (the revenues from which now significantly outstrip those from theatrical release).[10] Hence the destruction of the city as the third act of *Troy*: it is not the *Iliad* or even Greek myth being adapted here, but every recognizable popular cultural association with ancient Greece as a world. But long term sell-through potential is also important, so lovers of history receive consideration as a secondary target audience, a demographic in which women over 30 figure highly: hence the opening slug-line with date, location and map: familiar tropes of "history" films.

Indeed, the film industry skillfully exploits what are now established inherent paradoxes of adapting history. Marketing departments can explicitly foreground what they assume is the popularly-acknowledged "impossibility" of satisfying multiple audience agendas, or the conflicting needs of "truth" versus "story." In this they are served by ancient film historians Robert Rosenstone, who discusses such films in terms of the "true or false" debate.[11] Ever since D. W. Griffith claimed that "educators" told him a film "can impress upon a people as much of the truth of history in an evening as many months of study will accomplish" (qtd. in Rosenstone 11–12), comparison of the effectiveness of history films versus history has continued to the present day (White 1193–9). Natalie Zemon Davis argues film is a "source of valuable and even innovative historical vision" (11), and Rosenstone claims the central question of his 2006 book *History on Film/Film on History* is "How do you tell the past?" (9). But we would not ask this of, say, Shakespeare's history plays. We would not suggest that in *Henry V*, or *Richard III*, Shakespeare was trying to tell the past, or struggling to find the best way to do it. On the contrary, both Shakespeare scholars and popular audiences expect to look at the contextual politics of early seventeenth century Britain to explain what these gestures towards history might have meant in their Elizabethan context. Yet history films are still discussed as forms of historiography ("historiophoty," to use White's exploratory term [1193–99]) without much attention paid to the history brand as an aspect of selling. Few discuss period accuracy in terms of the producers' imperative to demonstrate concern for fidelity to the truth, while at the same time entirely disregard it in relation to a film's other, more economically significant, agenda.

There are many reasons why the ancient history brand, in the shape of such big-budget films, is on the upswing at present: none, however, requires the presumption of an increase in interest in ancient history *per se*. The fact there are currently six Pompeii films in development has more to do with the decline of talent-financed, character-driven narrative films (since the 1980s' heyday of $20 million payouts for Arnold Schwarznegger, Tom Cruise et al.) in favour of material-driven event films. These offer eventhood and maximum afterlife potential for the diverse exploitation of rights in multiple media and platforms, for which the film release is the advertising leader. The ancient world, because of the role of Greek mythology and Roman history in school curricula, is already associated with juvenile audiences: but so are most of the ancillary revenues (especially computer games and merchandising) behind such tentpole releases: it is a perfect match. Bill Broyles' current adaptation of *The Odyssey* is accordingly being developed without the (more adult) sexual relationships so central to Homer's original.

Keeping the focus on an apparent concern for authenticity distracts our attention not only from these types of economic determinants, but also from the film's ideological import: indeed, from the ideological import of this very true or false debate. Snyder, significantly, first defended the historicity of *300* in the context of what he called "huge sensitivity about East versus West with the studio" (qtd. in Crabtree) and the controversial reception of the film at its Berlin film festival premiere, when early commentators, both positive and negative, connected the jingoistic message to America, rather than Herodotus (Schnack, McCarthy). In this light, the apparent contradiction in his statement that the film is both "a work of fantasy" and "90% accurate" makes sense.

In conclusion, I have briefly ventured into what are obviously fraught and amorphous concepts—history and adaptation—for two reasons; first, to suggest how much we may have to gain by repositioning our perception of these concepts as an aspect of a specifically western popular culture, in tension with a specifically western intellectual tradition; and second, to suggest that precisely because adaptations of historical events reveal such intellectual tensions. There is such a vast range of potential participations in the actual, real or true, it is not whether such films are "true" or not, but rather what the claims to be "true" or not are performing for the work that we should examine.

Notes

1. Outreach projects for classics in general, especially in schools, celebrate films as a shot in the arm for a beleaguered subject.

2. In Britain recently there were 600 candidates for A-level Ancient History, compared to, for example, 80,000 in Psychology, a subject which did not exist 15 years ago; there was a single candidate from state schools taking A-level ancient Greek, which they had studied by correspondence course. It was only in 1920 that ancient Greek was abolished as a requirement for Oxford and Cambridge (Latin was abolished as a requirement in 1960).

3. Nor for others familiar with the role of Sparta in general in German nationalism and the third Reich (Roche 2012).

4. At Greenwich University, London, January 21, 2010. The learners were from a mixture of creative writing, media and film studies.

5. Translation, because it is a literal impossibility, is also more usefully viewed as a rhetorical, rather than empirical descriptor ("as close to the original as possible"). Both terms also have a separate legal function in intellectual property law which I do not address here.

6. Alternatively defined as "social legitimation" by Bordieu (491); or "normative excellence" by Schein (78).

7. For example, the sale of the Beckford collection (1823), followed by that of Horace Walpole (1842) Bernal (1855) and Rogers (1856).

8. For "intertextuality" in Roman literature, see Fowler; for wider context, Taplin.

9. The characteristic of classical art and literature as collegiate and knowing game-playing, an essentially social phenomenon about audience knowledge and identity, was correspondingly given short shrift.

10. The industry consequently distinguishes such tentpole releases, whose profitability depends on the diverse exploitation of rights in the concept or characters, from so-called "execution-dependent" films i.e., films which will make money or not according to what they are actually like to watch.

11. Kathleen Coleman believes that rendering the past accurately in film is "very hard to achieve" (47).

Works Cited

Beard, Mary, and John Henderson. *Classical Art: From Greece to Rome.* Oxford History of Art. Oxford: Oxford University Press, 2001. Print.

Bell, Barbara. "...taken from the original": Word, Image, and the Drive for Authenticity in Early Stagings of the Works of Walter Scott." *Shared Visions: Art, Theatre and Visual Culture in the Nineteenth Century.* University of Warwick. 11 Feb. 2012. Lecture.

Berger, John. *Ways of Seeing.* Harmondsworth: Pelican, 1972. Print.

Bordieu, Pierre. *Distinction: a Social Critique of the Judgment of Taste.* Trans. Richard Nice. Cambridge: Harvard University Press, 1984. Print.

Cabiria. Dir. Giovanni Pastrone. Perf. Italia Almirante-Manzini, Lidia Quaranta. Itala Film, 1914. Film.

Cleopatra. Dir. Cecil B. DeMille. Perf. Claudette Colbert, Warren William, Henry Wilcoxon. Paramount Pictures, 1934. Film.

_____. Dir. Joseph L. Mankiewicz. Perf. Elizabeth Taylor, Richard Burton, Rex Harrison. Twentieth Century–Fox, 1963. Film.

Coleman, Kathleen. "The Pedant Goes to Hollywood." *Gladiator: Film and History*. Ed. Martin M. Winkler. Oxford and Malden, MA: Blackwell, 2004. 45–52. Print.

Crabtree, Sheigh. "Giving 300 Movie a Comic Book Grandeur." *Los Angeles Times* 4 Mar. 2007. Web. 27 Mar. 2012.

Davis, Natalie Zemon. *Slaves on Screen: Film and Historical Vision*. Cambridge: Harvard Univerity Press, 2000. Print.

Forrest, Martin. *Modernising the Classics: A Study in Curriculum Development*. Exeter: Exeter University Press, 1996. Print.

Fowler, Don. "On the Shoulders of Giants: Intertextuality and Classical Studies." *Materiali e Discussioni per l'Analisi dei Testi Classici* 39 (1997): 13–34. Print.

"From Ruins to Reality." Extra feature on the DVD Release of *Troy*. Perf. Eric Bana, Devid Benioff, Lesley Fitton. Warner Bros., 2005. Film.

Gladiator. Dir. Ridley Scott. Perf. Russell Crowe, Richard Harris, Oliver Reed. Dreamworks SKG/ Universal Pictures, 2000. Film.

Goldhill, Simon. *Victorian Culture and Classical Antiquity: Art, Opera, Fiction and the Proclamation of Modernity*. Princeton: Princeton University Press, 2011. Print.

Gone with the Wind. Dir. Victor Fleming. Perf. Clark Gable, Vivien Leigh, Leslie Howard. Selznick International/ MGM, 1939. Film.

Hall, Edith. "Hollywood Versus Ahmadinejad: Conquering the East in the Third-millennial Western Cinema." University of London. 28 May 2008. Lecture.

The Last Days of Pompeii. Dir. Ernest B. Schoedsack. Perf. Preston Foster, Basil Rathbone. RKO Radio Pictures, 1935. Film.

_____. Dir. Mario Bonnard. Perf. Steve Reeves, Christine Kaufmann. Cinematografica Associati, 1959. Film.

Lifson, Amy. "Ben Hur: The Book that shook the World." *Humanities* 30.6 (Nov./Dec. 2009): n. pag. Web. 26 Mar. 2012.

Lister, Bob. *Changing Classics in Schools*. Cambridge: Cambridge University Press, 2007. Print.

Martindale, Charles. "Redeeming the Text: Latin Poetry and the Hermeneutics of Reception." *Arion* 3rd Series 1.3 (1991): 45–75. Print.

McCarthy, Todd. "300." *Variety* 9 Mar. 2007. Web. 23 Mar. 2012.

Miller, Frank. "Talk of the Nation." *NPR* 24 Jan. 2007. Web. 29 Mar. 2012.

_____. *300*. New York: Dark Horse, 1999. Print.

Moody, Rick. "Frank Miller and the Rise of Cryptofascist Hollywood." *The Guardian* (London) 24 Nov. 2011. Web. 28 Mar. 2012.

Rosenstone, Robert. *History on Film, Film on History*. London: Longman/Pearson, 2006. Print.

Ruehl, Martin A., and Karen Machtans, eds. *Hitler — Films from Germany: History, Cinema, and Politics Since 1945*. Basingstoke and New York: Palgrave, 2012. Print.

Salinger, J. D. *Franny and Zooey*. New York: Little, Brown, 1955. Print.

Schein, Seth. "'Our Debt to Greece and Rome: Canon, Class and Ideology.'" *A Companion to Classical Receptions*. Eds. Lorna Hardwick and Christopher Stray. Oxford and Malden, MA: Blackwell, 2007. 75–85. Print.

Schnack, A. J. "When Blogs Attack: Did *300* really get booed in Berlin?" *MCN Blogs* 20 Feb. 2007. Web. 28 Mar. 2012.

Settis, Salvatore. *The Future of the Classical*. Trans. Allan Cameron. Cambridge: Polity Press, 2006. Print.

Snyder, Zack. Interview with Rob Carnevale. *Indie London* (2007). Web. 28 Mar. 2012.
Taplin, Oliver, ed. *Literature in the Roman World*. Oxford: Oxford University Press, 2000. Print.
300. Dir. Zack Snyder. Perf. Gerard Butler, Lena Headey, David Wenham. Warner Bros., 2006. Film.
Troy. Dir. Wolfgang Petersen. Perf. Brad Pitt, Eric Bana, Orlando Bloom. Warner Bros., 2004. Film.
Wakabayashi, Judy. "Secular translation: Asian Perpectives." *The Oxford Handbook of Translation Studies*. Eds. Kirsten Malmkjaer and Kevin Windle. Oxford: Oxford Univerity Press, 2011. 23–36. Print.
White, Hayden. "Historiography and Historiophoty." *The American Historical Review* 93.5 (1988): 1193–99. Print.
"White House Meets with Hollywood Leaders to Explore Ways to Win War Against Terror." Public Radio Newswire, 11 Nov. 2001. Web. Feb. 24. 2012.

The Crisis of Adapting History in Zimbabwe

Sabelo J. Ndlovu-Gatsheni

The adaptation of history played a central role in how a nationalist hegemonic monologue has been inscribed by the Zimbabwe African National Union-Patriotic Front (ZANU-PF) on the Zimbabwean political landscape over the past three decades. In the recent years, this history has engaged with counter-hegemonic alternative histories emerging from civil society, opposition circles and pressure groups from the marginalized Matabeleland region. At the centre of these contestations are questions of what constitutes national history, who owns and authorizes it, who articulates it, how has history been deployed as a means to claim ownership of the nation, control of the state, power, belonging, citizenship, memory and the future of the country.

Arif Dirlik makes an important scholarly intervention on the complex subject of construction of identities. His core thesis is that many contemporary identities that are accepted and taken for granted as "civilizational" and "national" were not only hybrid, but products of prior processes of "colonizations, resistances, and encounters of various kinds, including oppression, exploitation, and forceful conversion, which are now buried under celebrations of historical emergence" (Dirlik 443). The issue of "historical emergence" has been addressed by Tony Bennett, who sees it as part of "nationing history" and "historicizing the nation" (141). This process is evident in Zimbabwean nationalism that emerged as an anti-colonial force while creating and articulating alternative national histories. The process of "historicizing the nation" involved dominant nationalist movements working tirelessly to blend their hagiographies into the history of the nation.

This essay shows how the Zimbabwe African National Union-Patriotic

Front (ZANU-PF) government has used a combination of history and politics to adapt the ideology of *Chimurenga* and to justify the strategy of *Gukurahundi* to build what Norma Kriger (72–76) terms a "party-nation" and a "party-state" as well as to maintain a hegemonic and monologic narrative of the nation. For the purposes of this essay we will define *Chimurenga* as the belief in the birth of a nation out of a history of revolution dating back to the 1890s, whereas the strategy of *Gukurahundi* entails the annihilation of all opponents and political critics of ZANU-PF. We begin by exploring how ZANU (before it became ZANU-PF in 1980) adapted the history of African resistance to construct the ideology of *Chimurenga* and thereby claim to be the divinely ordained heir to the nationalist revolutionary spirit. The ideology of *Chimurenga* has also been used to claim primal political legitimacy by ZANU-PF, and hence do away with general elections. It was this idea that inspired Mugabe to arrogantly tell the electorate in 2008.

> You can vote for them [MDC], but that would be a wasted vote. I am telling you. You would just be cheating yourself. There is no way we can allow them to rule this country. Never, ever. We have a job to do, to protect our heritage. The MDC will not rule this country. It will never, ever happen. We will never allow it [qtd. in Solidarity Peace Trust 12].

When ZANU-PF assumed state power in 1980, it made sure that the party was indistinguishable from the state and nation. This was done through selective deployment of history, memory and commemoration to establish hegemony and claim uncontested political legitimacy. The process involved the creative adaptation of ZANU-PF's hagiography and national history resulting in "rule by historiography" (Ranger, "Rule by Historiography" 217; Ranger, "Uses and Abuses of History" 1–15). The political use of memorialization and commemoration dated back to the time of the war of liberation. For example, the Chinhoyi Battle of 1966 (where seven Zimbabwe African National Liberation Army (ZANLA) cadres of ZANU's military wing were killed by Rhodesia forces), and the death of Leopold Takawira (a ZANU leader who died in detention due to diabetes) were commemorated annually in Mozambique in the late 1970s. The Chinhoyi Battle was celebrated as *Chimurenga Day*, marking the beginning of the armed liberation struggle (Ndlovu-Gatsheni and Willems, "Making Sense of Cultural Nationalism" 956). ZANU-PF wanted to be remembered as the originator of the armed struggle: as articulated by Robert Mugabe, the party was the carrier of the "burden of history" enjoying the oracular blessings of Nehanda and Kaguvi (Mugabe 48–56; Chitando, "Down with the Devil"1–8; Chitando, "In the Beginning Was Land" 220–239).

The essay is divided into five sections. The first explains the politics behind the ideology of *Chimurenga* as a central pillar in ZANU-PF's adaptation of national history. The second traces *Gukurahundi* as a strategy of annihilating all those opposed to the *Chimurenga* ideology and ZANU-PF hegemony. The third section explains the changing and additional adaptations of the nation-state ideology by ZANU-PF since 2000, while the fourth section focuses on the equally complex and ambiguous politics of counter-hegemonic initiatives. The final section assesses the impact of ZANU-PF nationalist monologue on the character of current national politics.

Chimurenga, "Nationing History" and "Historicizing the Nation"

The ideology of *Chimurenga* is a tale of the invention of a complex politically usable narrative by ZANU in its bid to construct a postcolonial nation, unite people, gain popularity, and assume political power at the end of settler colonial rule. It was and is premised on the doctrine of permanent nationalist revolution against imperialism and colonialism. The early historical work of the liberal British historian Terence Ranger (who was sympathetic to the cause of Zimbabwean nationalism), provided the historical raw materials for the nationalist adaptation of the ideology of *Chimurenga*. He argued that the risings of 1896–7 were informed by the creative strengths of Shona and Ndebele culture, as well as pre-colonial religious leaders, especially Shona spirit mediums (*Revolt in Southern Rhodesia* 10–12). These religious leaders provided prophetic and ideological inspiration — something also evident in the mass nationalism of the 1960s. These voices were populist and dismissive of all those who did not support them on the grounds of challenging the spirit of national unity. Their key tropes were consistent anti-colonial rhetoric and anti-western "bogus universalism" (Ranger, "Nationalist Historiography" 215).

Ranger argues that, in its early days, the ideology of *Chimurenga* drew its power from "nationalist historiography," which was informed by universal ideas of human progress and modernity; hence it espoused projects of modernization, reform and even socialist egalitarianism ("Uses and Abuses" 8). It matured into the historiography of nationalism that "raised questions about the nature of nationalism and about the course of its development" ("Uses and Abuses of History" 8). It also revealed "struggles within the struggle," by tracing the roots of rural and urban nationalism, and raising questions about nationalist violence. Ranger's ideas were appropriated by local leaders such as the Reverend Ndabaningi Sithole, the founder president of ZANU and first Commander-in-Chief of ZANLA, to motivate party members to fight against the white-dominated Rhodesian government. In 1976 at the Geneva Conference, Bishop Abel Muzorewa, leader of the moderate and internally-based United African National Council (UANC) used the same ideas to connect the liberation struggle to primary resistance (Ranger, "The People in African Resistance" 128).

The notion of *Chimurenga* became very popular with ZANU nationalists in particular. The term was derived from Murenga; the name of a spiritual medium that Ranger identified as actively involved in the 1896–7 war of resistance, providing desperately needed ideological support to the African fighting forces. Murenga is said to have administered some traditional war medicine to the African fighting forces that would make them invulnerable and immune to white forces' bullets (*Revolt in Southern Rhodesia* 217–220). The term *Chimurenga* began to be widely used in the 1970s by the nationalists— mainly in the ZANU and its fighting wing (ZANLA)— as a vernacular name for the armed liberation struggle against the settler colonial state. It was also used as an ideological thread capturing the undying spirit of African resistance to colonialism, running from the primary resistance of the 1890s to the fast-track land reform program that was christened by Robert Mugabe as the *Third Chimurenga* (Mugabe 10–14). In 1977 the ideology of *Chimurenga* was reinvoked as part of a call for a total transformation of Zimbabwean society and its people (ZIPA 1–8; Moore 73–103). As ZIPA (Zimbabwe People's Army) put it:

> The word drives its meaning from the national liberation war, fought by our fore-fathers in 1896–7 uprising in opposition to the British domination and occupation. The 1896–7 armed uprising by the entire Zimbabwe masses was one of the stiffest resistances registered by the African people in Southern Africa to colonial rule and imperial advance in the region [...] This was a total war to expel foreign capitalists and imperialists from the soil of Zimbabwe [...] This is a source of inspiration which guides us in our current struggle against the [white] Smith regime. [...] With the defeat of our forefathers in 1897 African resistance went underground up to the mid-fifties when African nationalism came to the fore [ZIPA 1–8; Ranger, "The People in African Resistance" 125–146].

In the ideology of *Chimurenga* the nation was born as a result of two violent conflicts of the 1890s and the 1970s. *Chimurenga* was adapted to justify any form of nationalist violence — even against citizens of the postcolonial state. It was also used to validate election-related unrest, beginning with the independence elections of 1980 (Kriger, "ZANU (FP) Strategies" 1–34). Every time when ZANU-PF was cornered politically by the opposition forces, it has tendentiously reminded people that *"Zimbabwe ndeyeropa"* (Zimbabwe came after a violent war of liberation), and that it would go back to the bush to fight another *Chimurenga* if defeated in an election (Sithole and Makumbe 133–135).

The ideology of *Chimurenga* was also mobilized to identify the enemies of ZANU-PF; those who participated in the liberation struggle (*Second Chimurenga*) were considered patriots, while those who remained on the outside, as well as white commercial farmers, were considered the enemies of the nation (Ndlovu-Gatsheni and Muzondidya, "Introduction" 2–5). Blessings-Miles Tendi argued in 2010 that *Chimurenga* was not just a "fabrication" or a "polemic," but played on real grievances and its "narrative must be taken seriously" (Tendi 2; Muzondidya, "Jambanja" 321–325; Muzondidya, "The Zimbabwean Crisis" 5–38). While the *Third Chimurenga* was popularly dubbed *Hondo Yeminda* (the war for land reclamation), President Mugabe articulated it broadly as the "conquest of conquest," marking the triumphalism of black sovereignty over white settlers (Ndlovu-Gatsheni, "Making Sense" 1139–1158). One of its core objectives was to mobilize the strategy of *Gukurahundi*, and thereby authorize a culture of violence. The ideology of *Chimurenga* and violence were closely interwoven, "because it sees itself as a doctrine of revolution" (Ranger, "Uses and Abuses of History" 8).

Gukurahundi and ZANU-PF Hegemony

The term *Gukurahundi* was a colloquial expression which in Shona language means "the storm that destroys everything" ("Elections in Zimbabwe" 133). This early storm often destroyed crops and weeds, huts and forests, people and animals, opening the way for a new ecological order. ZANU officially adopted *Gukurahundi* as a strategy in 1979 and that year was declared *Gore reGukurahundi* (*The Year of the Storm*) ("Elections in Zimbabwe" 133). This storm was presented in revolutionary terms as a destruction of the white settler regime, the "internal settlement puppets," the capitalist system and any other obstacles to ZANU ascendancy to power ("Elections in Zimbabwe" 133; *Breaking the Silence* 2–10). Sithole and Makumbe described *Gukurahundi* as "policy of annihilation; annihilating the opposition (black and white)" ("Elections in Zimbabwe" 133).

Eddison Zvobgo (the Information and Publicity Secretary of ZANU in the late 1970s), drew up a hit list comprised of high-ranking personalities of the "internal settlement" parties that were singled out for killing ("Elections in Zimbabwe" 133; Hudson 9–15; Ndlovu-Gatsheni, "Puppets" 345–397). In 2004, ZANU-PF produced another list that included Archbishop Pius Ncube, a severe critic of Mugabe; Trevor Ncube, owner of critical independent newspapers; Geoffrey Nyarota, a journalist critical of Mugabe regime; leaders of MDC including Morgan Tsvangirai, Welshman Ncube, Paul Themba Nyathi opposed to Mugabe regime; Wilfred Mhanda, leader of the Zimbabwe Liberators Platform that opposed ZANU-PF storm-troopers; and the critical public intellectuals including Brian Raftopoulos, John Makumbe and Love-more Madhuku (ZANU-PF 1–5; Tendi 87–90).

While the strategy of *Gukurahundi* was openly adopted as party policy in 1979, it is traceable to the formation of ZANU in 1963. Its philosophy of confrontation entailed embracing violence as a legitimate political tool in the fight for independence and the destruction of one's opponents. Zvobgo wrote of the "ZANU Idea" which he elaborated as the "gun idea" that was funda-mental to the party's ideology of confrontation ("The ZANU Idea" 23). The deployment of the strategy of *Gukurahundi* within ZANU was necessitated by internal crises of the 1970s such as the Nhari rebellion of 1974 that became the first major disciplinary case to be dealt with by the *Dare reChimurenga* (High Command) (Mazarire 571–591). Thomas Nhari and his comrades were eliminated through execution on the orders of Josiah Tongogara. By the end of that decade the strategy of *Gukurahundi* was used to eliminate counter-revolutionaries as well as exposing sell-outs. Parades were used to identify trai-tors, while *Pungwes* (night vigils) fulfilled a similar function in operational zones inside Rhodesia. Mazarire identified what was termed *chikaribotso* whereby pit structures were dug and built to keep prisoners underground (581).

Mugabe and his party were swept to power in 1980 through the strategy of *Gukurahundi* ("Elections in Zimbabwe"134). When ZANU-PF assumed state power, the state employed a *Gukurahundi* style of violence in Matabele-land and the Midlands regions. An estimated 20,000 civilians lost their lives as ZANU-PF pushed for a one-party state. Joshua Nkomo, PF-ZAPU, ex-ZIPRA and all supporters of PF-ZAPU had to be annihilated as they stood in the way of ZANU-PF's assertion and consolidation of hegemony through impo-sition of a one-party state (Shaw 373–394; Mandaza and Sachikonye 6–12).

ZANU-PF has continued to use the strategy of *Gukurahundi* each time its hegemony is threatened. Such military style operations as *Operation Murambatsvina* (*Operation Urban Clean-Up*) of 2005; *Operation Mavhoter-apapi* (*Where did you put your vote?*) in April-August 2008; *Operation Chi-mumumu* (that involved abductions of opposition and civil society figures) all testify to the popularity of the strategy (Ndlovu-Gatsheni "Do Zimbab-weans Exist?" 81–89). Stephen Chan argued that Mugabe was "refusing to allow the Chimurenga to die," and interpreted this as a sign that Zimbabwe "can never be cleansed because there cannot be an end to fighting and that for him [Mugabe] to fight is more important than to be cleansed" (183).

The Carnivalization and Commemoration of *Chimurenga*

When the ZANU-PF regime's popularity in the late 1990s and beginning of 2000 reached its lowest ebb, it resurrected the ideology of *Chimurenga* and celebrated the strategy of *Gukurahundi,* boasting that the party and its leaders had "degrees in violence" while at the same time trying to re-mobilize the populace around memories of the liberation struggle (Blair 8–13). The policy of reconciliation was repudiated and replaced by an adaptation of the discourse of cultural nationalism (Dorman 50; Ndlovu-Gatsheni and Willems, "Making Sense of Cultural Nationalism" 945–960; Ndlovu-Gatsheni, "Beyond the Drama" 37–79). The post–2000 nation was defined in autochthonic and nativist terms including attributing "new meanings to concepts such as independence, heroes, and unity in the changed political context of the 2000s" (Ndlovu-Gatsheni and Willems, "Making Sense of Cultural Nationalism" 945). President Mugabe popularized the idea of "Zimbabwe for Zimbabweans," including Occidentalizing white citizens (Muchemwa 505; Ndlovu-Gatsheni, "Africa for Africans" 61–78). Musical galas were introduced to reinforce this ideology.

Sabelo Ndlovu-Gatsheni and Wendy Willems suggest that "the national imaginary that was promoted through music galas was by no means an inclusive definition of the nation, but should be seen as the mediation of a 'party nation'" ("Making Sense of Cultural Nationalism" 964). One such gala was inaugurated to commemorate the achievements of Joshua Nkomo, who during the 1980s had been represented by ZANU-PF as "the father of dissidents," and had been forced into exile in 1983 (Ndlovu-Gatsheni and Willems, "Reinvoking the Past" 191–208).

Moses Chikowero saw the galas as epitomizing "the public construction and carnivalization of that nationalist project, utilizing the iconography of the country's departed and living patriarchs, matriarchs and heroes as well as the symbolisms of the 1987 Unity Accord and the achievement of independence in 1980" (Chikowero 323). The galas were introduced at a time when Zimbabwean society was not at peace with itself—the economy was crumbling and ZANU-PF's political fortunes were declining. Modern music such as "urban groove" tunes were mixed with old *Chimurenga* songs so as to convince the so-called "born-frees" (all those born after the end of colonialism) of the efficacy of the nationalist project. ZANU-PF thought it was these "born-frees" who supported and voted for the opposition MDC and needed to be adapted into patriotic citizens (Ndlovu-Gatsheni and Willems, "Making Sense of Cultural Nationalism" 964).

Memorialization and commemoration took a Stalinist form, dominated by what Guy Debord described as "the ruling order's non-stop discourse about itself, its never-ending monologue of self-praise, its self-portrait at the stage of totalitarian domination of all aspects of life" (8). By the year 2000, Zimbabweans were being exposed to adaptations of history that transported them back to the 1970s, a time when the ideology of *Chimurenga* had successfully established itself as the popular nodal point around which the anti-colonial struggle crystallized.

Memory Crisis and Counter-Hegemonic Articulations of the Nation

However there were signs that this ideology was being challenged. Internal critics of the party were regularly expelled, including Margaret Dongo in 1995, who went on to form Zimbabwe Union of Democrats (ZUD) and Lawrence Mudehwe in 1996 ("Elections in Zimbabwe" 135). The other internal critic of ZANU-PF was Eddison Zvobgo who in 1995 openly called for democratization of Zimbabwe through cutting the powers of Executive President (Zvobgo, "Agenda" 1–15). The seeds of counter-hegemonic adaptations of history took the form of internal party contestations that revolved around the definition of who constituted a "hero" in the party's struggle. There were tensions among elite nationalists who spearheaded the war from exile; those who actually handled the guns and operated inside Rhodesia against colonial forces; those who were incarcerated (ex-detainees, ex-prisoners and ex-restrictees) inside Zimbabwe, as well as those who were described as *mujibha* (male war collaborators) and *chimbwido* (female war collaborators).

What provoked most comment was the open elevation of those exiled nationalists into what Muchemwa terms "Chimurenga aristocracy," that displayed "vulgar opulence" and dominated the economic and political landscape of the country (509). The conflicts within ZANU-PF were exacerbated by the hierarchization of heroism into national, provincial and district heroes acres, with those buried in provincial and district heroes accompanied by less material benefits (Kriger, "Politics" 137–156). The Heroes Acre, which was meant to be a powerful source of national unity and strong source of legitimacy, became a site of contestation with two veteran nationalists from Matebeleland—Welshman Mabhena and Thenjiwe Lesabe—indicating before their death that they did not want to be buried at the national shrine. Despite President Mugabe's glorifying words of condolence following the death of Mabhena ("We have lost a true patriot *par excellence*"), the Mabhena family observed his wishes ("We Have Lost a True Hero.")

The formation of MDC in 1999 led to the open declaration by its leader Morgan Tsvangirai in 2000 that nationalism was "trapped in a time warp" and "was an end in itself instead of a means to an end" (*Southern Africa Report* 5–8). This was a direct attempt to depart from the ideology of *Chimurenga* as packaged by ZANU-PF. The MDC tried to counter ZANU-PF's rendition of *Chimurenga* by claiming that the liberation war was spearheaded by the working class and was subsequently hijacked by the nationalist elite (MDC,

Election Manifesto 5–12). As Richard Werbner remarks, "memory as public practice" was "increasingly in crisis" (Werbner 1). The MDC encapsulated its vision of another Zimbabwe through the slogans of "A New Zimbabwe" and "A New Beginning," that became very popular with young people and urban residents (MDC, *A New Zimbabwe* 1–10).

Finally, there are strong counter-messages from the Matebeleland region that was adversely affected by postcolonial state-sanctioned violence, generating a radical politics of secession spearheaded by such Diaspora-based political formations as the Mthwakazi People's Congress (MPC) and the Mthwakazi Liberation Front (MLF) (Ndlovu-Gatsheni, "Nation-Building" 27–55; Ndlovu-Gatsheni, "Do Zimbabweans Exist?" 149–188). During the Independence Day celebrations on April 18, 2011, members of the MLF marched through Johannesburg and publicly burnt the Zimbabwean national flag as a symbolic statement of their intentions. Those forces working for the secession of Matebeleland have gone further by establishing a fully-fledged virtual nation known as the United Mthwakazi Republic (UMR) complete with all trappings of a nation-state including a radio station and a national flag (Ndlovu-Gatsheni, "The Ndebele Nation" 5–14).

Conclusion

The acceptance by ZANU-PF to share power with the MDC political formations in September 2008 through signing the Global Political Agreement (GPA), and the installation of the inclusive government in February 2009, are clear indications that President Mugabe and his colleagues have realized the limits of adapting the ideology of *Chimurenga* and the strategy of *Gukurahundi*. But within the government such questions as the ownership of the nation, control of the state, exercise of power, and a lack of a unifying national narrative continue to be unanswered. The nation remains caught in a Gramscian interregnum, whereby the old history of nationalism and the old adaptations of *Chimurenga* and *Gukurahundi* are taking time to pass away, while new historical adaptations founded on tolerance, plurality, inclusivity, social peace and human security are taking time to be born. In the interim, the old order continues to polarize the nation, while an alliance of civil society organizations, opposition political formations and progressive intellectuals continue to struggle for democratization of historical knowledge as well as state structures. Non-state media continue to offer counter-narratives to the adapted history propagated by the state-owned media. But a "Zanufied" state retains a strong control over alternative historical narratives and alternative memories within a monologic framework whose leitmotif is *Chimurenga*.

Works Cited

Bennett, Tony. *The Birth of the Museum: History, Theory, Politics.* New York and London: Routledge, 1995. Print.

Blair, David. *Degrees in Violence: Robert Mugabe and the Struggle for Power in Zimbabwe.* London and New York: Continuum, 2000. Print.

Catholic Commission for Justice and Peace (CCJP) and Legal Resources Foundation (LRF). *Breaking the Silence, Building True Peace: Report on the Disturbances in Matabeleland and the Midlands Regions, 1980–1989.* Harare: CCJP and LRF, 1997. Print.

Chan, Stephan. *Robert Mugabe: A Life of Power and Violence.* London and New York: I. B. Tauris, 2003. Print.

Chikowero, Moses. *Struggles over Culture: Zimbabwean Music and Power, 1930–2007.* Diss. University of Dalhousie, 2008. Print.

Chitando, Ezra. "'Down with the Devil, Forward with Christ!' A Study of the Interface Between Religious and Political Discourses in Zimbabwe." *African Sociological Review* 6.1 (2002): 1–16. Print.

_____. "In the Beginning was Land: The Appropriation of Religious Themes in Political Discourse in Zimbabwe." *Africa* 75.2 (2005): 220–239. Print.

Debord, Guy. *The Society of the Spectacle.* Canberra: Treason Press, 2002. Print.

Dirlik, Arif. "Rethinking Colonialism: Globalization, Postcolonialism, and the Nation." *Interventions* 4.3 (2002): 428–448. Print.

Dorman, Sarah R. *Inclusion and Exclusion: NGOs and Politics in Zimbabwe.* Diss. University of Oxford, 2001. Print.

Hudson, Miles. *Triumph or Tragedy? Rhodesia to Zimbabwe.* London: Hamish Hamilton, 1981. Print.

Kriger, Norma. "The Politics of Creating National Heroes: The Search for Political Legitimacy and National Identity." *Soldiers in Zimbabwe's Liberation War.* Eds. Ngwabi Bhebe and Terence Ranger. London: James Currey, 1995. 137–156. Print.

_____. "ZANU (PF) Strategies in General Elections, 1980–2000: Discourse and Coercion." *African Affairs* 104.414 (2005): 1–34. Print.

Mandaza, Ibbo, and Lloyd Sachikonye, eds. *The One-Party State and Democracy: The Zimbabwe Debate.* Harare: SAPES Books, 1991. Print.

Mazarire, Gerald C. "Discipline and Punishment in ZANLA, 1964–1979." *Journal of Southern African Studies* 37.3 (2011): 571–591. Print.

MDC. *MDC Election Manifesto.* Harare: Information and Publicity Department, 2000. Print.

_____. *A New Zimbabwe: A New Beginning,* Harare: Information and Publicity Department, 2007. Print.

Moore, David. "The Zimbabwe People's Army: Strategic Innovation or More of the Same?" *Soldiers in Zimbabwe's Liberation War.* Eds. Ngwabi Bhebe and Terence Ranger. London: James Currey, 1995. 73–103. Print.

Muchemwa, Kizito Z. "Galas, Biras, State Funerals and the Necropolitan Imagination in Re-Construction of the Zimbabweans Nation, 1980–2008." *Social Dynamics* 36.3 (2010): 504–514. Print.

Mugabe, Robert G. *Inside the Third Chimurenga,* Harare: Ministry of Information and Publicity, 2001. Print.

Muzondidya, James. "Jambanja: Ideological Ambiguities in the Politics of Land and Resource Ownership in Zimbabwe." *Journal of Southern African Studies* 33.2 (2007): 321–325. Print.

_____. "The Zimbabwean Crisis and the Unresolved Conundrum of Race in the Post-Colonial Period." *Journal of Developing Societies* 26.1 (2010): 5–38. Print.

Ndlovu-Gatsheni, Sabelo J. "Africa for Africans or Africa for 'Natives' Only? 'New Nationalism' and Nativism in Zimbabwe and South Africa." *Africa Spectrum* 1 (2009): 61–78. Print.

_____. "Beyond the Drama of War: Trajectories of Nationalism in Zimbabwe, the 1890s to 2010." *Redemptive or Grotesque Nationalism? Rethinking Contemporary Politics in Zimbabwe.* Eds. Sabelo J. Ndlovu-Gatsheni and James Muzondidya. Oxford: Peter Lang, 2011. 37–79. Print.

_____. *Do "Zimbabweans" Exist? Trajectories of Nationalism, National Identity Formation and Crisis in a Postcolonial State.* Oxford: Peter Lang, 2009. Print.

_____. "Making Sense of Mugabeism in Local and Global Politics: 'So Blair, Keep Your England and Let Me Keep My Zimbabwe.'" *Third World Quarterly* 30.6 (2009): 1139–1158. Print.

_____. "Nation-Building in Zimbabwe and Challenges of Ndebele Particularism." *African Journal on Conflict Resolution* 8.3 (2008): 27–55. Print.

_____. *The Ndebele Nation: Reflections on Hegemony, Memory and Historiography.* Amsterdam and Pretoria: Rozenberg Publishers and UNISA Press, 2009. Print.

_____. "Puppets or Patriots: A Study of Nationalist Rivalry over the Spoils of Dying Settler Colonialism in Zimbabwe, 1977–1980." *Nationalisms across the Globe: An Overview of Nationalisms in State-Endowed and Stateless Nations: Volume II: Third World.* Eds. Tomasz Kamsuella, Wojciech Burszta and S. Wojciechowski. Poznan: School of Humanities and Journalism, 2006. 345–397. Print.

_____, and James Muzondidya. "Redemptive or Grotesque Nationalism in the Colony?" Introduction. *Redemptive or Grotesque Nationalism? Rethinking Contemporary Politics in Zimbabwe.* Eds. Ndlovu-Gatsheni and Muzondidya. Oxford: Peter Lang, 2011: 1–31. Print.

_____, and Wendy Willems. "Making Sense of Cultural Nationalism and the Politics of Commemoration under the Third Chimurenga in Zimbabwe." *Journal of Southern African Studies* 35.4 (2009): 945–965. Print.

_____, and Wendy Willems. "Reinvoking the Past in the Present: Changing Identities and Appropriations of Joshua Nkomo in Post-Colonial Zimbabwe." *African Identities* 8.3 (2010): 191–208. Print.

Ranger, Terence. "Nationalist Historiography, Patriotic History and History of the Nation: The Struggle over the Past in Zimbabwe." *Journal of Southern African Studies* 30.2 (2004): 215–234. Print.

_____. "The People in African Resistance." *Journal of Southern African Studies* 4.1 (1977): 125–146. Print.

_____. *Revolt in Southern Rhodesia 1896–7: A Study in African Resistance.* London: Heinemann, 1967. Print.

_____. "Rule by Historiography: The Struggle over the Past and its Possible Implications." *Versions of Zimbabwe: New Approaches to Literature and Culture.* Eds. Robert Muponde and Ranka Primorac. Harare: Weaver Press, 2005. 217–243. Print.

_____. "The Uses and Abuses of History in Zimbabwe." *Skinning the Skunk — Facing Zimbabwean Futures.* Eds. Mai Palmberg and Ranka Primorac. Uppsala: Nordic Africa Institute, 2005. 1–15. Print.

Shaw, William H. "Towards the One-Party State in Zimbabwe: A Study in African Political Thought." *Journal of Modern African Studies* 24.3 (1986): 373–394. Print.

Sithole, Masipula, and Makumbe, John. "Elections in Zimbabwe: The ZANU (PF) Hegemony and its Incipient Decline." *African Journal of Political Science* 2.1 (1997): 122–139. Print.

Solidarity Peace Trust. "Weekly Accounts of the Run-Up to 2008 Parliamentary and Presidential Elections." *Solidarity Peace Trust* 14 June 2009. Web. 30 Apr. 2011.

Southern Africa Report 15.3 (June 2000): 1–10. Print.
Tendi, Blessings-Miles. *Making History in Mugabe's Zimbabwe: Politics, Intellectuals and the Media.* Oxford: Peter Lang, 2010. Print.
"We Have Lost a True Hero." AllAfrica.com. 8 Oct. 2010. Web. 17 Aug. 2011.
Werbner, Richard. "Beyond Oblivion: Confronting Memory Crisis." *Memory and the Postcolony: African Anthropology and the Critique of Power.* Ed. Richard Werbner. London and New York: Zed Books, 1998. 1–34. Print.
ZANU-PF Department of Information and Publicity. *Traitors Do Much Damage to National Goals.* Harare: ZANU-PF Department of Information and Publicity, 2004. Print.
ZIPA. "Chimurenga — A People's War." *Zimbabwe News* March/April 1997. Print.
Zvobgo, Eddison. "Agenda for Democracy, Peace and Sustainable Development in the SADC Region." Meikles Hotel, Harare, 14 Nov. 1995. Conference Paper.
_____. "The ZANU Idea." *The Struggle for Zimbabwe: Documents of the Recent Developments of Zimbabwe: 1975–1980.* Ed. Goswin Baumhogger. Vol. IV. Hamburg: Hamburg University Press, 1984. 13–23. Print.

Adapting Archaeological Landscapes: Re-Presenting Ireland's Heritage

MANJREE KHAJANCHI

In an Ireland where heritage tourism is becoming the fastest growing aspect of Irish tourism of the future, critiques of heritage presentation serve an important purpose in enhancing and maximizing the economic and cultural benefits of this industry in all nations, in this case Ireland (O'Connor and Cronin 1; Camp 24). I will use first hand information and experiences witnessed on an archeology field trip to Ireland in April 2008 to conduct a discussion on why adapted historical sites—which have been restored or reconstructed since they were first made — should be interpreted in different ways. Such an investigation into the nature of heritage presentation and interaction is important not just to archeology, but to anybody involved in the creation and dissemination of histories. This essay argues that equal importance (Stewart and Strathern; Synnestvedt) should be given to a landscape's past, present and future, allowing for the whole site history and biography of a place to be treated equally. To achieve this goal, emphasis needs to be placed on a variety of adaptive processes, focusing on the following: the symbiotic nature of the past in the present and the present in the past; the concept of interpretive multi-vocal and multi-dimensional narratives; and the implications of such strategies for the future of Irish heritage.

Heritage landscapes are sites that include physical structures and monuments, which are "inherited from the past, for which we in the present are responsible" (Olivier 180). This implies a form of historical adaptation, whereby a portion of the past needs preserving outside of the present, irre-

141

spective of the passage of time (Pearson and Sullivan 1). Thus, heritage sites are often becoming frozen-in-time, encouraging past-centric adaptations. Yet, paradoxically, heritage is also intrinsically linked to tourism and present-day politics, as sites in history are promoted, packaged, and sold to the public with today's concerns in mind (Lincoln 220). Hence a rather problematic process ensues, in which heritage sites are being marketed for the present day while delineating a past-centric interpretation. This is especially evident in the case studies explored throughout this essay, arising from our visit as university students to various Irish historical sites.

Past in the Present, Present in the Past

Heritage sites are often demarcated as past spaces within the present landscape, even though tangible material remains of the past are scattered around most modern landscapes. They are seen as a physical connection to the past; spaces that must be cared for on behalf of the past for future generations (Olivier 180, Fagan 7). These sites are considered to be fixed by unspecialized visitors to historical sites, despite the frequent interactions with people throughout time, and the various repairs and conservation measures that occur throughout the sites' histories. Therefore, it is necessary to openly question upfront, as Hodder does, whether archeology is really only limited to the past, and whether it should continue to be viewed as exclusively past-centric (189). Or maybe we should look for a broader and more inclusive definition of an "archaeology of the present," one that redefines the discipline as the "materiality of life" (Hodder 191). The field trip taken by archeology students attending the University of Wales, Lampeter, to visit the Republic of Ireland's diverse heritage landscapes highlighted the unique inter-relationship between past and present. Not only did our class trip intend to study Ireland's adapted history, but it was designed to focus on how people from different socio-historical periods interacted with this history to construct their views on Irish heritage. These interactions in the present day put all such sites within the reach of the contemporary past, especially since archaeological heritage sites are situated in what Hodder calls a "public present" (189), making the past part of the here and now.

It is not an over-exaggeration to claim that adaptations of history are always changing, and while no such thing as "the past" or "the history" exists, "a past" or "a history" can refer to one of many possible options. Continually negotiated and re-negotiated, Brett makes a persuasive argument when he states that "history, truly considered, is a verb, not an abstract noun. We history" (186). Accordingly, history is considered an "active entity" that negotiates between power and identity at all times (Karlsson 26). It is not stationary as commonly assumed, making it one of many archaeological "universals" that have been taken for granted among practitioners over the years, but needs re-evaluating (Potter 36). History does not presume to have a beginning or origin, as its creation relies on the unstoppable process of interpretation and adaptation (Barrett 21). Viewing history as the expression of actions that continually shift in meaning is often a case of identifying who is doing the interpreting and who it is intended for, as each group molds history to meet their own goals and ideals, resulting in the formation of various adapted histories.

The site of Fourknocks (Co. Meath) visited during our Ireland trip offers an example of how every heritage site is situated within a political and contested present (Stewart and Strathern). It consists of three Neolithic mounds that were excavated by P. J. Hartnett in the 1950s (Cooney 104). Fourknocks I has been interpreted by archaeologists as being a passage tomb, while Fourknocks II and III are cremation sites (Harbison 261). Only Fourknocks I has been reconstructed after excavation (Cooney 106) and is open to the public (by permission), while Fourknocks II and III, which lie about 50 meters away, are neither accessible nor have been "restored" (Cooney 106). Apart from a signpost explaining the site's importance during the Neolithic, there are no other additions— benches, car parking facilities, souvenir shops— in the vicinity. Although the main site, Fourknocks I, is on private property (Branigan 188), the site is also managed by the Irish Office of Public Works (OPW). At present, a fence divides and separates Fourknocks I from Fourknocks II and III, which are under a different management. The question of who owns the past and benefits from the heritage industry can be raised here. The deliberate separation of Fourknocks I from the other two sites, with a physical barrier like a fence, guides our views as to the relationship of the tomb site to the cremation sites. The past historical landscape of Fourknocks would have been more open compared to its present-day counterpart, but the changes to the topography, with the addition of the fence in the last few decades, changes that outlook (Brett 188–189, 199). Moreover, the entrance into the passage grave is also barred by an iron door that can be unlocked by obtaining the key from the owner of the property who lives nearby. Issues such as ownership of the site, and entering the tomb freely, regardless of religious or socioeconomic status, are all present-day developments of Fourknocks I that may not have been relevant 5000 years ago. This is important because changing the tomb's previous state to suit present conditions involves adapting its history.

It is up to individuals who visit the Fourknocks landscape to experience this place of the dead, to decide for themselves whether they deem the site to provide a realistic experience of the Neolithic or not (Brett 199–200). The issues mentioned above are only a few examples of the efforts involved in trying to preserve a specific view of the Neolithic past, which inevitably prompts reflection on how the site is interacted with and experienced by site visitors in the present (Hodder 189; Potter and Chabot 53). Different experiences add yet another dimension to the history of the Fourknocks sites (Cooney 112), from a past view (where no barrier appeared between these sister sites), to the current view where ownership, architecture, and topography have all been altered.

From (Re)Living History to Equal Importance

The term (re)living history implies that someone can walk into a museum or reconstructed space and visually experience "the past" (Brett); it plays a significant role in guiding what individual visitors believe authentic past sites to look like. To achieve this goal, heritage practitioners must maintain a high degree of preservation in order to satisfy the visual appetite of individual visitors who wish to experience the site in its historical context. This is clearly evident at the site of Newgrange, the premier prehistoric monument in Ireland, located along the Bend of the Boyne Valley (Harbison 265). It is a reconstructed Neolithic passage tomb noteworthy for its roof-box above the entrance of the tomb, which allows sunlight to shine into the tomb floor on the morning of every winter solstice (Cochrane). This is due to the perfect alignment of the rising sun with the roof-box on this shortest day of the year. The central focus of a Newgrange tour involves being led inside the passage tomb to witness the "magic" of the roof-box through artificial means (Lewis-Williams and Pearce 228–229; Cochrane). Following this is a request for anyone interested in witnessing the "real thing" to sign up for the lottery at the Visitor Center to experience the actual event inside Newgrange during the winter solstice each year!

For the purposes of the heritage tour, importance is given to freezing Newgrange's existence into one specific time of the year (Olivier 183). Even the tour guide in Newgrange will reiterate the message that "you haven't really seen Newgrange until you've seen the solstice," as if a visit to this important monument would be nullified if the simulation of the rising sun entering the tomb through the roof-box were to be missed. However, for all the visitors who visit Newgrange to "experience" this historical phenomenon every day of the year (done two to three times each hour), the sheer amount of artificial fixtures and changes to the architecture of the site inevitably changes the experience itself (Olivier 183–184). Although visitors are able to see the phenomenon by way of simulation every day of the year, emphasis is still put upon experiencing the "real" unsimulated version during each winter solstice. Tour guides at Newgrange explicitly state that the solstice cannot be experienced identically in the present as it was in the Neolithic period, due to the change in the earth's rotation which slightly changes the alignment of the sun with the roof-box today. Thus, the emphasis on recreating the "perfect" experience — thereby (re)living a moment in history — overshadows the desire to experience the phenomenon anew in the present (Cochrane). However, whether the phenomenon is experienced in the present or during the Neolithic period, the past-centric tone used for promoting this event should not affect one's experience of the site; both are special in different ways.

The relative success of preserving and maintaining a constant influx of visitors to Newgrange is not surprising, because going back in time to enliven the past through simulation is an attractive strategy that results in high visitor satisfaction (Robertshaw 52). This is why (re)living history has been used as an interactive technique to link past and present, because experiencing history is difficult for today's visitors to understand unless viewed from the present point of view (Brett 200). However, (re)living history has been criticized for being a problematic form of heritage interpretation and has been linked to the "Disneyfication" of sites (Robertshaw 51). A multi-dimensional approach is perhaps more desirable, as so-called "living history" cannot transcend space and time (Brett 221). Perhaps it would be better to look for elements of the past within the present. To quote one example: when archaeologist Håkan Karlsson and his wife decided to resituate Sweden's late Neolithic gallery tomb Dwarf's House (Karlsson 29) in a new context — as a background for their wedding photos and a champagne cooler in 1997 — their (re)use of the site added to the site's historical layers (Karlsson 36). Another example of this strategy involves the transformation of castles and other "romantic" sites into hotels, which add another layer of meaning to the "existence of places and things that have often already known a long series of functions and uses" (Olivier 180). Such techniques of adaptation, whether in the past or the present, are all important parts of understanding a site's biography (Synnestvedt). More importantly, any form of human contact with a landscape, whether physical, emotional, permanent, or temporary, adds more meaning to that site's importance in the past, present, and future (Stewart and Strathern, Synnestvedt). In the case of the Dwarf's House, the series of staged events that took place around the tomb in 1997, involving Karlsson and his wife, play an important and equal role in the heritage landscape's place within history.

While insisting that all interpretations should be treated equally, I do believe that a fully-informed decision can only be made once all the information available has been taken into consideration. Once that process has been accomplished, it is then possible to accept that all interpretations can be treated with equal importance. This process is evident in the way the Fourknocks I site in Ireland has been adapted throughout history. Originally thought to be covered by a wooden roof, due to the remains of a post-hole found during excavation, the inside of the Fourknocks I tomb structure now has a "concrete dome, with shafts letting in enough light to see by and creating a suitably eerie atmosphere" (Harbison 261). The dome was created during the reconstruction phase executed by Hartnett in the mid–1950s, and has been a part of Fourknocks I for over half a century. Fourknocks I does not fossilize the site in an ancient past, but rather adapts its meaning to different socio-historical contexts by designing "hybrid constructions that belong as much to the present as to the past" (Olivier 183). The combination of past and present components is equally important in understanding the life history of the Fourknocks I site.

Interpretive Multi-Vocal Narratives

The technique of adapting meaning to differing historical contexts was evident in our trip to Ireland, and the ways in which we interpreted the sites visited. The two course leaders dissected the class into five groups: (1) Heritage, (2) Phenomenology, (3) Mythology/Politics, (4) Barrier/Routeway, and (5) Site Description, and encouraged us to make a structured interpretation, combining personal and collective viewpoints. Individual site-accounts were directly influenced by group discussions, alongside interpretations provided by the course leaders (Potter and Chabot). This strategy created what can be described as a context for a poly-vocal interpretation, based on plural accounts of the past. For any adaptation of the past in the present, questions of context and individual agency were found to be essential. The Dwarf's House site provides a good example of this process in operation (Karlsson). Karlsson believes that the site's biography showcased multiple uses and varied meanings, and this so-called inactive Swedish megalithic site "could be used for our specific purposes," referring to the recycling of the site for an important part of his wedding (36–37). The same process was evident in our work as we learned that sites could be adapted to our individual purposes. Archeology cannot and should not be univocal, but should accommodate a plurality of influential adaptations (Olivier 187), even if such adaptations might, in some cases, be considered "pseudo-histories" based on misinformation and misinterpretation (cf. Brett 184, 202). Let me illustrate this point with an example of an "adaptation" which was not produced by our group, but by a famous actor/director. During our guided tour around the grounds of Trim Castle in County Meath, the tour guide mentioned the recent re-use of the landscape for the filming of actor/director Mel Gibson's *Braveheart* (1995). Although the storyline was set in Scotland, the decision to film at the Irish location of Trim Castle was inspired by economic concerns, and by doing so, Gibson contributed to the castle's layers of meaning by investing it with the associations of the Hollywood film industry. He kept it grounded in current events. Therefore, it is important never to forget about the modern uses and context in which a site survives (Potter 39).

An interesting case study of the myriad adaptations associated with a particular site can also be seen in our visit to Mellifont Abbey (Co. Louth), the first Cistercian Abbey to be erected by the French in Ireland (Harbison 237–238). On the day we visited this heritage site, the visitor center was closed, so our group set out to spend the next few hours in various ways. This site has unrestricted access, and has been left in situ after excavation, with jagged ruins visible. However, it has also been well maintained, with clean-cut grass and an artistically created site floor of smooth pebbles. Different people in our group undertook a variety of activities including walking the site, eating lunch in the remains of the octagonal lavabo, posing for photographs (using the "ruins" of the site as their stage), posing "mummy-style" on the grave markers that were scattered on the floor of the monastery, and making miniature megalithic structures out of pebbles and stones that covered the site grounds. Not only were new meanings created through these various processes on the day, they were also extended through the use of online platforms such as Facebook. Strategies such as this allow for alternative forms of multi-dimensional historical adaptation to occur, even after our trip had come to an end. Personal photographs and albums were uploaded of the Ireland trip on individual profiles, while a more public "photo group" was also created for the purpose of sharing photographs between group members. Nearly a quarter of the students who participated in the Ireland trip were not part of the online Facebook community, but they could nonetheless construct their own interpretations by viewing the photos online.

Our case studies of Mellifont Abbey, and the subsequent Facebook dialogues in the aftermath of the trip, are good examples of how the "present form of a site" should be taken into account as part of the site's biography and life history, as much as its "original form in the past," or more importantly its "various forms in the past" (Synnestvedt). Such an approach allows for the representation of poly-vocality and multiple uses throughout history, time, and space to be considered, leading to a more comprehensive understanding of the different voices that make up the past, present, and future.

Future Directions for Archeology and Irish Heritage

From the beginning, archaeologists have not been against the idea of multiple narratives, and have tried to incorporate this concept into their work (see Schmidt and Halle 158–159). However this methodology has not been taken to its logical conclusion, especially in the heritage sector. It is still uncommon for "site interpreters" to openly admit to not knowing the answer to an interpretive question, or feel comfortable simply saying, "I'm not sure." Rather than interact with these "(pre)historic sites" in their current setting, a traditional tour guide would be more likely to ask the public to forget the modern landscape in which these monuments are situated, and imagine a world without the hordes of tourists, traffic and modern infrastructure obstructing the view of these pristine landscapes (Potter 39). This rhetorical strategy inhibits, rather than expands, the potential for multiple adaptations of the past in the present. Because the majority of heritage sites are still run in this manner, it is possible that archaeologists and other field specialists would prefer to "serve the public with the facts" (Schmidt and Halle 159), with only a minimal number of narratives and interpretations besides those the experts provided.

In order for people in the present to engage with heritage more directly, archaeologists need to remove themselves from the "primary interpreter" position, and allow for a diverse set of voices to be heard (Potter and Chabot 53). As Olivier suggests, archaeologists need only focus on the continuity and ongoing adaptation of a site's heritage through time, and into the present (180). Doing so will allow archaeologists to acknowledge the presence of "considerable stratifications of meaning over time" (Olivier 180). With regard to Ireland's heritage, small but important changes to heritage sites, and the form in which information is disseminated, can make a big impact on how a landscape is perceived and viewed by visitors (Camp). Within Fourknocks, the presence of Bronze Age human remains, deposited centuries after the Neolithic period ended, indicates that this is not exclusively a Neolithic monument (as popularly advertised), making it a multi-stage historical site. Also, the recent addition of roughly cut-in stairs at Fourknocks I implies that present meanings have been imposed on the past site. The decision to make stairs on top of a tomb, or reconstructing one archaeological site but not the others, are important indicators of which aspects of Ireland's heritage are given priority over others, and explicitly demarcates Fourknocks I, among many others, as a site of historical adaptation.

The same phenomenon can be found at the Newgrange site and its managing authority — the Newgrange Visitor Center, which is preoccupied with questioning Neolithic beliefs, while showing the reconstruction phases of the mound up to the present day. However perhaps this strategy of reinterpreting the past has not gone far enough: importance has been limited to experiencing the effects of the roof-box to compare it to the past (Cochrane), rather than promoting contemporaneous interpretations or recording new memories in the present. The control exercised on this landscape is time-sensitive and lacking the freedom to do what one wishes (Camp). This is seen through the trimmed grass, the pebbled walkway, and the guided signposts that warn visitors to not "use" the site for climbing and the no entry barriers—all put in place to allow visitors to see the past from afar, but not to interact with it.

At Trim Castle, the importance of the castle keep has been overemphasized, despite the associations of the site with *Braveheart*. Perhaps more emphasis should be given to the combination of contemporary light fixtures and wood and glass bridges alongside the original mossy structure of the building. Also, this is one of the few sites with litter scattered around the grounds, including picnic tables where many visitors get their free time to eat meals. What does this suggest about the relationship between Trim Castle and the way it is adapted and managed for today's visitors? Finally, Mellifont Abbey, while encouraging a multi-vocal approach, is still restricted in terms of its interpretive scope. The concept of sitting on real ruins from the Abbey's wall might have been discouraged if a guard or member of staff had been around while we were making our visit. If patrons are given the room to breathe in the landscape and experience the site without the feeling of claustrophobia, this might permit a greater breadth of historical adaptation and/or interpretation to evolve. While such adaptations will make any archaeological landscape more past- and present-minded, in the case of Ireland's sites, they might help make visitors' experiences more authentic by giving them the freedom to create new narratives.

This essay has endeavored to explain why a difference in perspective is needed among heritage presenters and managers, as well as archeologists with regard to views and thoughts on the adaption of a heritage site's history. The (re)construction of heritage narratives in the service of archeology prove that histories are indeed adapted, through time and space, to accomplish a variety of tasks. A comprehensive understanding of these processes is important for those involved in creating and consuming said historical narratives, whatever the subject-matter. Although this approach to archaeological heritage management will result in the past having a relatively closer emotional and political link to the present, it is believed that this will lead to a more holistic understanding of the complexities that dictate what "the past" really means.

Works Cited

Barrett, John C. "Chronologies of Landscape." *The Archaeology and Anthropology of Landscape: Shaping your Landscape.* Eds. Peter J. Ucko and Robert Layton. London: Routledge, 1999. 21–30. Print.
Branigan, Keith. "The Heritage Industry: Whose Industry, Whose Heritage?" *Writing the Past in the Present.* Eds. Frederick Baker and Julian Thomas. Lampeter: Saint David's University College, Lampeter, 1990. 188–91. Print.

Braveheart. Dir. Mel Gibson. Perf. Mel Gibson, Sophie Marceau, Patrick McGoohan. Icon Entertainment, 1995. Film.

Brett, David. "The Construction of Heritage." *Tourism in Ireland: A Critical Analysis.* Eds. Barbara O'Connor and Michael Cronin. Cork: Cork University Press, 1993. 183–202. Print.

Camp, Stacey Lynn. "Disjunctures in Nationalist Rhetoric at Ireland's Brú na Bóinne Visitor Centre." *Tourism Consumption and Representation: Narratives of Place and Self.* Eds. Kevin Meethan, Alison Anderson, and Steven Miles. Wallingford: Oxfordshire: CABI, 2006. 24–45. Print.

Cochrane, Andrew. "The Simulacra and Simulations of Irish Neolithic Passage Tombs." *Images, Representations and Heritage: Moving Beyond Modern Approaches to Archaeology.* Ed. Ian Russell. New York: Springer, 2006. 247–78. Print.

Cooney, Gabriel. *Landscapes of Neolithic Ireland.* London and New York: Routledge, 2000. Print.

Fagan, Brian. "Looking Forward, Not Backward: Archaeology and the Future of the Past." *Of the Past, for the Future: Integrating Archaeology and Conservation.* Eds. Neville Agnew and Janet Bridgland. Los Angeles: The Getty Conservation Institute, 2006. 7–12. Print.

Harbison, Peter. *Guide to National and Historic Monuments of Ireland.* Dublin: Gill and Macmillan, 1992. Print.

Hodder, Ian. Epilogue. *Archaeologies of the Contemporary Past.* By Victor Buchli and Gavin Lucas. London and New York: Routledge, 2001. 189–91. Print.

Karlsson, Håkan. "The Dwarf and the Wine-Cooler: A Biography of a Swedish Megalith and its "Effect-in-history." *Archaeological Conditions: Examples of Epistemology and Ontology.* Eds. Ola W. Jensen and Håkan Karlsson. Göteborg: Göteborg University Press, 2000. 25–40. Print.

Lewis-Williams, David, and David Pearce. *Inside the Neolithic Mind.* London: Thames & Hudson, 2005. Print.

Lincoln, Colm. "City of Culture: Dublin and the Discovery of Urban Heritage." *Tourism in Ireland: A Critical Analysis.* Eds. Barbara O'Connor and Michael Cronin. Cork: Cork University Press, 1993. 203–30. Print.

O'Connor, Barbara, and Michael Cronin, eds. *Tourism in Ireland: A Critical Analysis.* Cork: Cork University Press, 1993. Print.

Olivier, Laurent. "The Archaeology of the Contemporary Past." Trans. Vérène Grieshaber. *Archaeologies of the Contemporary Past.* Eds. Victor Buchli and Gavin Lucas. London and New York: Routledge, 2001. 175–88. Print.

Pearson, Michael, and Sharon Sullivan. *Looking after Heritage Places: The Basics of Heritage Planning for Managers, Landowners and Administrators.* Melbourne: Melbourne University Press, 1995. Print.

Potter, Parker B., Jr. "The Archaeological Site as an Interpretive Environment." *Presenting Archaeology to the Public: Digging for Truths.* Ed. John H. Jameson Jr. Walnut Creek, CA: AltaMira Press, 1997. 35–44. Print.

Potter, Parker B., Jr., and Nancy Jo Chabot. "Locating Truths on Archaeological Sites." *Presenting Archaeology to the Public: Digging for Truths.* Ed. John H. Jameson Jr. Walnut Creek, CA: AltaMira Press, 1997. 45–53. Print.

Robertshaw, Andrew. "Live Interpretation." *Heritage Interpretation.* Eds. Alison Hems and Marion R. Blockley. London and New York: Routledge, 2006. 41–54. Print.

Schmidt, Martin, and Uta Halle. "On the Folklore of the Externsteine — or a Centre for Germanomaniacs." *Archaeology and Folklore.* Eds. Amy Gazin-Schwartz and Cornelius Holtorf. London and New York: Routledge, 1999. 158–74. Print.

Stewart, Pamela J., and Andrew Strathern. Introduction. *Landscape, Memory and History:*

Anthropological Perspectives. By Stewart and Strathern. London: Pluto Press, 2003. 1–15. Print.

Synnestvedt, Anita. "Who Wants to Visit A Cultural Heritage Site? A Walk Through an Archaeological Site with a Visual and Bodily Experience." *Images, Representations and Heritage: Moving Beyond Modern Approaches to Archaeology.* Ed. Ian Russell. New York: Springer, 2006. 333–51. Print.

PART TWO: ALTERNATIVE HISTORY

Palimpsests of History in Sebastian Barry's The Secret Scripture

GÜLDEN HATIPOĞLU

"I have a story right, my wanderers,
That has so mixed with fable in our songs
That all seemed fabulous." — W.B. Yeats, *Deidre, The Collected Works of W.B. Yeats: Vol. II: The Plays*, 175–76.

Every nation adapts its own version of history according to different political and social imperatives. This was especially true of Ireland in the early twentieth century, at a time when it was trying to assert its identity and rebel against English colonial rule. Members of the so-called "Irish Literary Revival," also known as the Irish Literary Renaissance, which included poets and writers George Sigerson, J. M. Synge, George Moore and W. B. Yeats, were heavily involved in trying to restore what they perceived as the national memory. They set out to collect the myths, legends and folk stories, and to translate them into English in order to re-equip the Irish people with a common, unifying cultural agenda. The spirit of this movement was expressed by the future politician (and founder of the Gaelic League) Douglas Hyde's famous speech "The Necessity for De-Anglicising Ireland" (1892) which argued that the Irish should follow their own traditions in attire, customs, sport, language and literature, and abandon all things English (Hyde).

Like in all essentialist views of history, however, this collective adaptation consciously excluded minority groups. Frequently it manifested itself in "state censorship, intolerance towards minority views and introverted forms of nationalism and unionism" (Daly 94).[1] This was especially evident after the creation of the Irish Free State from 1922 onwards. The Irish Historical Society, founded in 1937, determined the progress of historical writing in Ireland until the 1980s, and fortified a tradition which "privileged official sources [...] over others such as folklore and literary records" (Daly 94). R. F. Foster, one of Ireland's leading historians, articulates this deliberate process of censorship in post-independence narratives in *The Irish Story*:

> So from independence a version of Irish history had to be constructed by the state which stressed the "Story of Ireland" in relation to the removal of the British: developments within the island, especially post–1921, tended to receive rather short shift. "Outstanding personages" and "striking incidents" were to be emphasized [...] The process of censorship worked on more subtle levels than merely erasing love scenes from films or fretting out books describing birth control [...] The historical record was itself subject to a policy of enforced silence [26].

It is ironic that many significant literary figures who contributed to the revitalization of the nation's memory were also the agents of censorship. However things have changed over the last seven decades: a revisionist movement has evolved, which tries to create new adaptations of Irish history that allow for "the recovery of repressed histories," in which "'myth' is mocked at rather than mapped out, 'nation' defiled rather than defined and 'violence' decried rather than described" (Maley 17).

This essay will show how this revisionist movement works through a discussion of Sebastian Barry's *The Secret Scripture* (2008). The novel offers an alternative adaptation of Irish history by portraying the lives of misfits whose lives do not conform to the accepted grand narrative of Irish history, and whose histories are either erased from memory or adapted into normative versions to fit in the national identity promoted and reinforced by the Church and State to create a homogenous nation: Catholic, Gaelic, pious and sexless.

The Secret Scripture has a double-layered narrative which reveals the testimonies of two major characters through first-person narrative voices. One is a 100-year old woman, Roseanne, who survived the traumas of the civil war in post-independence Ireland and spent most of her life in a mental institution, and who "claims a hold on her history" (Barry, *Secret* 239) by writing out her life on surplus hospital papers. The other is Dr. Grene, a psychiatrist in the same mental hospital, who tries to come to terms with his own personal history and with Roseanne's in his journal entries. While excavating their own past they also uncover Ireland's past in ruins, especially those fragments of Irish history that have been disregarded in or wiped out from official records, and they question and comment on how personal histories were adapted into constructed/fictionalized official history in order to create an

envisioned identity for the Irish Free State, and how in the process the archi-
tects of national identity "[wiped] out the records of the very nation they
were trying to give new life to, actually burning memory in its boxes" (Barry,
Secret 262).

Roseanne is loosely based on a member of Barry's own family whose fate
was revealed one day when the author was "driving through Sligo, and my
mother pointed out a hut and told me that was where my great uncle's first
wife had lived before being put into a lunatic asylum by the family. She
[Barry's mother] knew nothing more, except that she was beautiful" (qtd. in
Jeffries). Roseanne's reimagined story in the novel covers a period from the
1910s to the first decade of the twenty-first century, and recounts several
important points in Irish history including the Anglo-Irish War, the foundation of the Free State, the Civil War and the Emergence.[2]

Roseanne's tragedy begins in 1922, when the foundation of the Irish Free
State not only resulted in the division of the island into south and north, but
divided the citizens of the new nation into "Free Staters" who supported the
Treaty, and the rebels or irregulars who resisted it. Roseanne's father Joseph
feels dispossessed by this division:

> As a Presbyterian he might be thought to have no place in the Irish story. But he
> understood rebellion. In his bedroom in a drawer he kept a memorial booklet for
> the Rising of 1916, with photographs of the principals involved, and a calendar of
> battles and sorrows. The only wicked thing he thought that Rising enshrined was
> its peculiar Catholic nature, from which of course he felt excluded [Barry, *Secret*
> 37].

For the non-Catholic members of the Free State, freedom from British oppression came at a great price. According to official records Joseph is believed to
be a member of the RIC (The Royal Irish Constabulary), Britain's police force
throughout the Anglo-Irish War of 1919–21, that incorporated many Catholics
and Nationalists of tenant-farmer stock, particularly from the west of Ireland
(McMahon and O'Donoghue 702). Following British withdrawal, most members of the RIC either joined the new police force of the Free State or ran the
risk of being exterminated. The IRA executes Joseph, leaving the sixteen-
year-old Roseanne and a mentally disturbed widow behind—both Protestant.

The Catholic parish priest Father Gaunt assumes a paternal role by offering Roseanne religious and social salvation through marriage. She declines,
and commits herself instead to an independent life in the newborn nation
which has promised equality for all citizens. Article 3 of the 1922 Constitution
confirmed that "every person, without distinction of sex, shall [...] enjoy the
privileges and be subject to the obligations of such citizenship" (qtd. in Beau-

mont 96). However the truth proved otherwise: the Catholic Church assumed the role of a policing moral force in the Free State, reinforced by the government. According to O'Mahony and Delanty, there were three likely reasons for this: first, the government needed church support in the task of regime stabilization; second, given the fact that nationalist revolution had ended in a bitter civil war with thousands of casualties, the new state needed the support of the church for legitimation. Thirdly, since alternative adaptations of identity had failed to take root (linguistic nationalism, as propounded by the Gaelic League),[3] Catholicism provided a symbolic unity and power both in cultural and political spheres (133–4). The Church assumed immense power over family life and a strict control of sexuality, especially in "the subjugation of the female body" (135), as well as calling for collectivity, social conformity, and a respect for their own authority. To accomplish this process they introduced a kind of collective "amnesia," dismissing from the nation's memory and the nationalist constructs the misfits who failed or rejected to conform to their ideology.

The meanings attached to the female body and femininity in the national discourse is an extension of the poetic discourse of the Irish Literary Revival, which identified Ireland with the motherland, "calling her sons to shed their blood so that the nation be restored after centuries of historical persecution" (Kearney 95). The female body symbolically represented the purity, dignity and honor of mother Ireland, restored by her faithful sons as they freed the country from the colonial yoke. However that body also had to be "protected" against unwelcome intrusion; this task, it was believed, could be best accomplished by the Church. Those who challenged this belief, or constructed their own adaptation of Irish history, were inevitably marginalized.

This is precisely what happens to Roseanne, as she is consigned to live in a small hut, isolated from society, on the grounds that she is mentally unstable and suffering from nymphomania. Father Gaunt's advice to her is worth quoting at length:

> If you had followed my advice, Roseanne, some years ago, and put your faith in the true religion [of the Catholic Church], if you had behaved with the beautiful decorum of a Catholic wife, you would not be facing these difficulties. But I do appreciate that you are not entirely responsible. Nymphomania is of course by definition a madness [...] Rome has agreed with this estimate [...] So you may rest assured that your case was seen to with all the thoroughness and fairness of mind well-informed, disinterested, and with no bad intention of any kind [Barry, *Secret* 231].

Yet Barry is not content just to look at identity construction at the personal level; in a clever adaptation of his historical material, he draws a deliberate parallel between Roseanne's predicament and the fate of the Irish Free

State in its first few decades. Her isolation parallels the isolationist policies implemented during the government of President Éamon de Valera,[4] as well as the neutrality adopted by the Irish Free State during wartime. Dr. Grene strengthens this parallel as he likens Roseanne's deliberate erasure from the official adaptation of Irish history to "a forest fire, burning away all traces of her, traversing her narrative and turning everything to ashes and cinders. A tiny, obscure, forgotten Hiroshima" (Barry, *Secret* 238). He criticizes the policy of neutrality, which was designed to protect Irish citizens from external violence, at a time when the nation was still fighting its own internal demons. He observes:

> I had the unworthy thought that maybe de Valera's great desire to avoid the Second World War was not because he feared the enemy within, feared to split his new country, but that it actually constituted a further effort to expunge sexuality. A sort of extension of the intentions of the clergy [237].

Dr. Grene's remarks forge a connection between the political neutrality of the nation and the sterile female body; both have to be "protected" through isolation.

A few days after the Belfast bombing at the beginning of World War II,[5] Roseanne encounters her brother-in-law Eneas McNulty, another exiled figure whose story has likewise been erased from the nationalist adaptation of history. At the age of sixteen Eneas leaves Ireland to fight in World War I rather than join the War of Independence; when he returns, he joins the RIC and is immediately branded a traitor by the IRA with a death sentence on his head. Freedom spells disaster for Eneas because he "chose to be loyal to the Crown at a moment when that loyalty no longer paid off" (Cullingford 144). Like Roseanne, he becomes a stranger in his own country. In Barry's earlier novel *The Whereabouts of Eneas McNulty* (1999), Eneas describes the experience of living in mid-twentieth century Ireland as "a sort of madness, a ferocious dizziness and misery of the heart" (Barry, *Whereabouts* 136–7). Both Roseanne's and Eneas' omission from mainstream adaptations of Irish history has created a vast absence in the memory of future generations. Both of them narrate "stories" that need to be told: as Roseanne observes early on in *The Secret Scripture*, she understands that "[t]he terror and hurt in [her] story happened because when [she] was young, [she] thought others were the authors of [her] fortune or misfortune; [she] did not know that a person could [...] be the author [...] of themselves" (Barry, *Secret* 4). Her words mirror the author's commentary on the novel:

> [I'm] afraid of the damage caused by not speaking of people like Roseanne, the unmentioned first wife, like so many families' old uncle Jack who dies in the first world war fighting for England. I'm concerned these silences leave a gap in your-

> self which then leaves a gap in your children and can ultimately lead to a hole in the country's sense of itself. Ireland's history is so much more rich, exciting, varied and complicated that we had realized. What I'm trying to do is gather in as much as I can. It is not to accuse. It is just to state that it is so [qtd. in Wroe].

Roseanne's testimony reclaims ownership of her own story; it represents her transition from a narrated subject to a narrating object. Her desire to narrate her own story reflects a post-colonial critique of Irish culture, with the recognition that "as a nation Ireland has been defined from the 'outside' for most of its existence" (Miller 9). She is also aware that "a person without anecdotes that they nurse while they live, and that survive them, are more likely to be utterly lost not only to history but the family following them" (Barry, *Secret* 11). Rewriting her own history becomes a means of therapeutic rehabilitation for her.

In the other main narrative of *The Secret Scripture*, the psychiatrist Dr. Grene tries to come to terms with his past, while at the same time trying to confirm the validity of Roseanne's story from official documentations and letters. Roseanne likens him to "St Thomas, with his beard and balding crown" (Barry, *Secret* 4)—a comparison that suggests Grene's skepticism about what his patients tell him, and whether it is a "truthful" reflection of their mental condition. In terms of the novel as a whole, Grene's skepticism reflects his commitment to the official adaptation of Irish history; he can never accept alternative constructions unless they have been verified by government documents. He questions the validity of Roseanne's so-called "freedom" on the grounds that "creatures so long kennelled and confined find freedom and release very problematic attainments, like those eastern European countries after communism" (17).

However Dr. Grene's skepticism is soon subverted, as he digs up the hospital archives, and comes across a document signed by Father Gaunt that details Roseanne's early life. Grene realizes that Gaunt was "the man who became auxiliary bishop of Dublin in the fifties and sixties, taking from the hemming and hawing of the Irish constitution a clear statement of his powers of moral domination over the city, as did most of his brother clerics" (142). He digs deeper, and by doing so discovers a shocking "truth" about his own history. We already know that he was an adopted child of Irish origin who was raised in England by adopted parents. It eventually transpires that he is Roseanne's child, who had been given away at birth to the Nazareth House, the orphanage in Sligo.

With this knowledge in mind, Dr. Grene comes to understand the necessity of acknowledging an alternative adaptation of Irish history—one that challenges his beliefs as well as his conception of identity. For the first time he is presented with "competing histories" (291) about his past. His experiences exemplify Roseanne's observation that "no one has the monopoly on truth. Not even myself" (134).

Elizabeth Cullingford suggests that Barry's "desire to give voice to the historically occluded native collaborator is a literary extension of the project of historical revisionism" (122), as well as part of a more general humanist desire to heal what he believes are the "wounds" of Irish history. To do this he follows T. W. Moody's dictum of "facing the facts of the Irish past, however painful some of them may be" (71). Barry sides with those revisionist historians who offer alternative adaptations of Ireland's past, moving the discourse away from the struggle against the British, and focusing instead on the potentially destructive consequences of the nationalist myth — especially for future generations. He uncovers the buried strata of history, and reveals the palimpsest-like nature of history writing, which incorporates the narratives of the minoritized and repressed as well as different versions of the hegemonic metanarrative. *The Secret Scripture* reveals how literary productions create alternative adaptations of the Irish past, as well as exposing how displaced micro-narratives have been erased for the purpose of sustaining hegemony and claiming sole authorship on national identity formations. Yet Barry neither attempts to colonize the past, nor claims "a higher truth-value for literature;" he merely show his work can "complete the picture and at the same time draw attention to what the framer [in this case, the government and the Catholic Church] chose to exclude" (Kiberd 646). By suggesting that Irish history is a sedimented series of shifting adaptations, Barry shows how the act of remembering entails a constant questioning of the past, leading to the creation of alternative futures and alternative histories.

Notes

1. For instance, the Criminal Law Amendment Act of 1935, which prohibited the sale of contraceptives; the Public Dance Hall Act of 1935, which restricted the holding of public dances; the Censorship of Films Act of 1923; the Censorship of Publications Acts of 1929, 1946 and 1967.

2. Ireland remained neutral during the Second War World. The period is officially known as the "Emergence."

3. This failure in the language issue is reflected in the fact that the 189 branches of the Gaelic League of 1922 decreased rapidly to 139 in 1924.

4. The Emergency Powers Act of 1939 was enacted, for example, to maintain the state of neutrality during the war. The police force's power of search and arrest was extended, but most importantly, communication through media and mail was restricted and strictly controlled to eliminate foreign influence that could threaten the peace and integrity of the nation.

5. On 15 April 1941, German planes unloaded more than a hundred tons of bombs over Belfast's residential areas, killing at least 745 in one night.

Works Cited

Barry, Sebastian. *The Secret Scripture.* London: Faber and Faber, 2008. Print.
_____. *The Whereabouts of Eneas McNulty.* London: Picador, 1999. Print.

Beaumont, Caitríona. "Gender, Citizenship and the State in Ireland, 1922–1990." *Ireland in Proximity: History, Gender, Space.* Eds. David Alderson, Fiona Becket, Scott Brewster and Virginia Crossman. London and New York: Routledge, 1999. 94–121. Print.

Cullingford, Elizabeth Butler. "Colonial Policing: The Steward of Christendom and The Whereabouts of Eneas McNulty." *Out of History: Essays on the Writings of Sebastian Barry.* Ed. Christina Hunt Mahony. Dublin: Caryfort Press, 2006. 121–144. Print.

Daly, Mary E. "Forty Shades of Grey? Irish Historiography and the Challenges of Multidisciplinarity." *Ireland Beyond Boundaries: Mapping Irish Studies in the Twenty-first Century.* Eds. Liam Harte and Yvonne Whelan. London: Pluto Press, 2007. 92–110. Print.

Foster, R. F. *The Irish Story: Telling Tales and Making It Up in Ireland.* London: Penguin Books, 2001. Print.

Hyde, Douglas. "The Necessity for De-Anglicising Ireland: Delivered Before the Irish National Literary Society in Dublin, 25 November 1892." *Irish Writing in the Twentieth Century.* Ed. David Pierce. Cork: Cork University Press, 2000. 2–13. Print.

Jeffries, Stuart. "Interview with Sebastian Barry." *The Guardian* (London) 29 Jan. 2009. Web. 13 Jan. 2012.

Kearney, Richard. *Postnationalist Ireland: Politics, Culture, Philosophy.* London and New York: Routledge, 1997. Print.

Kiberd, Declan. *Inventing Ireland: The Literature of the Modern Nation.* London: Jonathan Cape, 1995. Print.

Maley, Willy. "Nationalism and Revisionism: Ambivalences and Dissensus." *Ireland in Proximity: History, Gender, Space.* Eds. David Alderson, Fiona Becket, Scott Brewster and Virginia Crossman. London and New York: Routledge, 1999. 12–27. Print.

McMahon, Sean, and O'Donoghue, Jo. *Brewer's Dictionary of Irish Phrase and Fable.* London: Weidenfeld & Nicolson, 2004. Print.

Miller, Nicholas. *Modernism, Ireland and The Erotics of Memory.* Cambridge: Cambridge University Press, 2002. Print.

Moody, T. W. "Irish History and Irish Mythology." *Interpreting Irish History: The Debate on Historical Revisionism 1938–1994.* Ed. Ciaran Brady. Dublin: Irish Academic Press, 1994. 71–86. Print.

O'Mahony, Patrick, and Delanty, Gerard. *Rethinking Irish History: Nationalism, Identity and Ideology.* Basingstoke and New York: Palgrave, 2001. Print.

Wroe, Nicholas. "A Life in Writing: Sebastian Barry." *The Guardian* (London) 11 Oct. 2008. Web. 11 Feb. 2012.

Yeats, W. B. *The Collected Works of W. B. Yeats: Vol. II: The Plays.* Eds. David R. Clark and Rosalind E. Clark. New York: Scribners, 2001. 175–200. Print.

Interpreting the Vietnam War from a Vietnamese American Perspective

YUKI OBAYASHI

"[N]othing that has ever happened should be regarded as lost for history."—Walter Benjamin, *Illuminations* 177

Historical films reflect their filmmakers' understanding of the past and hence operate in the realm of subjectivity. In Foucault's formulation:

> The successes of history belong to those who are capable of seizing rules, to replace those who had used them, to disguise themselves so as to pervert them, invert their meaning, and redirect them against those who had initially imposed them; controlling this complex mechanism, they will make it function so as to overcome the rulers through their own rules [151].

This issue of power politics is clearly evident in historical films, which reflect the directors' preoccupations rather than trying to include a variety of perspectives. In this essay, I will show the subjective selection of history at work through an analysis of films about the Vietnam War, the majority of which focus on American soldiers and do not reflect the experience of Vietnamese Americans who evacuated their homeland as a result of the war and immigrated to the U.S. as refugees. According to Ronald Takaki, only 604 Vietnamese, mostly students, teachers, and diplomats, lived in the U.S. in 1964 (448). However, with the fall of Saigon in 1975, that number increased to 130,000 (451). Since then, the Vietnamese American community has expanded. The U.S. Census Bureau reports that the Vietnamese American population reached 1,100,000 in 2000 (Barnes and Bennett 9).

For Vietnamese Americans, the war shapes the foundation of their identity; hence they often find it difficult to accept their portrayal in mainstream Hollywood films. In his memoir *A Sense of Duty* (2005), Quang X. Pham voices his discontent:

> I watched *Coming Home, The Deer Hunter, Platoon, We Were Soldiers,* all of [them], hoping to get a glimpse of what my father went through [...] The stories portrayed in the movies [...] usually ended [with] the U.S. withdrawal in 1973. Only a few even attempted to capture the painful evacuations of Vietnam [34].

Quang Pham's father was imprisoned at a "re-education" camp for more than a decade after the war because he had fought for South Vietnam: Pham did not see him for almost two decades. The new communist government branded them as traitors, and forced them to confess their "crimes" and "reform" their previous anti-communist ideology while undergoing forced labor and torture. The Vietnamese American community currently includes survivors from these camps.

However the opportunities to tell such stories are often difficult — especially in recent years, as the subject has lost popularity. According to Marilyn B. Young: "To fight the new war against terrorism, the films, literature and histories of Vietnam would have to be obliterated" (24). Hollywood now produces war films set in the Middle East. Nonetheless, the need for Vietnamese Americans to adapt the past, and thereby accommodate their idiosyncratic point of view, remains as urgent as ever. With this imperative in mind, I will survey Hollywood's Vietnam films through fresh eyes, and subsequently examine representations of Vietnamese Americans in the independent works *Green Dragon* (2002) and *Journey from the Fall* (2007). Both films retrace the underrepresented history of Vietnamese Americans, while deconstructing American subjectivity.

To a large extent, mainstream Hollywood adaptations of the Vietnam conflict concentrate on the mid–1960s rather than looking at the later years: *Go Tell the Spartans* is set in 1964; *Good Morning, Vietnam, We Were Soldiers,* and *Rescue Dawn* in 1965; *Platoon* in 1967; *Born on the Fourth of July* 1967–8; and *Hamburger Hill* and *Casualties of War* in 1969. Only a few films have been set in the 1970s, such as *The Boys in Company C* (in 1973), *The Deer Hunter* and *Heaven and Earth*, both of which narrate the fall of Saigon in 1975. By contrast *Green Dragon* and *Journey from the Fall* begin in 1975: *Green Dragon* depicts the lives of the South Vietnamese in a refugee camp; in *Journey from the Fall*, the central conflict revolves around a family torn apart by war. The husband (Long Nguyen) is imprisoned at a re-education camp, while the rest of the family travels to the U.S. as boat people. These differences in period setting reveal different objectives: mainstream Hollywood adaptations question the morality of war and its effect on American society; the two independent films concentrate more on personal stories to depict the experiences of those most at risk from the conflict. These issues will be explored more fully in the next section.

Healing from Trauma

Judith Herman argues that "the core experiences of psychological trauma are disempowerment and disconnection from others. Recovery, therefore, is based upon the empowerment of the survivor and the creation of new connections" (153). Her arguments are especially applicable to all Vietnam War films, even though they are approached in different ways. In mainstream Hollywood adaptations American war veterans try (but sometimes fail) to achieve redemption through self-reliance. For example, in *First Blood* (1982), Rambo, a decorated Vietnam War veteran (Sylvester Stallone), is treated unfairly by a sheriff (Brian Dennehy) in a provincial area. Rambo's frustration leads him to commit murder and destroy the town. Just before surrendering, Rambo observes,

> Nothing is over. Nothing. You just don't turn it off. It wasn't my war. You asked me. I didn't ask you. I did what I had to do to win. And I come back to the world and I see all those maggots at the airport, protesting me, spitting. Calling me baby killer and all kinds of vile crap. Who are they to protest me? Who are they?

In *Born on the Fourth of July* (1989), Ron Kovic (Tom Cruise) is inspired by a wave of patriotism to fight in the war. However he returns to his homeland paralyzed from the waist down, and almost completely ignored by his one-time friends. Cooped up in a hospital ward, Kovic shouts: "I want to be treated like a human being." When no one listens to his pleas, he responds by joining the anti-war movement. Both films suggest that in a meritocratic society the invalid and the psychologically disturbed are perpetually marginalized. The only way that Rambo and Kovic can recover is on their own: Rambo reenacts the Vietnam War in the American countryside, and thereby believes that he has regained the power he used to exercise during the conflict. Kovic also finds a degree of independence by participating in the anti-war movement.

One of the main problems lies in the American soldiers' inability to relate to the world around them, either at home or abroad. In *Apocalypse Now* (1979), Captain Benjamin Willard (Martin Sheen) is ordered to assassinate Colonel Walter Kurtz (Marlon Brando), who turns out to be a psychopath who has created his own kingdom deep in the jungle. When Willard is captured and put in a cell, the children in the kingdom innocently gaze at him, while Willard stares into space, as if feeling completely out of place in an alien world.

Green Dragon and *Journey from the Fall* offer different perspectives on the same issue, as the children in both films Minh (Troung Nguyen) in *Green Dragon*, and Lai (Nguyen Thai Nguyen) in *Journey from the Fall* try to make sense of the trauma of separation. In her article "The 1.5 Generation: Thinking about Child Survivors and the Holocaust," Susan Suleiman looks at the experiences of the "1.5 Generation"—in other words, those who emigrated from their homelands during their childhood, and received education in their host countries. She suggests that this age-span of this generation normally runs from birth to eleven years old; in her view,

> children under the age of eleven have a different way of understanding what is happening to them from those who are older; the older child possesses the capacity to think hypothetically, to use abstract words appropriately and with understanding, as well as a vocabulary to name the experience that the younger child lacks [282].

According to Suleiman, younger children are often prevented from coming to terms with traumatic situations by a lack of suitable vocabulary; hence it is the adult's responsibility to help them come to terms with new experiences. If that task proves difficult, then the children are highly likely to experience the kind of emotional torment characteristic of the Hollywood adaptations. For example, Minh in *Green Dragon* is forced to part from his mother: Uncle Tai (Duong Don), who is assumed to have a strong connection with the U.S. government, is provided with only three tickets to fly to the U.S. and allocates two of them to Minh and his sister Anh (Jennifer Tran). Unable to understand this situation, Minh continues to look for his mother in the American refugee camp. In *Journey from the Fall*, Lai does not understand the potential danger of his family's evacuation from Vietnam; they have to move stealthily, even if Lai does not like it. He loses his sandal and attempts to find it in the dark; he does not understand that to spend too much time in one place might lead to instant death. The portrayals of these children's perspectives emphasize the brutality of war.

Although they struggle with their own trauma and sense of loss, the adults in the attempt to help their children deal with their suffering. In *Green Dragon*, Tai looks after the children while their mother is left behind and their father is missing. Once he learns of their father's death, he sits next to the children and tells them the news. His decision to place a blanket over them suggests his desire to make the news bearable and to protect them. This is a difficult task; in the next scene he is shown taking a shower alone in the darkness and breaking down crying. In *Journey from the Fall* Lai's mother, Mai (Diem Lien) occupies herself by working as a seamstress in a factory, caring for her child, and studying English at a vocational school in the U.S. However, the scar on her neck visibly represents her deep, repressed trauma: she was scalded during an assault by pirates during her evacuation by boat. In a later sequence, Mai slowly touches her scar while looking in a mirror at work. The camera zooms in as she looks away from the mirror towards the photo of her husband. In a private space apart from her family, Mai takes the opportunity to mourn for her husband. Meanwhile Lai's grandmother Noi (Kieu Chinh) attempts to help Lai compensate for the absence of his father by asking him to write letters and draw pictures, both of which provide a means for him to express his feelings.

However, the difference between Noi's and Mai's ways of adapting to the past produces a rift in the family. For Noi and Lai, Mai's silence suggests that she has forgotten her husband. Mai responds thus: "Do you think your mother is still alive? She's dead already. Dead already. I died the day they took your father. I died again out on that ocean. This person you call your mother is nothing but a corpse, living only to take care of you." Although emotionally shocking, this sequence helps to restore that sense of collectivity and mutual trust that differentiates the Vietnamese Americans' process of adapting to recent history from their Euro-American counterparts. Both films propose familial units that help the new emigrants to survive. In *Green Dragon*, the family initially consists of Tai and his nephew and niece, but subsequently encompasses Tai's his new wife Thuy (Hiep Thi Le), her sister (Linda Tran), and Tai's brother (Tuan Tran), who rejoins them in the refugee camp. In *Journey from the Fall*, the family of a mother, son, and grandmother is augmented by Nam (Khanh Doan), who helps them in their new country. Nam's devotion to the family suggests another type of family that extends beyond blood relations.

Adapting Stereotypes

Green Dragon and *Journey from the Fall* give Vietnamese characters a voice; non–Vietnamese speaking audiences can understand their speech through English subtitles. In contrast, in American films, the audience can only understand Vietnamese characters who speak English. In *Heaven and Earth* (1993), the main character, a Vietnamese woman named Le Ly (Hiep Thi Le), speaks English almost exclusively. Only when Le Ly's friend schemes to obtain money from an American GI does their language suddenly switch from English to subtitled Vietnamese. Except for this scene, the film suggests that Le Ly communicates with her family in English. *The Green Berets* and

Good Morning, Vietnam also contain Vietnamese figures who speak only English. In the latter film, DJ Adrian Cronauer (Robin Williams) falls in love with a Vietnamese girl Tuan (Tung Thanh Tran), and disguises himself as a teacher at an ESL school that she attends. Tuan and the other students have to communicate with him in broken English. The choice of language emphasizes the colonialist mentality: Cronauer's fast speech contrasts with Tuan's slow, imperfect, and thickly accented English. Yumiko Murakami believes that this deliberately stereotypical rendering reproduces the dominant American perspective (234).

In many other mainstream American films, Vietnamese characters speak their own language, but without subtitles. In *Casualties of War*, Sergeant Tony Meserve (Sean Penn) and other soldiers kidnap a female villager, Oanh (Thuy Thu Le) and imprison her as a sex-object. Her utterances are never subtitled. In *Platoon*, Chris Tylor's (Charlie Sheen's) platoon patrols a village and interrogates villagers; their pleas for mercy are again not subtitled. Such techniques are deliberately designed to denigrate the Vietnamese, as well as summing up the confusion experienced by many Americans faced with an alien environment.

More significantly, the Vietnamese in American films are the victims of racial abuse, being described as "gooks," whether they are from the North or the South, soldiers or civilians (Desser 89, 94). In *Good Morning, Vietnam* Cronauer takes Tuan's brother, Trinh (Chintara Sukapatana), to a bar that American soldiers frequent. One of the soldiers starts a fight with Cronauer, saying, "Who brought in the fuckin' gook?" The bar owner, Jimmy Wah (Cu Ba Nguyen), tries to settle the fight, saying, "Everybody say gook, but it's all right." In *Go Tell the Spartans*, the racial epithet is applied to South Vietnamese soldiers: objecting to the way Nguyen's (Evan Kim's) interrogates a suspicious Viet Cong, Major Asa Baker (Burt Lancaster) says to Captain Alfred Olivetti (Marc Singer), "I'm gonna zap that goddamn gook." In response Olivetti replies, "Which gook, sir? ... Well, you can't shoot that goddamn gook, sir. He knows English, French, Chinese, [and] 75 Viet[namese] dialects." Nguyen's linguistic proficiency does not permit him to transcend the racial barrier.

Vietnamese women are also victims of racial prejudice, being cast mostly as sexual objects existing solely for the white American soldiers' benefit (Williams 221). In *Good Morning, Vietnam* prostitutes crowd around American soldiers at Jimmy Wah's bar; even those women who are not members of this profession are consciously exoticized. On the way to an American base soon after landing in Vietnam, Cronauser shouts excitedly: "Mayday! Mayday! Dragon Lady with incredible figure at 11:00 A.M. Stop the car. Oh! There she is again! How'd she get ahead of us?" Vietnamese women are seldom distinguished from one another, but generalized as "dragon ladies." Even in Oliver Stone's *Heaven and Earth* (1993), the only film that casts a Vietnamese woman as the main character, the American soldier Steve Butler (Tommy Lee Jones) proposes marriage to Le Ly Hayslip thus: "I need a good Oriental woman like you. I want you to be my wife." Arriving in Vietnam after a traumatic divorce from his American wife, Butler hopes to find an obedient Asian partner.

Some American Vietnam War films portray Americans as generous; in *The Green Berets*, a Vietnamese orphan named Hamchunk (Craig Jue) lives on the American base, after a missionary who cared for him has been murdered. This is not his real name, however, but one that has been given to him by the American soldiers: orientalism is part of their way of life. However they provide medical care to anyone in need: when a girl steps on a Viet Cong trap and is injured, their humanitarian treatment of her contrasts with the Vietnamese brutality in battle. But for most American directors and their audiences, the entire Vietnamese nation represents the antithesis of the "desirable, homey, and 'good'" west (Christopher 5). Such representations "reinforc[e] the myth of American benevolence while suppressing the truth of U.S. genocidal activity throughout Southeast Asia" (Hamamoto 150). The representation of the Vietnamese as inferior emphasizes the positive aspects of American subjectivity.

Both *Green Dragon* and *Journey from the Fall* set out to deconstruct mainstream Hollywood historical adaptations of the Vietnamese people. In *Journey from the Fall* Lai's teacher (Robert Beck) in the American school is portrayed as an ignorant American, who proclaims that "[Lai] has no made effort to make friends, [and] doesn't take class work seriously." He takes no heed of Lai's situation: "I don't get you. You are all immigrants. You leave your home country because of war. And you come here, start a gang fight." Noi tries to find out why Lai is becoming involved in fights with other students. She notices that he is bullied because of the absence of his father; in the next sequence, the camera captures Lai standing in front of a mirror and looking at bruises all over his body. The film suggests that Lai is actually victimized in the U.S.; no one bothers to listen to him or takes any real interest in the emotional difficulties he experienced while coming to the country in the first place. This adaptation of contemporary American history stands in direct contrast to the benevolent American in mainstream Hollywood Vietnam War films.

Green Dragon portrays a reciprocal relationship between Americans and Vietnamese; in so doing, the film challenges hierarchical representations of them. The Americans begin by attempting to control the newly arriving Vietnamese according to their own social and behavioral standards. General Sergeant Jim Lance (Patrick Swayze) announces the camp rules through a loud-speaker in English, although most of the refugees do not understand him. Tai is hired as a camp manager because of his linguistic skills, and he teaches English to the other refugees. Eventually, Tai confronts Jim over the camp organization; Jim tries to ameliorate the situation by announcing: "I can only imagine just how difficult this must be for you and your people. But you need to know that we are trying to help. And we are friends." However Jim's offer of help is determined by liberal American standards; Tai suggests, in contrast, that he should "try speaking to us without your bullhorn." In the process of becoming acquainted with their differing value-systems, they share their mutual sorrow for their losses, as Jim reads the final letter from his brother — who died during the conflict — and shows a softer side to his nature. The shared act of mourning provides the basis for a more equal racial relationship. The film depicts another cross-cultural relationship between Minh and Addie (Forrest Whitaker), a volunteer cook in a mess hall for refugees. Despite the language barrier, he sees his situation reflected in Minh; his mother's death, his father's abuse and subsequent abandonment of him when he was four years old. Addie shows Minh sketches of his parents and suggests that the two of them draw together as a way of healing one another's sorrow and suffering.

In his "Theses on the Philosophy of History," Walter Benjamin states his notion of the past: "The true picture of the past flits by. The past can be seized only as an image which flashes up at the instant when it can be recognized and is never seen again" (255). The American mainstream cinema has to date focused on colonialist historical adaptations of the Vietnam War and the Viet-namese people. However, in *Green Dragon* and *Journey from the Fall*, the directors Timothy Bui and Ham Tran adapt untold stories from a Vietnamese American standpoint. Both films challenge the master narratives, especially the representation of the Vietnamese as "others," by investing all the charac-ters, Vietnamese and Americans alike, with humanity. By doing so, they emphasize the importance of filmmakers' responsibility towards the kind of histories represented in their work. As Marita Sturken argues: "Despite their role as fictional narratives, these [mainstream Vietnam War] films rescript the war and subsume documentary images. Indeed, many deliberately restage documentary images, blurring the boundaries between the reenactment and the original event" (94). As time passes, so these distinctions between "fiction" and "reality" become more and more blurred: what becomes more important is how the directors adapt their material.

Works Cited

Apocalypse Now. Dir. Francis Ford Coppola. Perf. Martin Sheen, Marlon Brando. Zoetrope Studios, 1979. Film.

Barnes, Jessica S., and Claudette E. Bennett. The Asian Population: 2000. U.S. Dept. of Commerce. Feb. 2002. Web. 1 Dec. 2007.

Benjamin, Walter. *Illuminations: Essays and Reflections.* Trans. Harry Zohn. New York: Schocken Books, 1969. Print.

Born on the Fourth of July. Dir. Oliver Stone. Perf. Tom Cruise, Caroline Kava. Ixtlan, 1989. Film.

The Boys in Company C. Dir. Sidney J. Furie. Perf. Stan Shaw, Andrew Stevens. Golden Harvest Company, 1978. Film.

Casualties of War. Dir. Brian De Palma. Perf. Michael J. Fox, Sean Penn. Columbia Pictures, 1989. Film.

Christopher, Renny. *The Vietnam War, The American War: Images and Representations in Euro-American and Vietnamese Exile Narratives.* Amherst: Univeristy of Massachusetts Press, 1995. Print.

Coming Home. Dir. Hal Ashby. Perf. Jane Fonda, Jon Voight, Bruce Dern. Jerome Hellman Productions, 1978. Film.

The Deer Hunter. Dir. Michael Cimino. Perf. Robert De Niro, Christopher Walken. EMI Films, 1978. Film.

Desser, David. "'Charlie Don't Surf': Race and Culture in the Vietnam War Films." *Inventing Vietnam: The War in Film and Television.* Ed. Michael Anderegg. Philadelphia: Temple University Press, 1991. 81–102. Print.

First Blood. Dir. Ted Kotcheff. Perf. Sylvester Stallone, Brian Dennehy, Richard Crenna. Elcajo Productions/ Anabasis NV, 1982. Film.

Foucault, Michel. *Language, Counter-memory, Practice: Selected Essays and Interviews.* Trans. Donald F. Bouchard and Sherry Simon. Ithaca: Cornell University Press, 1977. Print.

Go Tell the Spartans. Dir. Ted Post. Perf. Burt Lancaster, Craig Wasson. Spartan Productions, 1978. Film.

Good Morning, Vietnam. Dir. Barry Levinson. Perf. Robin Williams, Forrest Whitaker, Tung Thanh Tran. Touchstone Pictures/ Silver Screen Partners, 1987. Film.

Green Dragon. Dir. Timothy Bui. Perf. Patrick Swayze, Forrest Whitaker. Franchise Classics, 2001. Film.

The Green Berets. Dir. Ray Kellogg, John Wayne. Perf. John Wayne, David Janssen, Jim Hutton. Batjac Productions, 1968. Film.

Hamamoto, Darrell Y. *Monitored Peril: Asian Americans and the Politics of TV Representation.* Minneapolis: University of Minnesota Press, 1994. Print.

Hamburger Hill. Dir. John Irvin. Perf. Anthony Barrile, Don Cheadle. RKO Pictures, 1987. Film.

Heaven and Earth. Dir. Oliver Stone. Perf. Hiep Thi Le, Tommy Lee Jones. Alcor Films/ Ixtlan, 1993. Film.

Herman, Judith L. *Trauma and Recovery: The Aftermath of Violence — from Domestic Abuse to Political Terror.* 1992. New York: Basic Books, 1997. Print.

Journey from the Fall. Dir. Ham Tran. Perf. Kieu Chinh, Long Nguyen, Diem Lien. A Fire in the Lake Productions, 2006. Film.

Murakami, Yumiko. *Iero Feisu (Yellow Face).* Tokyo: Asahi Shimbun Sha, 1993. Print.

Pham, Quang X. *A Sense of Duty: My Father, My American Journey.* New York: Ballantine, 2005. Print.

Platoon. Dir. Oliver Stone. Perf. Charlie Sheen, Tom Berenger, Willem Dafoe. Hemdale Films, 1986. Film.

Rescue Dawn. Dir. Werner Herzog. Perf. Christian Bale, Steve Zahn. MGM, 2006. Film.

Sturken, Marita. *Tangled Memories: The Vietnam War, The Aids Epidemic, and the Politics of Remembering.* Berkeley: University of California Press, 1997. Print.

Suleiman, Susan R. "The 1.5 Generation: Thinking About Child Survivors and the Holocaust." *American Imago* 59.3 (2002): 277–295. Print.

Takaki, Ronald. *Strangers from a Different Shore: A History of Asian Americans.* 1989. New York and London: Penguin, 1990. Print.

We Were Soldiers. Dir. Randall Wallace. Perf. Mel Gibson, Madeleine Stowe, Greg Kinnear. Paramount Pictures, 2002. Film.

Williams, Paul. "'What a Bummer for the Gooks': Representations of White American Masculinity and the Vietnamese in the Vietnam War Film Genre 1977–87." *European Journal of American Culture* 22.3 (2003): 215–234. Print.

Young, Marilyn B. "Now Playing: Vietnam." *OAH Magazine of History* 18.5 (2004): 22–26. Print.

Re-Inscribing Sovereignty: History, Adaptation, and Medicine in the Poetry of Deborah Miranda

ROSE GUBELE

In the "Author's Note" to her book of poetry, *Indian Cartography*, Deborah Miranda of the Ohlone-Costanoan Esselen Nation recounts a conversation with another American Indian woman she had just met. When Miranda told the woman that she was Esselen, a California tribe, her new acquaintance responded "California! I heard all those Indians died!'" (ix). Miranda then turned and looked at one of her friends, who was also a member of a California tribe. The two of them said, "'Well, here we are!'" (ix). From this anecdote we understand how many people, both Native and non–Native, view California Indian tribes. The colonial history of each tribe in North America is unique, and each must find ways to come to terms with their particular historical circumstances. As Miranda writes:

[T]he truth of the matter is, for many tribes in California the words "All those Indians died" are horribly real. Our lives, and our ability to assert our identities as tribal people, remind me of ingenious, stubborn plants cracking through the thick pavement of history. We disturb the façade of conquest — challenge the myth of extinction — but though we still exist, we are not undamaged or unchanged [Miranda, *Indian Cartography* ix].

Miranda's poetry disinters a past that was unseen after her ancestors were silenced by the colonizing forces of Spain, Mexico, and the United States. She gives voice to the descendants of California tribes who live with this

171

legacy; at the same time her poetry helps surviving generations to adapt to the ongoing imperial paternalism imposed upon them by the United States government.

The purpose of this essay is to demonstrate the ways that Miranda's poetry addresses California Indian history, and the way that this process brings healing to her Nation, and other California Indian Nations. The natural tendency is to forget a traumatic past, but only through remembering and accepting the past can a people move forward. As a trauma survivor, Miranda understands the importance of accepting the past. It is essential to the process of healing. So, Miranda's poetry works like "medicine" in the Native American sense; it helps people heal both physically and spiritually. Her work does this by persuading people not to forget their past. It works cathartically, like the oral tradition, and it connects Nations with their memories. It persuades Indian peoples to keep going, to reclaim what they have lost.

Land-Line Adjustment[1]

> Once I dreamt that the truth was inscribed
> in bone, sacred skeletons waiting to be found —
> [Miranda, "Without History" 74].

In order to understand Miranda's rhetoric, it is important to understand the historical context from which it originated. She is Esselen and Chumash on her father's side and European and Jewish on her mother's side (Miranda, *Indian Cartography* x). Her father's ancestors were Native Californians originating from the "Monterey/ Big Sur/ Carmel River area" and the "Santa Barbara/ Santa Ynez River area" (xi). Although twenty thousand inhabitants still survive, the tribe as a whole suffered unspeakably from the violation of colonization. The Spanish arrived in California in 1769, although they had previously been on brief explorations (Borah 6). They tried to establish a protective barrier for Mexico against the Russians and the British, who were beginning to show interest in the Pacific coasts and islands (7). In addition, they hoped to protect the area from Southwestern Indians who resisted colonization. To consolidate their power, the Spanish set up a mission, designed to handle Indians and harness aboriginal societies to the state. Local people were "encouraged" to attend the missions and thereby accommodated into a new social structure, furnishing labor and services for the Mexican people, while living in their own settlements under the guidance of Christian missionaries.

For the most part the native Indians were appallingly treated. Punishments included whipping with a barbed lash, solitary confinement, mutilation, use of stocks and hobbles, branding, and even execution for both men and women (Castillo 929–930). Disease was rife: at the Santa Clara Mission in 1777, pneumonia and diphtheria broke out, while a measles epidemic decimated native peoples from San Francisco to Santa Barbara in 1806. Resistance to the colonial power was impossible: most people mounted individual acts of defiance, but were brutally crushed by the Spanish army. The soldiers would catch the women with their lassoes to become prey for their unbridled lust. At times some men would try to defend their wives, only to be shot down with bullets (Tibesar 362–63). Native Indians who chose to work in pueblos and ranchos were ruthlessly exploited by their employers, who often paid them with alcohol alone.

In 1848, the Treaty of Guadalupe Hidalgo placed California under the power of the United States (Castillo 935), whose government saw Indians as obstacles to the country's progress. Two years later a law entitled "An Act for the Government and Protection of Indians" was passed, binding Indians to labor contracts upon approval of the justice of the peace, while indenturing children to be up to the age of majority, a provision that condemned them to sexual slavery as well as excluding them from formal education (Fernandez 917). Many tribes had land taken away from them: the first reservation was established in 1852, but they failed to cater for the local people's needs. Nearly eight decades later, only thirty-six reservations had been created; these were "mostly home sites or rancherias between five and a few hundred acres each. In southern California none of the many landless bands or individuals were provided with home sites as a result of these appropriations" (Castillo 946). Some California tribes, including the Ohlone-Costanoan Esselen nation — Miranda's father's tribe — were simply ignored. Ever since the mid-nineteenth century they have been clamoring for federal recognition. Although the tribe was never terminated legally by Congress, they have been deliberately discriminated against by Bureau of Indian Affairs agents, who neglected to purchase lands for California tribes, even though they were officially ordered to do so. One agent stated that it was "his personal belief that land should not be purchased for California Indians" (Ohlone Costanoan Esselen Nation). As a result, one hundred and thirty four tribes were removed from the list of recognized tribes by the year 1927.

History is not a thing of the past for American Indians; it is lived daily. Each Native person must carry around his or her colonial history. The fact that Miranda's tribe does not have Federal recognition is one current consequence of their history. But also, Miranda's personal history is linked inextricably with her people's history. Poetry works cathartically for Miranda, to help her deal with past traumas, both personal and historical, and offers medicine to help others.

Compilation[2]

[Blood] is ink, like faith,
indelible
[Miranda, "Without History" 74].

Miranda's personal history and the history of her nation are inextricably intertwined. Born in California, Miranda suffered a traumatic childhood; her father had a drinking problem and engaged in physically abusive behavior (Miranda, "Silver" 130). The tumultuous relationship between her parents did not last long; they separated, and her father went to San Quentin, where he spent the next eight years (127–30). At age seven, Miranda was raped by her mother's boyfriend; her best friend was also abused and Miranda had to witness the incident (128–29). Miranda uses poetry as a way of dealing with her personal history, as well as the suffering of her tribe. In an essay published in 1998, she attributes the development of her poetic sensibility to a dream, in which she volunteered "to be a part of a memory experiment in which scientists lock up a bunch of Indians in a mission" to monitor their responses. During the experiment, the doors of the mission were closed, and "each of the people present [...] simultaneously and without volition, opened their mouths and began to scream." As Miranda felt her own mouth open in a scream, she realized that "It was somebody else's scream." This dream made her realize that she could be "a voice for others," while helping her to accept that her own pain "was at once personal and universal," and making her aware that she had a right "to be a survivor, to be a witness (Miranda, "Lunatic or Lover..."). Miranda observes that in the past "the Indians of California were never meant to survive;" their "demise was legally and officially planned, executed, and very nearly carried out" (*Indian Cartography* ix). Her poetry is more than just testimony to her and her people's endurance, more than a celebration of survival; it disinters the often willfully hidden history of her tribe in an attempt to heal the wounds of the past.

The idea that a poet could rewrite history and promote healing may seem unlikely. However, Craig Womack suggests that poetry is a continuation of the oral tradition. Speaking about the connection between storytelling and poetry, Womack writes:

> Many times, the poems [written by Native authors] are autobiographical, and there is not as great a fictive distance between the speaker of the poem and the author of the poem as there is in poetry at large. This is not a derivation of the Plath and Sexton school [of confessional poetry] but a natural evolution from the oral tradition where a performed story is very close to the person who tells it. First of all, the oral tradition, the story literally emanates from the speaker's body. The story is never performed as a fixed entity but is personalized through

the speaker's voice and movements. And the story, passed down from generation to generation, is communal property, the history of the people, so the story explains the teller's place in the scheme of things; it incorporates both "I" and "we." Because of the performative dimension and the passed-down dimension of the stories in an oral community, all stories are autobiographical to varying degrees [...] Oral stories tell the history of individuals and their communities [249].

Robert Warrior also sees this poetry in this way, as a continuation and re-development of traditional storytelling (118). Miranda's poetry, then, can be seen as an act of re-claiming history and tradition in an attempt to persuade California tribes not to forget their history. Poetry helps people reconnect with ancient stories and remember the past without being overwhelmed by it.

Coordinates³

> Once I believed my account survived, written
> on my heart — a secret fragment
> [Miranda, "Without History" 74].

Deborah Miranda's first collection of poetry, *Indian Cartography*, inter-twines her personal history with the history of her nation. The title, *Indian Cartography*, contains multiple implications for Native Americans. Cartography is a science that has served the imperial illusion that the colonized land is empty, devoid of humanity:

Colonization itself is often consequent on a voyage of "discovery," a bringing into being of "undiscovered" lands. The process of discovery is reinforced by the construction of maps, whose existence is a means of textualizing the spatial real-ity of the other, naming or, in almost all cases, renaming spaces in a symbolic and literal act of mastery and control. In all cases the lands so colonized are lit-erally reinscribed, written over, as the names and languages of the indigenes are replaced by new names, or are corrupted into new and Europeanized forms by the cartographer and explorer [Miranda, *Cartography* 32–3].

Through the act of creating maps, the colonizers renamed and forever changed the landscape, and the people with it. In the "classic" scenario, a postcolonial people are those who have been colonized by an imperial force that later departed, leaving the country ostensibly liberated, but still in thrall to the former invading power. As Malea Powel notes, "it is difficult to describe American Indians as either "postcolonial" or "neocolonial" peoples. The occu-pying force has not been, nor will it ever be, withdrawn" (399). Perhaps we should characterize Native Americans as "paracolonial" rather than "postcolonial" people: "paracolonial" is a term coined by Gerald Vizenor, denoting multiplicity, indicating the many ways a people have been colonized and recolonized since the late eighteenth century (77). In addition to the initial act of colonization by the Spanish, the Mexicans and the Americans, Native people have been recolonized each time they are declared extinct by dominant discourses—for example, those early map-makers who claimed that the lands in America were "unoccupied," or "virgin," in spite of the fact that they had been peopled for centuries beforehand (Ashcroft et al., 32).

Throughout *Indian Cartography*, Miranda draws a connection between land and the Native Indian body. In the title poem, Miranda looks at a map with her father as he "traces mountain ranges, rivers, county borders/ like family bloodlines" (77). Here, Miranda's image shows the parallel between the people and the land; the bloodlines of the tribe are etched into the range of mountains. The land is not something to be owned; it is the foundation of a culture. As her father looks at the map, he sees "Places he was happy,/ or where tragedy greeted him/like an old unpleasant relative" (76). He looks at a lake that was "created when they/ dammed the Santa Ynez, flooded/a valley," and he is overcome by memories that require him to seek "the solace of a six pack," so that he can return in his dreams to "lands not drawn on any map" (76). In the process of colonization, lands were remapped, and California Indians have been remapped like the land itself.

The link between cartography and rape is also at work in Miranda's poetry. As stated previously, cartographers saw vast, "virgin" areas of wilderness, ignoring the native populations. These "virgin" areas were seen as "open and inviting" spaces "into which the European (usually male) explorer [...] [tried to] penetrate" (Ashcroft, et al. 32). Cartography in the hands of a colonizing power could be seen as the rape of the land. Tragically, this mindset translated itself into reality as well. As the cartographers inscribed the land, erasing Native place names, the colonizers inscribed bodies through rape— especially the children who were indentured after the mid-nineteenth century. However rape was a daily consequence of colonization in earlier times: in a biography of Christopher Columbus, Samuel Eliot Morison writes: "Never again may mortal men hope to recapture the amazement, the wonder, the delight of those October days in 1492 when the New World gracefully yielded her virginity to the conquering Castilians" (113). The colonizers extended this view to Native women, who they considered available for the taking, like the land itself:

> While I was in the boat I captured a very beautiful Carib woman, whom the said Lord Admiral [Columbus] gave to me, and with whom, having taken her into my cabin, she being naked according to their custom, I conceived desire to take pleasure. I wanted to put my desire into execution but she did not want it and

treated me with her finger nails in such a manner that I wished I had never begun. But seeing that, (to tell you the end of it all), I took a rope and thrashed her well, for which she raised such unheard of screams that you would not have believed your ears. Finally we came to an agreement in such manner that I can tell you she seemed to have been brought up in a school of harlots [Cuneo 49].

The idea that Native Americans deserve to be colonized is similar to the idea that a woman who wanders out alone (without an escort) or who wears a certain kind of clothing asks to be raped. Both colonialism and rape are exercises in power (Brownmiller 256).

Miranda's most poignant poems in *Indian Cartography* are ones in which she integrates her own personal rape trauma with the colonization of her nation. In "Looking for a Cure," she recalls the experience of abuse, comparing it to the eruption of a volcano:

> In this country that is and is not
> hers, a woman sees a stream of bloody sparks
> racing along an obsidian-slick channel
> Cut out of heat and desperation,
> she can never map or anticipate
> this path. She is always just on the other
> side of knowing, separated by a wall
> of flesh or maybe layers of bone,
> marrow thick at the center.
> Bleeding is too small a word [3].

In this stanza, the "country that is and is not/ hers" is her own body, colonized by an imperial force. She "cannot map" her own path. The lava flowing down the channel is analogous to the flow of her blood after the rape.

The significance of Deborah Miranda's use of her body to represent land lies in the connection between cartography and rape. As a rape survivor, she is forever changed; as a member of a colonized people, her nation also changed. Her response to the change is to fight for survival, and thereby try to change the course of American history. Native Americans in general and California Indians in particular, are constantly referred to in the past tense. It is difficult for many people to "see" living Indians because too many people envision Indians as a part of an idealized past. Similarly, rape survivors are often constructed as "victims," "damaged" by their experience, and prone to suicide.[4]

By entwining her own personal story with the story of her Nation, Miranda disinters a hidden history: "Rape and gendered violence are invisible in most histories of California; certainly, sexual assault is not a topic commonly thought of by most Americans when they visit or learn about California

Missions" ("Saying the Padre Had Grabbed Her" 98). However, she also enacts the healing power of story. Storytelling works like medicine for the author, as the act of telling can bring catharsis, but also for the listener (or reader) who sees her own traumas, both personal and National, reflected in the words of a story.

In a 2010 essay, "Rape Is the Weapon, Story Is the Cure," Miranda argues that "California Indian women have still not healed from the tragedy of Missionization, colonization, and the violence it inflicted on our bodies" (104). She continues:

> Silence solves nothing. Even if a rape victim goes through the long process of reclaiming his or her body and processing the most intimate kind of invasion there is, healing is not guaranteed and is not immediate. And no matter what kind of justice occurs, nothing can bring that person back to who they were before the rape. How we raise our children, how we walk down the street, how we dress, how we form or don't form friendships, even how well we sleep or how well we do or don't take care of our bodies, is affected by the experience of rape. The ripples of a rape spread in every direction. How we respond to rape determines whether those ripples continue to be destructive, or move towards restoration [105].

Miranda offers statistics from "Maze of Injustice: The Failure to Protect Indigenous Women from Sexual Violence in the USA"—a study of American Indian women and rape conducted by Amnesty International. She points to the report's findings that one in three native women will be sexually assaulted in their lifetimes, which puts them at a 2.5 times greater risk of rape than any other socio-economic or racial group. Eighty percent of men who commit rape are nonnatives, attesting to the strength of the colonial legacy (Amnesty 2). Miranda observes the probability of under reporting, and argues that the numbers of Native women who are raped are much higher ("Saying the Padre Had Grabbed Her" 104). The logic of sexual violence constructs the colonial mindset. In her book *Off the Reservation*, Paula Gunn Allen argues that: "The ubiquitous concept of evolution, deriving as it does from the "civilized" belief that the strong must prevail over the weak, the superior over the inferior, the violent over the peaceful, and the order of patriarchy over all, leads inexorably to rape" (66).

This is the most important point of Miranda's poetry. Not only does it deal with buried history, but it addresses the ways that history affects current Native women. As Miranda argues: "the rape of a Native woman in the United States is almost as invisible to the eyes of the law now as it was in 1835, or during Missionization" (104). We are all affected by the history of colonization. The message in Miranda's poetry is clear: non–Native men and women must become aware of Native America and its impact on the present, while realizing that by denying it, they perpetuate the culture of violence. Meanwhile, Native women should not be silent: "by telling our stories, Native women can move past survival and into the role of healers" (105).

> Nothing remains—
> only my cupped hands
> [Miranda, "Without History" 74].

Miranda views her own existence as a miracle; she is not a victim, but a survivor. In "Waking" she writes: "When I braid my hair,/ whole tribes recite genealogies/between the strands" (98). This statement clearly names her own existence as proof of her tribe's legacy. She doesn't retreat into despair, or escape reality, because in her own body she is "never homeless" (99). Yet she doesn't pretend that the past didn't happen. She sees herself and her people as changed and newly created: as she notes in "A Walk In the Forest:" "old roots anchor deep in survival,/yet my soul is newly leafed: tender, turning,/opening toward light" (49). The significance of her new self is that it is one she has forged herself. In "Looking For a Cure," she writes: "She feels a path incised into her palm,/ a course that flows directly/into the heart's homeland" (4). Her past was inscribed by colonizers, but she inscribes her own future.

While rape and colonialism are both exercises in power, writing is also a manifestation of power. Storytelling can work as medicine, and as a part of the new oral tradition, Miranda's poetry is medicine to Native people. Peoples adapt their histories by shaping them into stories. It is only then that they can move forward as a people. Trauma cannot be buried; survivors must weave their trauma into stories so that healing can begin.

Note

1. A cartographic term: "Positioning land lines on a map to indicate their true, theoretical, or approximate location relative to the adjacent terrain and culture, by reconciling the information shown on Bureau of Land Management plats and field records with the ground evidence of the location of the lines" (Thompson).
2. A cartographic term, denoting the "preparation of a new or revised map or chart, or portion thereof, from existing maps, aerial photographs, field surveys, and other sources" (Thompson).
3. A cartographic term, denoting the "linear and (or) angular quantities that designate the position of a point in relation to a given reference frame" (Thompson).
4. See Brownmiller.

Works Cited

Allen, Paula Gunn. "Father God and Rape Culture." *Off the Reservation: Reflections on Boundary-Busting, Border-Crossing Loose Canons.* Boston: Beacon, 1998. Print.
Amnesty International. *Maze of Injustice: The Failure to Protect Indigenous Women from*

Sexual Violence in the USA. New York: Amnesty International, 2006. Web. 21 Mar. 2012.

Ashcroft, Bill, Gareth Griffiths and Helen Tiffin. *Key Concepts in Post-Colonial Studies.* 1998. London and New York: Routledge, 1999. Print.

Borah, Woodrow W. "The California Mission." *Ethnology of the Alta California Indians: II Postcontact.* 2 vols. Eds. Lowell John Bean and Sylvia Brakke Vane. Spanish Borderlands Sourcebooks 4. New York and London: Garland, 1991. 5–24. Print.

Brownmiller, Susan. *Against Our Will: Men, Women and Rape.* 1975. New York: Fawcett Columbine, 1993. Print.

Castillo, Edward D. "The Impact of Euro-American Exploration and Settlement." *Ethnology of the Alta California Indians: II Postcontact.* 2 vols. Eds. Lowell John Bean and Sylvia Brakke Vane. Spanish Borderlands Sourcebooks 4. New York and London: Garland, 1991. 927–955. Print.

Cuneo, Michele de, and Tzvetan Tordorov. *The Conquest of America: The Question of the Other.* Trans. Richard Howard. New York: Harper & Row, 1984. Print.

Fernandez, Ferdinand F. "Except a California Indian: A Study in Legal Discrimination." *Ethnology of the Alta California Indians: II Postcontact.* 2 vols. Eds. Lowell John Bean and Sylvia Brakke Vane. Spanish Borderlands Sourcebooks 4. New York and London: Garland, 1991. 911–925. Print.

Miranda, Deborah. "Silver." *"Bad Girls"/"Good Girls": Women, Sex and Power in the Nineties.* Eds. Nan Maglin and Donna Perry. New Brunswick, NJ: Rutgers University Press, 1996. 125–33. Print.

_____. *Indian Cartography.* New York: Greenfield Review, 1999. Print.

_____. "Lunatic or Lover/ Madman or Shaman: The Role of the Poet in Contemporary Culture(s)" *Cultural Geography: A Raven Forum.* Ed. Michael Hueaux-Perez. *The Raven Chronicles.* Mar. 1997. Web. 12 Sep. 1998.

_____. "'Saying the Padre Had Grabbed Her': Rape Is the Weapon, Story Is the Cure." *Intertexts* 14.2 (2010): 93–112. Print.

Morison, Samuel Eliot. *Admiral of the Ocean Sea: A Life of Christopher Columbus.* New York: Little, Brown, 1942. Print.

Ohlone Costanoan Esselen Nation. *Official Tribal Website: Ohlone Costanoan Indians of the Greater Monterey Bay Area.* n.d. Web. 25 Dec. 2011.

Powell, Malea. "Rhetorics of Survivance: How American Indians Use Writing." *College Composition and Communication* 53 (2002): 396–435. Print.

Thompson, Morris Mordecai. *Maps for America: Cartographic Products of the U.S. Geological Survey and Others.* 3d ed. Reston, VA: U.S. Dept. of the Interior; Geological Survey, 1988. Print.

Tibesar, Antonine, OFM, trans. and ed. *Writings of Junipero Serra.* 4 vols. Washington, D.C.: Academy of American Franciscan History, 1955. Print.

Vizenor, Gerald. *Manifest Manners: Postindian Warriors of Survivance.* Hanover, CT: Wesleyan University Press, 1994. Print.

Warrior, Robert Allen. *Tribal Secrets: Recovering American Indian Intellectual Traditions.* Minneapolis: University of Minnesota Press, 1995. Print.

Womack, Craig S. *Red on Red: Native American Literary Separatism.* Minneapolis: University of Minnesota Press, 1999. Print.

Recuperating, Re-Membering and Resurrecting the Old South: Historical Adaptation in Caroline Gordon's Penhally and None Shall Look Back

TANFER EMIN TUNÇ

With over 620,000 casualties, the Civil War (1861–1865) was the deadliest war ever fought by the United States. It resulted in a major social paradigm shift — one that radically changed southern economics, politics, and cultural life. The Confederate defeat, emancipation, and Reconstruction, which brought with it urbanization, industrialization, and the abandonment of large-scale plantation-style agriculture, gave birth to a new genre of writing — 'Lost Cause' literature — which enshrined the Old South and the Confederacy's "noble loss." Lost Cause literature remained a popular literary type until the end of World War I (1918) and was reinforced by the writing of historians such as William Archibald Dunning, who during the early twentieth century promoted the idea that the South was ruined by Reconstruction; segregation was necessary to protect white values; and the antebellum period was the golden age of southern culture (Current 213). Works such as Lyon Gardiner Tyler's *A Confederate Catechism*, which was reprinted numerous times throughout the first half of the twentieth century, reinforced concepts already circulating in the intellectual realm by attempting to explain to the common citizen, in simple question and answer format, that the Civil War as a "war of northern aggression" upon a peace-loving civilized society with which it differed philosophically. The pamphlet, which was distributed by

Confederate veteran groups and the United Daughters of the Confederacy as a way to instruct children about the war, idealized the antebellum South and its lost culture, speculating about "what could have been" had the South won (Tyler).[1] This had the net effect of perpetuating the Lost Cause myth well into the twentieth century, which prompted a wide assortment of literary reactions, ranging from sympathy, to resistance, to outright rejection.

The appearance of works by writers such as Thomas Wolfe, William Faulkner, and Tennessee Williams between the 1930s and 1950s helped establish a southern literary "Renaissance" which began the slow dismantling of the Lost Cause myth and its literature. These writers focused on the peculiarities of southern culture; the individual's place within the community; the dual burdens of history and race; and the shift away from "traditional" social values (i.e., the Protestant work ethic, with its emphasis on ingenuity, honesty, and determination) by exploring corrupt worlds, the empty pursuit of wealth, superficial status, and meaningless commodities. The Southern Fugitive or Agrarian branch of the Renaissance, which included writers and critics such as John Crowe Ransom, Robert Penn Warren, Allen Tate, and Donald Davidson who banded together under the manifesto *I'll Take My Stand: The South and the Agrarian Tradition* (1930) (*I'll Take My Stand*),[2] also critiqued modernity and urbanism through their poetry, prose, and essays, which emphasized how industrialization was impacting southern traditions. They promoted a regional literature that rejected local color in favor of broader conservative social and political concerns such as agrarianism (i.e., they believed that the independent farmer would be the building block of the South), while ventriloquizing a longing for the Lost Cause of the South — or life as it "once was" — which sets them apart from a great deal of Southern Renaissance writers. Consequently, many Agrarians seemed as if they were perpetual fugitives, trapped between the pull of the past (the Old South) and their ambivalence towards the present (the New South) — somehow displaced, "fleeing" from the horrors of both. Invariably, their writing is framed by recreating the southern pastoral, an adaptation of "old-fashioned agricultural values," and, to a certain extent, escapism through re-membering history.

Although she was never considered an "official" member of this male-dominated literary movement, as Allen Tate's wife, Caroline Gordon (1895–1981) was an "unofficial" member of the group. Not only did she incorporate their ideas into her works, but she collaborated and interacted with the Agrarians both personally and professionally. This essay will discuss how two of her most prominent novels, *Penhally* (1931) and *None Shall Look Back* (1937), adapted favorable historical representations of the Old South in order to recuperate, re-member, and resurrect the Lost Cause of the Confederacy according to Agrarian values. While, traditionally, adaptation refers to the transformation of literary texts into different forms of media (e.g., films and television programs), the concept of adaptation can also be applied to other disciplines, such as history. Historians who pose as novelists, and novelists who pose as historians, engage in process of negotiating or subjectively adapting various histories, or dialogues, when they tell the story of a nation. They are usually not objective recorders of facts, but quite frequently scholars with specific socio-political agendas. Consequently, when "the truth" challenges myth, the process of historical *dis-membering* and *re-membering* can only occur in the literary realm of fiction. Southern Agrarians engaged in this practice through their writing, namely by adapting those elements of "History" (with a capital H) that best suited their manifesto (i.e., a nostalgic return to "traditional values" such as farming "the land"), reflected their subjective contexts, and contributed to a historical "reality" that complimented their world-view. Gordon's novels reinforce this movement by merging family myth with southern history to construct a "cultural memory of the war and a postbellum identity for the region" which reclaimed History through personal stories and interpretive strategies (Gardner, *Blood and Irony* 263). By providing a close textual analysis of *Penhally* and *None Shall Look Back*, this essay will show how Gordon positively adapted the values of the Old South to recuperate, remember, and resurrect its history vicariously through fiction, in the process exhibiting, as Paul V. Murphy notes, "a southern nostalgia as strong as any member of the group, including [Donald] Davidson, the most unreconstructed of the Agrarians" (Murphy 9).[3]

Penhally: Penning Plantation Life and the Old South

According to Louis Rubin and Robert Jacobs, the decades following the Civil War were so "suffused with a sense of tragedy and frustration that it was almost impossible for [Southerners] to take a 'normal' view of anything" (32). The ghosts of the Confederacy hung over the political and social life of the South for at least fifty years; thus the Civil War was not an event obscured by the past but rather a lived, and living, experience. To a southern child — even one who was born years after the end of the war as were Faulkner, Tate and Gordon — the abstractions of war were very real. They "knew that history was not merely something in books [...] [and] it was this kind of atmosphere [...] into which [...] the writers of the Southern Renaissance were born" (33). As the Old South gave way to the new, industrialization and urbanization displaced the agrarian lifestyle of the plantation system. Those who were previously members of the southern planter aristocracy were now the genteel poor, having lost much of their wealth during the war, and their remaining assets to northern industrialists and developers in the decades that followed. The powerbrokers of the New South were these investors, as well as the immigrants, who through their labor, sustained factories and entrepreneurial enterprises. Part of this new world yet rooted in their historical past, the writers of the Southern Renaissance were trapped in an age of transition, limbo, and for many purgatory. They were fighting a new war — a war of survival (37).

As Allen Tate remarked, when the South entered this world of modernity, it "gave a backward glance as it stepped over the border: that backward glance gave us the Southern Renaissance, a literature conscious of the past in the present" (qtd. in Millichap vi). Consequently, members of this movement — and in particular the Agrarians — used their literature as a means of searching for the past in the present and resolving the tension between old conventional values and new standards of behavior. Endowed with "two-way vision" or a "double consciousness" (Rubin and Jacobs 37), the early Fugitives (Ransom, Warren, Tate, and Davidson, the first three of whom would later establish New Criticism) felt as if they were displaced Southerners who were "fleeing" the "high-caste Brahmins of the Old South [...] and the mint julep South of Thomas Nelson Page" (38), as well as the "modern" and "progressive" New South, which in reality achieved only "faddishness, unbelief, and a tawdry commercialism." As Rubin and Jacobs convey, "in the South's eager race to emulate the rest of the country, all the things they had been taught were good were being cast aside [...] the South was callously throwing out cherished ways of faith and life," and in their opinion, southern tradition was being debased in the name of modernity (40).

The Agrarians sought an impossible place in between and perceived history as a continuing dialogue that united the poles of the past and the present. They maintained that many of the problems of modernity could be solved with a return to the simple, pastoral values of the antebellum world — the values of the good farmer and the gentleman planter. History inevitably informed the Agrarians' writing, with the Civil War, Reconstruction, the Industrial Revolution, modernity, and the conflict between the values of the Old and the New South serving as important foci. For Gordon, *Penhally* became a therapeutic space to reconcile the two poles of her past and present, coming to terms with her family history and the conflict between the Old South of her ancestors and the New South in which she lived. No fictive retelling of the Old South would be complete without a timeless reconstruction of pastoral plantation life (which if conveyed effectively can transcend, and even substitute, for history) and the impact of the "War Between the States." In *Penhally*, like in many of the retellings of the antebellum south that emerged from Agrarianism, defeat was replaced by personal experience and interpretive strategies, which, in turn, helped recuperate, re-member and resurrect the idyllic landscape of plantation life and the Lost Cause.

In the case of *Penhally*, the experiences in question emerge from the saga of a Southern aristocratic family (the Llewellyn-Crenfrew-Allard family connection, modeled on Gordon's own Meriwether-Barker-Ferguson connection), who inhabit a large plantation on the Kentucky/Tennessee border near the Cumberland River Valley (Arbery 3). *Penhally* was inspired by Gordon's family, including one ancestor who played a major role at the Virginia Convention of 1788, which ratified the US Constitution on behalf of the state; her mother's great aunt "Aunt Cal" (Caroline Douglas Meriwether Goodlett), who established the Daughters of the Confederacy in 1894 (and served as the basis of *None Shall Look Back's* Aunt Cally); Elizabeth Meriwether Gilmore (also known as Dorothy Dix); explorer Meriwether Lewis; Charles Nicholas Meriwether (her great-great-grandfather), who was the legendary master of the Woodstock plantation; and her favorite uncle, Robert Emmett Meriwether, who, in her mind, best exemplified the "ancient virtues" of the gentleman farmer (Lewis 183; Rodenberger 78). Nicholas Douglas Meriwether (Charles Nicholas Meriwether's brother) served as the model for patriarch Nicholas Llewellyn in *Penhally* (with Charles Nicholas represented by Ralph Llewellyn); Gordon's grandfather, Douglas Meriwether, is fictionalized through John Llewellyn, who inherits Penhally from Nicholas Llewellyn; and Gordon's aunt, Caroline Ferguson Meriwether, shares a great deal in common with *Penhally's* Miss Carrie (Gordon, *Penhally* ix). Clearly, the complicated "structure of the Meriwether connection [with cousins marrying each other] furnishes a model for the family organization of much of what she wrote"—an organization which not only provided order to Gordon's world but also negotiated the threat of change through familial solidarity and generational continuity (Rodenberger 79–80). Moreover, it was from these and other female relations that Gordon learned the tenets of the Lost Cause, learned "to love the South, hate the North, and lament the passing of [her family's] glory days" (Warren 54; Jonza 12). Gordon's well-known family history lent credence to her ability to adapt national history by allowing her to use personal stories to interpret official versions of the past.

By preserving her version of southern tradition through her works, Gordon simultaneously functions as an interpreter, translator and adapter of history. As Molcie Lou Rodenberger observes, she "turns to her family history for material because she remembers her past as part of an orderly society maintaining traditional values she herself still holds valid" (5). In the process, she "transforms family legend and lore into written tradition [...] [and] her strong loyalties to her heritage [...] ultimately affect her fiction" which engages in the mission of dealing with loss by freezing time (Rodenberger 14). Her female kin, who excelled in the southern folk tradition of oral storytelling, and her father, who instilled in her a love of classical heroes, also provided Gordon with the historic tools that allowed her to cope with change through ancestor veneration (especially Civil War veterans) and a nostalgic worshipping of the past. Consequently, her work is full of allusions and references to Greek and Roman gods, orators, playwrights, and literary/mythic figures. In fact, she often compares the Old South to these fallen civilizations, adapting elements of the latter to reinforce the myths of the former.[4] David Davis contends that this is typical of Southern Renaissance and Agrarian writing: "Modern southern writers [...] venerated classical culture. [Those] who idealized the Lost Cause often used the pro-slavery rhetoric of ancient orators to justify the black codes, and many ... identified with fallen ancient empires" and neoclassical architecture. Southerners even named their cities after those in the ancient world, such as Rome, Athens, Sparta, and Smyrna, all of which are located in Georgia, and "the southern educational system also drew heavily upon classical learning" (145). Gordon adopted these social and historical tenets liberally, incorporating myths, legends, ancient culture, as well as detailed descriptions of the neo-classical architecture of southern plantation homes, into *None Shall Look Back* (hereafter referred to as *NSLB*) and *Penhally*. The epic and dynastic framework of her novels further reinforces the historic image in Gordon's work, as well as her belief that ultimately, history is tragic since it inevitably results in the decline of civilization (Jonza 2; Brown 19).

As Richard King delineates, "the Agrarians' great good time was the antebellum South, a felicitous, harmonious balance of yeoman and planter, [which, according to them, was] culturally the bastion of non-materialistic values, and economically opposed to the expanding capitalism of the North" (55). They depicted the Old South in a way that allowed them to retain ideological control: through romanticized adaptations of history that elide issues such as abolitionism (in *Penhally*, Gordon depicts anti-slavery activists, such as John Brown, as "crazy") and class difference (poor whites are contemptuously dismissed as diseased trash). Gordon privileges aristocratic white male planters, and when she does include women in her narrative — such as Mrs. Robert E. Lee in *Penhally* or Susan Allard in *NSLB* — they are as belles of the same elite social class who either sacrifice for the southern cause, or perish because they fail to do so. Most plantation masters in Gordon's fiction are "described as southerners seem to like their plantation owners remembered. [They] love their plantations," are beneficent towards slaves, and unquestioningly generous with their families. Many of these plantation masters styled themselves as country squires, or landed gentry who were "direct descendents of the English Cavaliers [...] a combination of the natural aristocrat and European gentleman, nature and civilization [...] freedom and restraint" (Roden-berger 158–159).

The grand patriarch of *Penhally* is plantation master Nicholas Llewellyn, whose father Francis left Virginia as a young man to seek his fortune in what was then considered the backwoods. Living in a world of gentlemen, chivalry, duels, romantic paternalism, primogeniture, and the entailment of property (Francis did not inherit any land since he was a younger son), Nicholas is determined to follow these traditions despite the fact that Thomas Jefferson criminalized primogeniture decades before (Gordon, *Penhally* 37). His attempts to maintain tradition become the narrative arc of *Penhally*, which spans roughly a century (1826 to the beginning of the Great Depression) and three historic phases: the antebellum years to the Civil War; the decline of Penhally from Reconstruction to the turn of the twentieth century; and the 1920s, which deals with the displacement of the Old South by the New South, and northern industrialists who invade the agrarian idyll.

In the novel, Nicholas and his nephews become the self-appointed pro-tectors of southern agrarian values—especially honor and land—thus con-veying the idea that "those who uphold the legend of the Old South after the war [...] are heroic [even] though their ideals are imperfect. In the advent of industrialism, even a flawed agrarian society [with primogeniture and entail-ment for example] seems preferable, and consequently, those who sacrifice themselves to ceremony and order are admirable" (Fraistat). Southern identity and honor are derived from one's community and family standing, which also determine one's debt to the past. The best means of reconciling these poles—of identity/honor, community/family, and past, present and future—is to, if necessary, fight for one's values (as the Agrarians did). Placing one's personal battles into historical perspective historicizes them and renders them part of History. For example, John, who inherits Penhally after Nicholas's death, is willing to sacrifice himself for the Great Cause because "he saw his own personal misfortunes monstrously shadowed [in] those of the nation" (Gordon, *Penhally* 196; McDowell 16). However, because patriarch Nicholas Llewellyn's descendants, brothers Nicholas Jnr. and Chance, spend more time arguing and competing with each other than farming the land, they ultimately lose Penhally, the tie that binds the family for decades.

Tragically like the South itself, Penhally is overrun by outsiders, such as Douglas and Joan Parrish, who do not understand the rooted history of the South. Although she is married to Douglas (a Llewellyn relative) and is from Baltimore, Maryland (often considered part of the South), Joan, who wishes to buy Penhally, is characterized as a capitalist "agent from the East"—a destructive force with little sensitivity to southern heritage, including agrar-ianism (Arbery 23–24). She is not interested in Penhally as an historic plantation and family home; rather, she wants to fashion her own mythic vision of the Old South in the New South by buying a remnant of the antebellum world and turning it into a hunt club where racial hierarchies could continue and she could preside over the estate and its black caretakers like a plantation mistress. Similarly, Douglas is a student of history — he studies Native American tribes as a hobby — but does not have a genuine interest in the past. As a capitalist opportunist who is diametrically opposed to agrarian values, he manipulates history because he believes there is profit to be made in it. Although his parents are southerners, "Parrish was raised in France, and thus he knows the South mainly through reading and second-hand accounts. Despite his wish to recover the South's history, he keeps it in the past, as artifacts that he can catalogue in his collection" which he is certain will one day become monetarily valuable. Douglas is not interested in the family's patriotic stories, but is concerned with ransacking Penhally before the decorators come — he "searches through the house, borrows old books, and records dates from tombstones in the family graveyard [...] [in essence, he is] a menace to what is valuable in the southern past:" history and honor (Fraistat).

Once a steadfast marker of aristocratic and genteel southern living, by the end of the novel, Penhally is in ruins due to neglect — a tragic ghost of what it once was. The townsfolk in nearby Gloversville also no longer value land and convince Nicholas Jr. to sell Penhally to Joan because they think that the influx of her wealthy friends will improve the local economy. Chance assumes the role of agrarian hero and kills his brother to avenge the sale of Penhally. However, fratricide will not bring order or resolution, since Nicholas has already sold the estate. Chance, his aging relatives, and his grandmother Lucy, whose memory "seemed to have stopped with the Civil War," will now have to live the rest of their lives exiled from Penhally (Gordon, *Penhally* 231). Detached from its past and rich historical roots, in the end Penhally becomes a "glorified hunt club" which "revives the sports of the Old South" in the capitalist realm of the New South — complete with paintings of deceased Llewellyn family members to lend it credibility, charm, hospitality, and history (265).

Looking Back on History
Through *None Shall Look Back*

As Gordon expressed: "As a child, I felt that the fact that we lost the Civil War was a calamity for the South. When I attained my majority and began to read history for myself, I came to the conclusion that it was a calamity for the whole world" (Gordon, "Cock-Crow" 558). She blamed the biased history books of her youth, many of which were written by northern historians sympathetic to the Union, for this disjuncture, and was determined to set the record straight about the Civil War through *NSLB*: "Our history was miswritten and our children were taught lies ... the northerners could not bear the image of us as we were" (qtd. in Magee 55). Unfortunately for Gordon, the novel was published shortly after the release of *Gone with the Wind* (1936), which overshadowed *NSLB*'s success. Nevertheless, Gordon was determined to tell her version of the war or, more accurately, the version she had constructed for herself based on the memories and recollections of veterans and elders who could remember life in the antebellum South: "'When my brothers and I were children, one of our favorite pastimes was to get into a hammock, three deep, and swing and sing.' Their songs were not the popular ragtime songs of the day but those that celebrated famous Confederate heroes, notably Nathan Bedford Forrest. Their grandmother punctuated their singing with stories of bloodied battle fields and home front heroics" (Gardner, *Blood and Irony* 252). Clearly for Gordon, "the war infiltrated family life and childhood play." Yet, as she remarked, "'I do not think that my childhood experiences were very different from those of any Southerner who is over thirty years old' [...] [After all], she grew up surrounded by former soldiers [...] [they] lived (and died) at Merry Mont, Gordon's childhood home" (Warren 54; Jonza 11–12).

These experiences, as well as her familial ties to the Confederacy, shaped the ways in which Gordon adapted history to recuperate, re-member, and resurrect meaning through fiction. Forrest was not only a childhood hero, but also the major war hero of *NSLB*, and her great uncle, Captain Edward Meriwether (who she fictionalizes through the character Rives Allard in *NSLB*), was killed in the Civil War while under Forrest's command (Rodenberger 78). Gordon reinforces this historical continuity — of past/present and the family/nation — by incorporating elements of the Trojan War and the fall of an ancient city (which could be Troy or Nineveh) in the epic novel (Brown 21; Young 785). In fact, the title of *NSLB* comes from the Book of Nahum in the Old Testament — "But Nineveh is of old like a pool of water; yet they shall flee away. Stand! Stand! *Shall they cry*, but none shall look back" (Nahum 2:8) — which links directly to the closing battle scene of the novel. In this scene, the Confederates are retreating and Forrest shouts at the soldiers to "'Rally, men, rally! For God's sake, rally!' But they would not listen" (Gordon, *NSLB* 373). As Rose Ann Fraistat contends, the "biblical description of the fall of Nineveh is also important for the implicit parallel between the fall of the Assyrian empire and the fall of the Old South [....] Furthermore, the biblical allusion is significant for its prophetic tone: like Nahum who foretells the end of an empire that has subjected other nations, the narrator of *NSLB* describes the ruin of a [civilization] whose economic system is based on slavery" (Fraistat).

Heroism is a constant theme in *Penhally* and *NSLB*, and reinforces the historical unity of both novels, binding fact with fiction and creating continuity that blurs the line between the two. Gordon wrote her novels in the style of the grand epics of antiquity and even used Tolstoy's *War and Peace* (1869), which also deals with aristocratic culture and its disruption by war, as her guide (McDowell 21). Gordon rendered Forrest a god-like figure, and much like Napoleon in *War and Peace*, he is always on horseback, ready to go into battle to sacrifice his life for the Great Cause of the Old South. In order to make her depiction of Forrest as dramatic, historically accurate, and plausible as possible, Gordon "studied Civil War histories, papers of Confederate leaders, and *The Century Magazine's* [four volume] '*Battles and Leaders [of the Civil War]*' series published [in the 1880s] [...] She also studied classical accounts of war by Homer, Plutarch, and Thucydides." Moreover, in an effort to write a novel that was as entertaining as Tolstoy's work, Gordon deliberately treated "each battle [...] in a different way [to avoid] monotony [...] I treated Ft. Donelson in Plutarchian style, reserving my personal impressions for Chickamauga" (Gardner, "Every Man" 30). She contextualized the Civil War through allusions to previous American wars (such as the War of 1812 and the Mexican-American War of 1846–1848) while critiquing the social importance placed on the individual at the expense of History. As she suggests through a conversation between Rives and Fontaine Allard, after wars are fought, very few remember the details, and fewer still retain their allegiance to the causes that drove them to fight in the first place; however, everyone remembers who was killed and injured on the battlefield (Gordon, *NSLB* 32).

In an attempt to add credibility to her depictions, Gordon resorted to "just lifting sentences" from the works that she read, including John Allan Wyeth's *Life of Lieutenant-General Nathan Bedford Forrest* (1899). While these "verbatim borrowings" troubled many of her critics (as well as the publishers involved), for others they simply added to the authenticity of her battle scenes (Warren 82). The Chickamauga section of *Battles and Leaders*, which was authored by Confederate General Daniel H. Hill, was almost adapted into her fictional text in total. Moreover, "once alerted to Gordon's use of Hill's *Battles and Leaders* article, readers can easily find dozens more examples of where she borrowed observations, descriptions, and dialogue from the seminal collection of veterans' remembrances" (83–84). Gordon also adapted other historical texts into her novel, including Allen Tate's biographies of Stonewall Jackson (1928) and Jefferson Davis (1929); Tate's poem "Ode to the Confederate Dead"; and Andrew Lytle's biography of Nathan Bedford Forrest, *Bedford Forrest and His Critter Company* (1931). Lytle's work was such an influence that according to Charlotte Beck, "without Lytle's previous work on Nathan Bedford Forrest [...] [*NSLB*] would have been a very different book. Forrest

[...] [had to be] Gordon's heroic paradigm because several of her relatives actually served in his 'critter company' at Shiloh and Chickamauga and the battles around Clarksville and southern Kentucky were a part of her family saga. It is remarkable how much intertextual relationship exists between *Bedford Forrest and His Critter Company*, published in 1931 [...] and *NSLB*" (160–161). Interestingly enough, in depicting Forrest, both Gordon and Lytle chose only to adapt his heroic, historically-constructed image, marginalizing the fact that he was originally a slave trader (though she mentions it a number of times) and later a member of the Ku Klux Klan (Jonza 90).

As Jane Gibson Brown notes, "unlike [Thomas] Jefferson in *Penhally*, [Forrest] is not an allusion but rather a living [historic] character. He is Rives' commanding officer, and he comes to know him quite intimately as a member of his special corps of spies" (96–97). Forrest looms larger than life as a colonel (and later general) and is the only character whose letters and personal appeals to the South are printed, in full, in the text. Unlike his bureaucratic superiors who have been trained in northern textbook strategies of war at West Point, "Forrest is an instinctive soldier and an embodiment of virtues lacking among the more refined generals." Gordon makes it clear that the only reason why he loses his battles is not because of mistakes on Forrest's part but because his superiors "outnumber him, they prevail, and the South loses the war for want of sufficient heroes" (Brown 96–97). Nevertheless, Forrest is able to maintain his honor because he is a timeless, traditional, virtuous hero who embodies chivalry: even though he lives in a flawed word, he is willing to die for it (Gardner, "Every Man" 28). Rives Allard also embodies these virtues and adopts the southern cause in the fictional realm, once again blurring the line between fact and fabrication, which Gordon mythologizes through her depiction of the Lost Cause and its cavalry/ cavaliers. Rives internalizes the message that only through death can he acquire honor, and waving his arms crazily, shouts, "Everyman. Got the right. To get killed" (Gordon, *NSLB* 319). He "pursues death like a lover consumed with passion" because he knows that if he survives, he will not be able to handle life in the postbellum South (Arbery 70–71). As Gordon conveys, "if the Confederate cause failed [...] there could be no happiness for him except in the grave" (Gordon, *NSLB* 286). Rives dies a hero's death, transcending history by gaining immortality as a human sacrifice to the Lost Cause. Thus even in death, Rives pursues the concerns of the southern gentleman — romantic nobility and chivalrous honor.

Like *Gone with the Wind*, *NSLB* begins with a barbecue and the reminiscences of a "benevolent" plantation master, Fontaine Allard, who treats his slaves well and believes that blood sometimes must be shed to protect cultural values and freedom (at least for those of his own social class). In fact, he conveys the notion that a man has "got to take a stand" (8), echoing the title of the Agrarian classic *I'll Take My Stand*. Gordon uses Fontaine's thoughts as a vehicle to convey the connection between the southern pastoral (land) and family (heritage), which form an integral part of this Agrarian stand: "Walking along through those trees over ground covered by their dead leaves he had had the strange feeling, as if a voice had said to him: 'These are your father's and your father's before him' [...] He [...] [was] overcome by his attachment for that earth, those trees" (10–11). The southern agrarian order of his plantation, Brackets, is challenged by the war, which brings Union soldiers to the plantation's doorstep. They come to search the premises for ammunition — they know that Fontaine gave horses to Nathan Bedford Forrest's cavalry, and that his son Ned enlisted under the military leader. Their casual rudeness and ownership of Brackets offends Fontaine deeply. However, he cannot defend his honor for fear that his actions might spur retaliation on the estate or his family (there are women on his property and his son Ned and nephew Rives are on furlough at Brackets). The soldiers burn Brackets, and as the walls come down, the Allards see the original log cabin — the heart of the plantation and their agrarian identity — emerge from the melting structure. Fontaine mumbles "something indistinct that sounded like 'My child,' [and] then fell face downward," suffering a stroke (physical and psychological collapse) as his home came tumbling down around his feet (social collapse) (159). The Allards' way of life is suddenly "gone with the wind," and while such destruction often dictates that in order to survive, "none should look back," the Allards cannot help but look back to their former glory days as part of the planter-aristocracy for the rest of the novel.

After their world collapses, Fontaine's children — Jim, Cally, Ned and his granddaughter Lucy — struggle to pick up the pieces. Jim, like the Parrishes, comes to represent the merchant class of the New South and shuns the "honorable" agricultural lifestyle of his predecessors. Like Scarlett O'Hara, he conducts business with "Yankees" after the war because not only are they the victors but they also have money. Thus, he literally and figuratively "sells out" his heritage and identity. Although the women — Cally and Mrs. Allard — who carry the burden of cultural identity, morality, and honor, wish to return to and restore Brackets, they end up living in a house owned by Joe Bradley, who worships materialism and wealth, and has so little faith in the southern cause that he converts his Confederate money into US bonds and deposits them in a Cincinnati bank before the war comes to an end. Cally despises this new order, and is "governed entirely by the instincts and prejudices of [her father's] class, that of the landed proprietor" (30). Cally voices the reasons why the South chose to fight, thus serving as the mouthpiece of the Confederate Lost Cause and historian by proxy. When an emaciated Ned is released from Johnson's Island, a northern prison camp, he conveys the belief that true freedom can only come through self-reliance (especially with respect to food) and "farming the land," becoming determined to transform Brackets into the productive plantation it once was. As he conveys, "I reckon the land's still there. The Yankees couldn't burn that and they ain't strong enough to cart it off" (337). As the protector of traditional values, this agrarian-warrior gathers what remains of his family and returns to Brackets to start all over again, building a log cabin just as his ancestors had done decades before him.

According to David Goldfield, since the Civil War, southerners have struggled with these burdens of "history and memory." As a result, they have become "either fixated upon the past and therefore immobilized by it, or [...] total amnesiacs and therefore destructive" (298). Southern Agrarians like Gordon certainly acknowledged this burden of history and memory through their fiction, which seeks to recuperate the southern past by adapting it for social purposes; namely, the perpetuation of the pervasive Lost Cause myth and the restoration of the former glory days of the plantation South. Even though the Confederacy surrendered in 1865, many southerners are still fighting a metaphoric Civil War — a "Lost Cause" to reconcile a history "woven from wishes, lies, and necessity, and passed off as gospel" (Goldfield 31). To a certain extent, the South remains a "nation within a nation," still searching for its place in the world and for a civilization that has "gone with the wind." A hundred and fifty years later, southerners "are not altogether free agents in the here and now [...] the past is part master" (Rubin and Jacobs 57). As *Penhally* and *NSLB* elucidate, many Agrarians were certainly trapped in this impasse of past, present and future, forever hoping that their re-membrances of the Old South would somehow help resurrect a more idyllic, land-based, New South. "Alluding to the title of one of Flannery O'Connor's most famous short stories," Gordon ended a lecture in 1974 with an excited optimism that one day their Lost Cause would be realized: "Everything that rises must converge but everything that converges must have risen. Hold [on to] your Confederate money, boys! The South [will] rise again" (Gardner, *Blood and Irony* 263).

Notes

1. For more information, see Lyon Gardiner Tyler, *A Confederate Catechism*, 3d ed., 21 Nov. 1929. Web. 7 Mar 2012.

2. "I'll take my stand" is originally a line from the "de facto" Confederate anthem "Dixie": "I wish I was in Dixie, hooray! hooray! In Dixie Land I'll take my stand to live and die in Dixie."

3. In 1974, Gordon even admitted that as a "totally unreconstructed Confederate" she had become a rarity. Peter Bridges, "The Lost Cause's Female Champions," *The Washington Times*, 24 Jul. 2004: D–05.

4. In *Penhally*, Gordon alludes to several ancient myths "including those of Orion-Arion, the Pleiades, the House of Atreus, and Aphrodite" as well as the biblical Cain and Abel (Brown 20). An analysis of the plethora of classical references in Gordon's works is beyond the scope of this essay. See Brown and Millichap for a complete consideration of mythology in her works.

Works Cited

Arbery, Virginia Lombardo. "The Stony Path: Ethos, Land and History in Caroline Gordon." Diss., University of Dallas, 1984. Print.

Beck, Charlotte H. *The Fugitive Legacy: A Critical History*. Baton Rouge: Louisiana State University Press, 2001. Print.

Bridges, Peter. "The Lost Cause's Female Champions." *Washington Times* July 24, 2004: D–05. Print.

Brown, Jane Gibson. "The Early Novels of Caroline Gordon: The Confluence of Myth and History as a Fictional Technique." Diss., University of Dallas, 1975. Print.

Current, Richard N. "From Civil War to World Power." *Legacy of Disunion: The Enduring Significance of the Civil War*. Eds. Susan-Mary Grant and Peter J. Parrish. Baton Rouge: Louisiana State University Press, 2003. 207–222. Print.

Davis, David A. "A Backward Glance: The Southern Renascence, the Autobiographical Epic, and the Classical Legacy." *The Thomas Wolfe Review* 33.1/2 (2009): 144–147. Print.

Fraistat, Rose Ann C. "The Early Novels." *Caroline Gordon as Novelist and Woman of Letters*. Baton Rouge: Louisiana State University Press, 1984. 37–95. Rpt. in *Twentieth-Century Literary Criticism*. Ed. Lawrence J. Trudeau. Vol. 241. Detroit: Gale, 2011. Literature Resource Center. Web. 2 May 2011.

Gardner, Sarah E. *Blood and Irony: Southern White Women's Narratives of the Civil War, 1861–1937*. Chapel Hill: University of North Carolina Press, 2004. Print.

_____. "Every Man has got the Right to Get Killed? The Civil War Narratives of Mary Johnston and Caroline Gordon." *Southern Cultures* 5.4 (1999): 14–40. Print.

Goldfield, David. *Still Fighting the Civil War: The American South and Southern History*. Baton Rouge: Louisiana State University Press, 2002. Print.

Gordon, Caroline. "Cock-Crow." *Southern Review* 1 (1965): 554–569. Print.

_____. *None Shall Look Back*. 1937. Nashville: JS Sanders, 1992. Print.

_____. *Penhally*. 1931. Nashville: JS Sanders, 1991. Print.

I'll Take My Stand: Twelve Southerners. 1930. Introduction by Louis D. Rubin, Jr. Baton Rouge: Louisiana State University Press, 1977. Print.

Jonza, Nancylee N. *The Underground Stream: The Life and Art of Caroline Gordon*. Athens: University of Georgia Press, 2010. Print.

King, Richard. *A Southern Renaissance: The Cultural Awakening of the American South, 1930–1955*. New York: Oxford University Press, 1982. Print.

Lewis, Nghana Tamu. "Politics from the Pedestal: Modernity, Cultural Intervention, and the Myth of Southern Womanhood, 1920–1945." Diss. University of Illinois at Urbana-Champaign, 2001. Print.

Magee, Rosemary M. *Friendship and Sympathy: Communities of Southern Women Writers*. Jackson: University Press of Mississippi, 1992. Print.

McDowell, Frederick P.W. *Caroline Gordon*. Minneapolis: University of Minnesota Press, 1966. Print.

Millichap, Joseph. *A Backward Glance: The Southern Renascence, the Autobiographical Epic, and the Classical Legacy*. Knoxville: University of Tennessee Press, 2009. Print.

Murphy, Paul V. *The Rebuke of History*. Chapel Hill: University of North Carolina Press, 2001. Print.

Rodenberger, Molcie Lou. "Caroline Gordon, Teller of Tales: The Influence of Folk Narrative on Characterization and Structure in her Work." Diss., Texas A&M University, 1975. Print.

Rubin, Louis D., and Robert D. Jacobs. *South: Modern Southern Literature in its Cultural Setting*. Garden City, NY: Doubleday, 1961. Print.

Tyler, Lyon Gardiner. *A Confederate Catechism*, 3d ed. 21 Nov. 1929. Web. 7 Mar. 2012.

Warren, Craig Andrew. "Regimental Memory: Veterans' Narratives and Civil War Fiction." Diss. University of Virginia, 2004. Print.

Young, Walton. "The Cup of Fury: The Preferred Title of Caroline Gordon's *None Shall Look Back*." *Mississippi Quarterly* 58.3/4 (2005): 785–794. Print.

Looking Beyond the Moving Moments: Adaptation, Digitization and Amateur Film Footage as Visual Histories

HEATHER NORRIS NICHOLSON

In Orhan Pamuk's *My Name is Red* (2001), two visions of artistic perfection challenge Sultan Murat III's reign in the late sixteenth century. The brilliance of Venetian painting and novelties of Renaissance perspective collide with the art of classic miniaturism as perfected by Persian illustrators. Stylized image, rooted in illustrative practice as an art of recording in service to Allah, and a higher realism meets the individual experimentalism of Frankish painters, as the Ottoman Empire encounters and responds to influences from East and West. The intellectual silk road on which _stanbul sits as a meeting point for cross-cultural exchange has long been contested, but from those encounters arose alternative ways of seeing as traditions evolved. Notwithstanding their aesthetic differences, Pamuk's protagonists deal with different kinds of remembering: illustration as an act of memory committed to passing on inner truths contrasts with interpretative, artistic practice informed by individual expression and remembered fleeting moments of passing shadow or light. The chasm between faithful replication and transformative interpretation seems unbridgeable, and yet the author's ultimate purpose is one of reconciling difference and bringing renewal. That message had particular resonance, given the novel's publication in September 2001, but has broader application to the notion of adapting history and its relationship to visual histories in an age of digitization.

As Pamuk's illustrators work surrounded by intrigue, suspicion and guilt, there are accusations of betrayal and loss. Their morality is rooted in notions of good and bad aesthetic technique and their rhetoric juxtaposes infidelity with being faithful to an idealized "original." Importantly, they do not function in isolation, nor is their activity seen as an abstract process. Pamuk's readers encounter different stakeholders, decision-makers and agents involved in the complex interconnected processes of illustration, that include the rival miniaturists themselves (dead and alive), a tree (source material for pages), a coin (involved in multitudinous transactions) and the eponymous color red of the book's title. The materiality, the institutional settings (court, workshop, apprenticeships) and the visceral, competitive world of the Ottoman miniature painting business form the backdrop for Pamuk's battle over aesthetic adaptation. Our gaze is led beyond the miniaturists to consider the vested interests, politics and passions that underlie how an image appears on a page.

Pamuk's polyvocal narrative readily links to debates about fidelity and adaptation. Likewise, in the historical and yet fictionalized reconstruction of _stanbul, materialities and economies affect how illustrators accommodate processes of adaptation (Murray). Fast forwarding five hundred years to processes affecting contemporary forms of visualization, this exemplification of adaptation at another crossroads in intellectual history has relevance to debates on working with archive film in an era of digitization, especially over issues of disappearance, loss and betrayal linked to denying future generations the historic texts inherited by their predecessors. Yet concerns over the transformative power of the digital turn inform various aspects of archive film activity. From the first stage of film acquisition, through cataloging, preservation and storage, to online electronic access or transfer to DVDs for wider viewing, archival practice is being redefined. Such changes affect not only how historic film is handled but interpreted and understood.

Long considered a poor relation to other aspects of the film business, the archival branch of film preservation, particularly away from commercial studios, occupied a marginal niche for many years. Set up to safeguard film, the very existence of public film archives challenged received wisdom about valuing text and artifact as being historically significant. Much neglected by film scholars and historians of film alike, these archives—mostly comprised of amateur cinema—occupy an emerging territory of critical interest in the areas of social history, cultural studies, geography, anthropology and more recently film studies (Norris Nicholson, *Amateur*; Craven; Shand). Recent scholarship is now putting amateur activity within a more nuanced understanding of past visual practice, but still relatively little attention focuses upon the processes of taking privately produced materials out of their archival settings and storing them in an archive for public consumption (Norris Nicholson, "Framing"). This might be seen as a suggestive process of historical adaptation, involving a reworking of the past into hitherto undiscovered present and future meanings that merits further examination.

This essay thus considers such meanings change, as amateur archive footage increasingly journeys beyond the archive for scholarship, educational, exhibition or broadcasting purposes. Arguably, such traveling involves a process of historical adaptation, and each journey contextualizes the imagery differently and reshapes its reading as a text. This kind of analysis permits individual, subjective and personalized views captured by the amateur lens to co-exist alongside more official versions of past experience. Personal stories interweave with broader narratives of change informing each other. The resultant intertextuality fosters more inclusive and nuanced visual histories. Amateur film reclamation from obscurity owes much to individual efforts: our attention turns next to how film archives as institutions have also undergone transformation in this exploration of multiple forms of adaptation.

From Wilderness to Market Place

Film archivists were long regarded as "keepers of the frame" in their remit to safeguard and preserve for future generations the historical legacy of early moving image (Houston). Their role as protectors of historical sources entrusted to them for future posterity was not dissimilar to that of archivists in other and far older realms of archival preservation. As with Pamuk's classic miniaturists, traditional archivists were chroniclers and transmitters of unquestioned "truths." Cataloging and careful storage had inherent value. The deposited records or artifacts contributed evidential proof for official adaptations of history. In their custodial role as careers, archivists helped to control an archive's contents: what it kept and who gained access. Just as archival contents reflected the power inequalities of who could and could not leave historical traces, archivists themselves had a far from neutral role in their own decisions on routine tasks of gathering, selection, cataloging and prioritizing for conservation, display or sharing with users.

Long before the analogue era turned digital, the archivists' role of agency in the production and consumption of historical narratives had begun to be questioned (Derrida; Schwarz and Cooke 171–85). Calls for more inclusive forms of archive that would validate other voices, and not simply privilege the rich and powerful in society may be traced back to demands for more inclusive historical forms of adaptation from the 1960s onwards. Different groups within different societies have come forward, demanding that their histories be told, their voices be heard and that archives reflect their lives and experiences too.

Transforming the historical record beyond dominant groups on the basis of gender, class, education, status, politics, sexuality, race, language or faith produced more representative adaptations of historical experience. Profound changes in archival practice occurred too. Archives could no longer be "passive storehouses of old stuff, but active sites where social power is negotiated, contested, confirmed" (Schwartz and Cook 1–19). Archival practice reinvented itself as it adopted new types of acquisition, alternative interpretative frameworks and different ways of reaching out to ever wider audiences. The changing roles, perceptions and expectations of archives pose many challenges for their staff (Lane and Hill 3–22), as daily activity prompts outreach and forms of public engagement, collaboration with different partners, individuals and interest groups, as well as increasing levels of contact with broadcast media and popular culture.

Public film archives exemplify such transformations and Britain's network of regional archives have their origins in the broadening of historical interests and growing awareness of visual texts as suggestive sources. While holdings usually span the entire range of newsreel, film genres and sometimes television collections too, over half of the items held at regional level are usually non-professional productions made by amateur film enthusiasts. This figure exemplifies inclusive approaches to acquisition, yet masks the significant underrepresentation of some groups, whose histories have still to be more clearly identified within past visual practices.

Naremore's call for the study of adaptation in general to acknowledge studies of "recycling, remaking and every other form of retelling in the age of mechanical reproduction and electronic communication" (15), seems particularly apposite in contemporary archive film interpretation. A typical day in a regional film archive reflects the pervasive nature of recycling moving image in the contemporary world: as staff acquire, conserve, catalog, shortlist and make footage accessible, write funding bids and reports, while dealing with a multitude of enquiries from (amongst others) producers, museum curators, festival directors, or community workers seeking stimuli for intergenerational memory work. As archival film footage has gained visibility and a reputation for being popular and accessible, demands upon archival collections have grown. Finding new audiences and new uses for old film helps to validate archival existence in an era of financial retrenchment, in which cultural organizations and the arts are required to justify their existence in terms of adding value to society. Inevitably, footage has become a market resource too.

Digitization and new media technologies have also transformed archival activity: users may edit, enhance, mix and rework film footage to create new historical adaptations. Images, once accessible only for viewing on site during opening hours by prior arrangement may be watched available freely and globally. No longer constrained by paper-based recording systems and filing cabinet space, shot-listing (the detailed shot by shot description of film footage) has expanded and links are available to metadata (the associated contextual details of production, producer, location and content). The study of archive film frequently now occurs in a climate of data abundance rather than scarcity, as online sources proliferate and changing information technologies redefine how information is made available. If this "democratisation of the archive" (Flinn) has influenced content, policy and practice in bringing new dynamism, openness and accessibility, it has also shifted the production of historical knowledge by offering the possibility for alternative adaptations of the past. Dynamism is the watchword: "After many years in the wilderness and discussed only by a handful of archivists and historians, archives are finally on the larger agenda" (Lane and Hill 6). Footage is not simply repositioned neutrally in a news bulletin or report, interactive public display, educational resource or creative piece of work. The adaptive processes that archive footage undergoes, as it travels out from the archives should now be examined more closely, by reference to amateur footage that itself reflects the broadening remit of archives as "keepers of our collective memories" (Bunch qtd. in Flinn).

The World in Home Movies

Amateur film footage readily leans itself to many kinds of visual investigation. For some it is the uncensored visual testimony taken by people at a given moment — a persuasive lens through which to adapt historical events and experiences unmediated by subsequent memory. For others, its appeal lies less in what it offers as evidential history and visible proof of observable details: what it does not show in its selective chronicling of past experiences is instructive. Attention focuses on visual omissions and gaps that disclose the silences of historical adaptations and visual memories. Alternatively, amateur footage might attest to the experts' objectifying gaze, and the unequal power relations of those framed by the lens and those holding the camera, or the under-representation of families that reflect the migration histories and profound social and cultural changes of twentieth century Britain. Aesthetic interests might be of paramount interest: how did cine-camera users negotiate the visual novelty of motion capture, and what lingering influences of still photography may be discerned in the camera technique of the enthusiast?

For others, amateur film occupies a transitional niche in the archeology of media communications — a precursor to the highly personalized recording systems available to contemporary users of self-generated data (life-loggers restricted by film reels four minute long). Links between professional visual and media production during the formative years of film and television are traceable too, as are the newly emerging interests that chart more differentiated examples of amateur cine technologies—women, children, ethnic minorities, disabled filmmakers. As a flexibly used medium that first appeared in Britain during the early 1920s, and then became relatively cheaper and affordable to wider sections of society during the second half of the last century, amateur film has an infinite potential to be explored in different ways. Many historical adaptations of experience can be analyzed through films shot by amateurs in the past, which continue to be shot today (Craven). Here the focus is less on the content *per se*, but how readings and meanings of footage alter over time, in and away from an archival setting.

Home movies showing family and domestic scenes are perhaps the best known examples of amateur film footage. Easily dismissed for their clichéd content and poor quality camera work, their seemingly untroubled images of relationship and home life have often deterred serious historical analysis. Yet the very appeal of capturing "baby on the lawn" type imagery—which prompted one American scholar to suggest that Auguste Lumière's shots of his wife and infant daughter having breakfast in the garden were possibly the world's first home movie (Katelle 51)—is evident in the wealth of material produced over the decades of changing camera technologies. Such plentifully consistent scenes that show families together, children playing, holidays and special occasions are too frequent in the archive to simply ignore (Norris Nicholson, "Seeing;" "Moving;" *Amateur*). Readily studied for what they visibly show about childhood, parenting, family and home life, alternative ways of questioning might also focus on their selectivity: their visual omissions and what is left unsaid or un-shown about family experience. Ostensible scenes of happy childhoods are seen through adult eyes. Childhood memories, recalled one interviewee, were full of holidays spent in front of a father's cine camera, as if on constant location (Norris Nicholson, *Amateur* 158). Her elderly reflections contrast with idyllic scenes of youngsters running happily across flowery meadows screened by one proud parent over sixty years ago.

Most family scenes concentrate on special rather than everyday occasions, but it seems likely that the camera's presence would affect behavior, however ordinary the activities taking place. One filmmaker's record on color film of domesticity as his wife combines the roles of being cook, cleaner and career, in an apparently effortless flow of activity highlights predictable gender roles and the performative quality of recording mundane details in early postwar Britain. The featured household appliances in *Domestic Scenes at 30 Devonshire Road* (1949) not only reveal a materially comfortable and modern home, but hint at the filmmaker's familiarity with the current advertising of such goods.[1] Much footage deliberatively memorializes special occasions for future recollection; birthdays, seasonal occasions, family gatherings, holidays and days out. When such events, seen only through the filmmaker's eyes, were screened later for family and friends, impromptu remarks would typically add humor, extra unseen details and broaden the vision and version of family history captured on camera. Here the cinematic gaze of much silent home movie footage functioned as part of more collective familial adaptations of history, as part of a negotiated process of retelling shared experiences.

Relocating family footage from its original private into more public spaces alters its significance. Individual moments within family memories—learning to walk or ride a bicycle, the first day going to school, a sports day, wedding or holiday—acquire different value: the implicit histories of contextual details lose their significance for a wider audience. Family memories, trapped in visual obsolescence as camera technologies change and projectors stop working, may regain visibility for later generations if transferred to newer viewing formats and returned to relatives. For other independent viewers, family footage in an archive is redefined by new eyes and different questions: the strikingly colorful scenes of *Norma's Birthday Party and Family Get-Together*, with its beaming-faced young man in new RAF uniform who shakes hands with different people, silently captures the significance of this special celebratory meal.[2]

While familial pride is clearly observable, contemporary viewers ask different questions as they witness the lavish spread on the table. How could food be so plentiful under Britain's wartime rationing? How strange to see familiar brand names on the sauce bottles amidst the unfamiliarity and distinctive period style of the fluked china, embroidered table cloth and napkins? With the benefit of hindsight, questions about what happened to the young man in uniform, his admiring younger brother, and the two generations of people captured on camera in the early 1940s have very different significance.

Family footage discloses how personal lives interweave with broader adaptations of history. The amateur lens unwittingly magnifies and informs the tissue and rhythms of change through its capacity to particularize, individualize and modify more official reconstructions of the past. Whether in domestic settings, or late colonial and expatriate encounters in distant overseas locations, recreational cine footage offers more than simply an alternative adaptation of historical experience. Its intentionality is different too from a professionally recorded moving image; its flexibility, spontaneity and whimsicality offer an immediacy and sense of bearing witness that are unfettered either by censorship or commercial or professional requirements.

Relocating Meanings

Amateur film offers specific forms of visible historical evidence. It would be reductive to think of it only in this way, but its historical content and context readily differentiates it from other forms of material. But when it is recycled or reworked in other productions, or viewed through different media, does its meaning change significantly? Clearly the scope for contrast — whether the film is grainy black and white as the putative signifier of authenticity and eye-witness recording, or shot in the vibrant colors of Kodachrome cine-reels — is apparent in the edits that re-contextualize old footage. Other visual and technical transformations sometimes occur: archive footage is made to look older or younger for effect, colors change, as do aspect ratios when images move between different sized screens. Sound is also added, removed or altered. Alongside these changes, images shed and gain new adaptive meanings as they are understood differently. Their reframing within a television program fuses a generic and indicative sense of time and place, with the producer's intentions and the more individualized ways of understanding brought by each viewer. How do we accommodate these new meanings that occur through re-use? Rather like written quotations inserted to support or illustrate a point, amateur footage may be seen as bringing the strength of visual proof (in other words, proving the truth of an event as it "it was caught on camera," as if the camera's capacity to lie has been forgotten). Evidential truth occurs, but the popularity of archive footage for producers suggests that more is at stake. Perhaps amateur footage acts as a conduit that helps to forge new kind of historical adaptations for viewers that are less concerned with intellectual verification and more drawn into watching footage unconsciously as a touchstone to a collective past. What might be labeled dismissively as nostalgic visual consumption of accessible evocations of earlier twentieth century life is more problematic than at first sight. Superficially appealing to a conservative yearning for lost times, or perhaps the loss of what once was *thought* possible — a wish "for past thoughts rather than past things" in Lowenthal's words (8) — much amateur film offers innumerable visual evocations of aspects of life swept away or transformed into museum pieces by subsequent societal changes. Unlike the recreations of fictionalized historical adaptations (that require a suspension of disbelief to look beyond the minutiae of historical imagination and reconstruction) amateur footage has no need to prove its credentials. It simply exists as a material record of different times. There is not the same credibility gap present even in oral history — another seemingly democratic route into more collective understandings of past experience. The pull of the past exerted by amateur film relates in part to its direct link to the past; it is not a contemporary reminiscence about past events.

However much it is knocked around in the reworking process of adaptation, its longevity imbues it with status even if what is shown is fairly ordinary. The images on screen not only connect past and present but provide a surrogate memory for those who may remember differently, or not at all.

As footage journeys differently, its adaptations change. Some relocations offer more fluidity than others; multiple meanings may be rapidly contested and re-negotiated within teaching time and space. Archives may be able to log the specific contexts into which archive footage might be placed, but most archival teams have little time to document the individual meanings prompted by imagery that travels from their collections. However when amateur footage leaves the archive as part of deliberate outreach to specific audiences, visible traces of past experience may be valued by those who have been more usually omitted from historical record (Norris Nicholson, *Screening*). Sharing archive amateur films taken informally at local level in areas with rich migration histories helps to heighten youngsters' awareness of previous generations' immigration experiences. In such instances, the adaptive process involves generating new meanings through screening footage in new situations: archive practice adapts too as it compiles and finds ways to bring relevant footage in appropriate community-related and culturally sensitive ways (Norris Nicholson, "Manchester's").

The stories and meanings generated by projects that seek to reconnect imagery made by outsiders in contexts where visual material has not been readily available are some of the most challenging forms of historical adaptation. However this can be a beneficial process, especially when the visual texts are memories that may sit alongside other kinds of memory-making within a given socio-political or cultural setting.

Acts of virtual relocation give new possibilities to archive footage of many kinds. Amateur footage is among various categories of film that now travel freely via electronic online access for varied use. Despite its amateur status and popular appeal, non-professionally made material is as protected by copyright as other archived material, and permission for its reuse should be always traced via the archive. Yet digitized images can be recycled easily with no obligation for their contextual details or metadata to travel too. Arguably electronic means should enhance access to, rather than reduce, the contextual information available, but users are selective and the clipart-potential of online material is very seductive. The integrity of the historical researcher may be very different from the online downloader and re-mixer. Watermarks (distinguishing logos that safeguard and authenticate footage like marks on a banknote) may offer some protection to an individual image, but reworking may enable such markers to be squeezed and stretched off the screen. Manipulation rather than adaptation can arise from such interventions, more precisely defined as the exploitative misuse of raw archive material. Extending the argument beyond whether retelling produces good, bad or indifferent adaptations, this focus on reusing archived amateur film highlights some of the inherent risks of distortion and misrepresentation. Reducing imagery available on line to the status of "found" or "orphan footage" stripped of pre-existing roots or identity is disingenuous. Visual literacy at all levels must be cognizant of these risks: convenient and accessible sites that offer readily available visual solutions are fundamentally different from locations where archive material has undergone careful contextualization. Adjusting to new globalized ways of making and sharing knowledge across medias and technologies, and the changing notions of authorship and audience involves finding how to negotiate the multiple forms of visual and historical adaptations that are made, distributed, interpreted and remade during processes of relocating archive film.

Digitization makes material available in unprecedented ways. Access to an abundance of moving imagery exists on line, but more material does not necessarily mean better adaptive historical practice or becoming better informed. Our visual literacy and that of the learners and others we work with is ever more challenged by the unbounded availability and reach of visual material. The study of historical adaptation may help us to negotiate the pluralities of texts that result from how we relate to the moving image. The complexities embedded in amateur film footage and their relationships with material and less tangible aspects of past experience are, like historical interpretation more generally, best situated within the socio-cultural and geopolitical specificities of time and place. These micro- and macro narratives interconnect dynamically in their processes of retelling, yet they may be fragmented, inconsistent and sometimes contradictory. As digitization increasingly mediates our film heritage, being more critically aware of the adaptive processes that shape and re-shape the visual histories told by footage in our archives seems too important to ignore. Like Pamuk's miniaturists, how we negotiate the cross-currents in the digital turn will affect the visual histories that will pass to those who come after us.

Notes

1. Peter Sykes, *Domestic Scenes at 30 Devonshire Road*, North West Film Archive at Manchester Metropolitan University, Film no.4371 (color, silent, 6 min. 11 sec.), 1949.
2. Ernest W Hart, *Norma's Birthday Party and Family Get-Together*, North West Film Archive at Manchester Metropolitan University, Film No.4426 (b/w & color, silent, 9 min.35 sec.), 1940–42.

Works Cited

Craven, Ian, ed. *Movies on Home Ground: Explorations in Amateur Cinema*. Newcastle-upon-Tyne: Cambridge Scholars, 2009. Print.

Derrida, Jacques. *Archive Fever: A Freudian Impression*. Trans. Eric Prenowitz. Chicago: University of Chicago Press, 1995. Print.

Domestic Scenes at 30 Devonshire Road. Dir. Peter Sykes. North West Film Archive at Manchester Metropolitan University. No.4371 (color, silent, 6 min. 11 sec.). 1949. Film.

Flinn, Andrew. "An attack on professionalism and scholarship? Democratising Archives and the Production of Knowledge." *Ariadne* 62 (Jan. 2010). Web. 14 Feb. 2012.

Houston, Penelope. *Keepers of the Frame: The Film Archives*. London: British Film Institute, 1994. Print.

Katelle, Alan D. *Home Movies: A History of the American Industry, 1897–1979*. Nashau, NH: Transition, 2000. Print.

Lane, Victoria, and Jennie Hill. "Where Do We Come From? What Are We? Where Are We Going? Situating the Archive and Archivists." *The Future of Archives and Recordkeeping: A Reader*. Ed. Jennie Hill. New York: Neal-Schuman, 2010. 3–22. Print.

Lowenthal, David. *The Past is a Foreign Country*. Cambridge: Cambridge University Press, 1985. Print.

Murray, Simone. *The Adaptation Industry: The Cultural Economy of Contemporary Literary Adaptation*. London and New York: Routledge, 2011. Print.

Naremore, James. *Film Adaptation*. New Brunswick, NJ: Rutgers University Press, 2000. Print.

Norma's Birthday Party and Family Get-Together. Dir. Ernest W. Hart. North West Film Archive at Manchester Metropolitan University. No. 4426 (b/w & color, silent, 9 min.35 sec.). Film.

Norris Nicholson, Heather. *Amateur Film: Meaning and Practice, 1927–1977*. Manchester: Manchester University Press, 2012. Print.

_____. "Framing the View: Holiday Recording and Britain's Amateur Film Movement c.1925–1950." *Movies on Home Ground: Explorations in Amateur Cinema*. Ed. Ian Craven. Newcastle upon Tyne: Cambridge Scholars, 2009. Print. 93–127.

_____. "Manchester's Moving Memories: Tales from Moss Side and Hulme: Archive Film and Community History-Making." *Tourists and Nomads. Amateur Images of Migration*. Eds. Sonja Kmec and Viviane Thill. Marburg: Jonas Verlag, 2012. Print. In press.

_____. "Moving Pictures; Moving Memories: Framing the Interpretative Gaze." *Private Eyes and the Public Gaze. The Manipulation and Valorisation of Amateur Images*. Eds. Sonja Kmec and Viviane Thill. Trier: Kliomedia, 2009. Print. 69–78.

_____. "Seeing It How It Was? Childhood, Memory and Identity in Home-Movies." *Area* 33:2 (2001): 128–40. Print.

_____. *Screening Culture: Constructing Image and Identity*. Lanham, MD: Rowman and Littlefield/ Lexington Books, 2003. Print.

Pamuk, Orhan. *My Name is Red*. Trans. Erdağ M. Göknar. London: Faber and Faber, 2001. Print.

Schwartz, Joan M., and Terry Cook. "Archives, Records, and Power: From (Postmodernism) Theory to Archival Performance." *Archival Science* 2 (2002): 171–85. Print.

Shand, Ryan. "Theorizing Amateur Cinema: Limitations and Possibilities." *The Moving Image: The Journal of the Association of Moving Image Archivists* 8.2 (2008): 36–60. Print.

Recasting the Past
in the Personal Present:
History, Film, and Adaptation

GERALD DUCHOVNAY, ERIC GRUVER,
CHARLES HAMILTON and HAYLEY HASIK

When members of a film audience view a film, some let it wash over them, some intellectualize its ideas, some read its aesthetics, and some experience it. Sometimes there is a synthesizing effect: a viewer will go beyond passive viewing to rekindling knowledge, memories or experiences. What transpires in a movie theatre (or watching a film in a classroom or on a small screen) is a form of adaptation. Viewers adapt or "translate" what is passing before their eyes by making it their own.

In an academic environment, what is personal might turn into something shared if there is an opportunity to exchange responses with fellow learners and instructors. A sharing of ideas and personal responses is what happened in three linked courses taught at Texas A&M University-Commerce in Spring 2011. One, taught by Eric Gruver, a member of the history faculty and undergraduate advisor to the university's honor program, focused on the history of the 1960s: readings of primary documents, viewing a few films, and extensive discussions and responses to the material; two other courses, one undergraduate and one graduate, taught by Gerald Duchovnay, focused on the films of the 1960s and early 1970s and provided students with opportunities to view feature films in their entirety and clips from many others, with readings and analytical responses focused on the films, aspects of 1960s' culture, and personal reflections on those turbulent years.

With a total of nearly sixty students in these classes, all taught in collaborative rather than lecture format, instructors and students were able to gain a better understanding of what the history was like then, how filmmakers in the 1960s and later presented those years on film, and how our perceptions of that time have been shaped by personal experiences, age, and what we were taught about the period in our formative years. As a result of these classes most of the learners had epiphanies about what the 1960s were about. What follows are comments by learners (Chuck Hamilton, graduate; Hayley Hasik, undergraduate) and instructors and also learners (Eric Gruver, history; Gerald Duchovnay, film studies) about what we experienced as students and faculty in studying the films and history of the 1960s and what these classes meant to us.

Gerald Duchovnay

When Eric Gruver, a colleague in the history department at my university, approached me about doing an honors course for first-year learners using films that would be linked to a history section, we discussed several options. Based on his experience with learners, and a seemingly general lack of knowledge about "recent" history (history after World War II), in part because high school curricula in Texas seems to stop there, we decided that doing a course on the Sixties would be the focus. In film history, a renaissance of U.S. filmmaking overlapped into the 1970s, so I opted to focus on a period of approximately 1959–1974. In addition, that semester I was offering a graduate course on the history of narrative film, and while I almost never teach linked graduate-undergraduate courses, I thought it might be insightful to see how the overlap might work at both levels.

The undergraduate course consisted of eighteen first-year learners, mostly 18–20 years old, who had never studied film before. Three honors learners were juniors or seniors, one of whom had studied film before. At the graduate level, the sixteen learners ranged in age from twenty-two to about sixty, including three international learners (one from the Middle East, one from Europe, and one from Africa), which met twice a week for two and one half hours for sixteen weeks.

Not knowing much about individual backgrounds, on the first day of class, learners in both classes were asked to respond to a questionnaire listing thirty-seven key names or dates to see what they could identify or what they remembered from those decades. As previous learners at this Texas regional university have said to me on numerous occasions, in high school they were being taught names and dates, and not asked to do analysis or "critical thinking" about what they were studying, so here was an opportunity to see if any of those names or dates stuck. The results of the survey were eye-opening.

The most recognized or identified items in the survey amongst undergraduates were Rosa Parks (all), Jimi Hendrix (17), Mahatma Gandhi (14), Bob Dylan (13), and Andy Warhol (8). Items that not one could identify included: Marshall McLuhan, Timothy Leary, Haight Ashbury, Betty Friedan, Stonewall Riots, Daniel Ellsberg, what happened at Kent State in 1971, Gulf of Tonkin, My Lai, or the significance of the organization NOW. Only one could identify the significance of the date November 22, 1963. In the graduate course, where generational differences could be expected, the results were somewhat better, with all but one knowing who Gandhi was, followed by Rosa Parks (13), Jimmie Hendrix, and the Black Panthers, and then Andy Warhol, Malcolm X, and Bob Dylan (12). Only one knew Gulf of Tonkin or Daniel Ellsberg and no one knew about the Stonewall riots. The international learner from Europe was better versed on these matters than many of his U.S. counterparts, and the learners from the Middle East and Africa were unfamiliar with almost the entire list.

The graduate class, part of a film studies certificate, focused on the films, with some readings and references to cultural and historical events, but the undergraduate course linked the readings and discussions in the history class to the films the learners were seeing in the English class. I began each segment of the course with a documentary. The first day the learners watched the PBS documentary *The Sixties*, and for the Seventies part of *The Decade Under the Influence*. Both films helped ground the work we were doing in the course, along with readings from anthologies that dealt with films from those decades, as well as a general primer for the undergraduates on aspects of film studies.

Both courses were learner-centered and collaborative, with the graduate learners presenting on specific films they chose to focus on. For the first part of the undergraduate course, specific films were assigned, and learners were asked to respond in writing to "talking points" or "study questions." While I would share some background information on films or filmmakers, or aspects of culture, for each presentation, much of the discussion (I do not lecture) was directed by learner responses of their analysis of the film at hand and aspects of culture. The responses to specific questions on each film were done individually, with some questions being answered by everyone, with others linked to designated groups. So when we met the class after seeing a film, the learners would break into groups and discuss their individual responses to their questions and then one member of the group would share the group's consensus view (if there was one) with the rest of the class. While some questions drew consensus, many times the individuals in the groups saw and understood the films (and their readings) differently, and thus they negotiated their answers with one another, saw diverse ways of looking at and understanding events and filmic presentations. Discussion ensued following each response.

For their formal papers for the class (two for undergraduates, one for graduate learners), they were given the option of choosing the texts to study. Each learner was required to present an aspect or two of the films chosen in presentations that included clips. Thus, how texts were negotiated and presented to their peers remained an individual, not instructor choice. The specific elements stressed varied from presentation to presentation, thus suggesting something about each film, but also avenues the individual learner wanted to explore and share.

While many in both classes had a vague sense of what the period was about prior to entering the class, most were blank slates. As a result, there were not many preconceived ideas about what they were seeing. As we progressed in the courses, the undergraduates were able to make links and connections between the ideas and events they were reading about in the history class and the films they were seeing. As they became more familiar and at ease about talking about film (form and content), they were using higher level cognitive skills in analyzing the material.

It did not matter if the learners saw the canonical films of the 1960s or 1970s; the aim was to get them to read the films in ways that went beyond mere narrative — to understand how form relates to content, how certain films of, say, Italian Neo-Realism or the French New Wave influenced filmmakers, and how things such as color or the *mise en scène* are useful tools in reading films. Most of the films they saw were easy enough to follow, but to be able to see how the films connect to the historical, social, and cultural milieu, both of the time the film was made and how it influences their lives, even today, was central to my approach to the course. The courses then, for the students and for me became a voyage of discovery, to see how as French historian Pierre Sorlin has noted, we always look at the past from the perspective of the present. As one student noted, for example, looking at *American Graffiti* (1973) today, we can see that George Lucas was appealing to an audience "worn out" from assassinations and years of conflict in Vietnam and that we craved nostalgia for the music and life of a more innocent time. But was that as apparent to audiences in 1973? Or, as Chuck Hamilton suggests elsewhere in this essay, in 1967 the word "plastics" was shorthand for rejecting middle class values, while today's traditional learners (under the age of 25) might think of plastics in terms of recycling or how plastic products are made from oil and what that means to our current economy.

Seeing new "things" for the first time, looking at and considering an influential time in world history in new ways (especially in U.S. history), and seeing how the events and films of fifty years ago (some of which could not or would not be made today given the "business climate" of moviemaking) connect to our lives today were key to the goals of the course. While some in our culture like to claim that our students are guilty of collective amnesia, they are not because for the most part they have never been taught to think critically about the past and as a result, when they confront it as history or film, they recast the past in their personal present.

The learners were also asked to respond at the end of the course on how it impacted them. One of the graduate learners commented: "As a product of American public schools, my knowledge of the more controversial parts of our history during the 1960s and 1970s was severely lacking. I didn't know too much about the sorts of political corruption that took place during this time, such as Watergate, nor was I knowledgeable about civil rights issues — namely, the specific riots that were most influential in social change — or Vietnam. This class helped to clarify through film, these issues, as well as helping me understand how film can act as an agent of social change, rather than a purely aesthetic statement. Even films that were not overtly about the 1960s and 1970s, such as *To Kill a Mockingbird* (1962), made me realize how film can take certain events out of their exclusive contexts in order to speak to an audience about similar, universal issues, such as racism and war, as well as how history tends to repeat itself. As a result, I can clearly see how many of these films apply even to events of today."

Cinema (and television) helps us to understand and adapt our ideas of history, culture, and texts. Having taught these courses for the first time, I am now anxious to revisit the material with new ideas about "ways in" to the material, but knowing that future classes will bring somewhat different lived memories and different knowledge to each class. The courses reconfirmed that one can never assume anything about the knowledge or "baggage" our learners bring to our courses. Each semester, each course, each day, we are on a voyage of discovery about what we thought we knew and did not know about the world around us, our learners and the background and analytical skills they bring to our classes, and ourselves as instructors.

Eric Gruver

Teaching a course about U.S. history during the 1960s (hereafter the Sixties) to a classroom of undergraduates born in the early 1990s presents a natural series of challenges, but offering an interdisciplinary history course on the period in conjunction with a film course presented both additional hurdles and tremendous opportunities to enhance and reinforce learner learning. As with any course a professor cannot presume learners' academic familiarity with an historical era for fear of moving too quickly in the course without adequate explanation and understanding, but I developed the history course with the expectation that learners had encountered disparate elements from the Sixties era — particularly music — but without an understanding of the historical context of the broader events, ideas, and issues of the era. All learners enrolled in the courses were members of the University's Honors College and nearly all of them attended public secondary schools in Texas where the studying of history consists of memorizing names, dates, and facts — what I amusingly call "dead, rich, white guy" history — to accommodate the high stakes assessment model used to evaluate public schools and educators. Because the assessment tests contain multiple choice items, Texas high school learners are trained to recall information rather than engage in conceptual and/or causal analysis of history or in an examination of multiple interpretations of historical events. Not surprisingly, given their mis-education in high school, the learners had no foundation with the terms "interdisciplinary" or "humanities," so the professors expected and planned to devote adequate time during the early weeks of the courses reminding learners of the mission of the clustered, conjoined courses: to examine the human condition during the Sixties era in the U.S. via historical contexts illustrated in writing by the era's participants and historians and on the screen by film writers, directors, and producers.

Given the aforementioned factors, we expected learners to be able to recall — what we considered "knowing" — the "stars" of the Sixties era (e.g., Martin Luther King, Jr., Malcolm X, Lyndon Johnson, Vietnam, and especially Woodstock), but we did not expect learners to possess an "understanding" of the context of the people, places, and concepts. In order to facilitate learners' exploration of the Sixties from multiple perspectives and ideologies, learners needed to read different types of sources from people of all leanings, both those who lived during the era and those who have studied the period. I quickly jettisoned the idea of utilizing a textbook because they typically contain the same repository of names, dates, and facts with which learners are accustomed and because no textbook contains the variety of perspectives learners needed to understand the Sixties. Thus, learners read two primary document collections and several journal articles that provided a wide array of philosophical viewpoints, including a lengthy examination of "when the Sixties began" as well as the variety of definitions attributed to terms like liberal, conservative, radical, fundamentalist, socialist, feminism, equality, justice, and hippies. Each primary source was preceded by a brief but thorough description of the circumstances under which the document appeared during the era, and learners commented throughout the course that they appreciated the editors' explanations because learners learned why the document, its author, and the subject(s) therein were significant to the Sixties.

During the first class meeting learners identified their "knowledge" about the Sixties, listing items that included names of presidents, domestic economic and social issues, international crises, and cultural icons. When pressed to provide a brief explanation for the items listed on the board, learners could provide only rudimentary comments about a president or an international incident. Learners readily admitted that they "knew stuff"—the aforementioned disparate collection of facts—because they had viewed a popular film or television program, their parents had taught them what they should think or believe, and they heard stories from parents' friends and other family members. To further impress upon learners the importance of historical context, I asked them to consider that the events, ideologies, and concepts of the Sixties originated in previous decades and that the events of the Sixties affected people long after the end of the decade. Thus, I asked, "When did the Sixties begin?" Not surprisingly, learners were perplexed when I selected 1954 — the *Brown* court decision, hydrogen bomb testing, and mid-term elections—as the "start date" for this course on the Sixties, and their intellectual angst increased further as they noticed that the course would end with President Richard Nixon's resignation in 1974. Casting the Sixties beyond the bounds of the actual decade caused learners to re-examine their own interpretations of history and their understanding of the era.

Learners' re-casting their personal knowledge with their new discoveries is not a novel concept, but learners' ability and willingness to modify their understanding of historical events might have diminished: our history and film learners, however, gradually embraced the need to adapt what they thought they knew and understood about the Sixties, particularly when we encountered the terms "liberal" and "conservative." Learners admitted that their understanding of or context for these terms originated from parents and media sources, and they offered similar comments regarding other terms throughout the course, including radical, fundamentalist, socialist, containment, feminism, counterculture. Two episodes from the history course stand out as exemplary of learners re-packaging what they comprehended about the Sixties. First, during the first few weeks of the course, learners read primary documents and a journal article on Presidents John Kennedy's and Lyndon Johnson's efforts to work with big business in order to stimulate a sluggish economy during the first two years of their administration. Acknowledging that Kennedy and Johnson had been Democrats associated — in learners' minds—with civil rights and other "liberal" ideas, learners read with perplexing interest how JFK and LBJ forged relationships with corporations that simultaneously enabled them to achieve many of the social program successes. Most learners knew that big business typically aligned itself on the conservative end of the spectrum within the American system of politics, so studying how left-leaning politicians allied with right-leaning businessmen who understood that their support of the presidents would facilitate the advancement of social programs presented learners with a cognitive challenge.

Woodstock and the hippie movement provided the subject for a second major episode of learners' cognitive dissonance. Learners presumed they understood hippies, the free speech movement, and free love ideology, given the popularization of the period in film, music, and the media. Upon reading primary accounts of non-drug users, casual attendees to the New York music festival and the profit-seekers planning the event, as well as others who participated in commune and other hippie-attributed experiments across the U.S., learners became confused as the authors explained that they rejected drug use along with the free love and other anti-establishment campaigns, and that they did not understand the goals of the "hippie movement." Learners asked: why had historians omitted these people from mainstream books, how could such contradictory information from media and popular culture accounts have been hidden from people for so long, and was the Woodstock generation as radical as the conservative backlash of the 1970s suggested? This pair of examples, culled from several similar learning episodes during the semester, provided the professors and learners opportunities to reassess what they thought we knew and understood about the Sixties and allowed learners to adapt their own perceptions and interpretations of the period.

Perhaps the most revealing learning event, however, did not occur in a singular moment or class meeting, but instead was achieved in cumulative terms from week to week as the semester progressed. Working in tandem and pairing films with historical content — frequently changing which films to show a day before a class meeting — the professors allowed learners to adapt their knowledge, understanding, and learning of the Sixties by offering an opportunity to consider the role of government in society (not necessarily limited to the U.S., but that was our focus). A majority of learners reported that they had grown up in conservative households, with their families adhering to Christian religious teachings and conservative social and economic philosophies that rejected the idea of big, intrusive government; while a significant number of learners admitted a disdain for politics and analyzing government affairs of any kind. By the end of the course, however, learners understood that the social progress of the Sixties — an increase in equality of several types, a safety net for the poor and/or disabled, the emphasis on education for everyone — could not have occurred without government agencies intervening in situations unseen in U.S. history. Learners read several documents and articles in the history course about segregation in the South and about African Americans' push for equality and justice across the nation, but learners were unprepared for the visual realities of *Mississippi Burning* (1988), a film inspired by the story of three civil rights workers murdered in the South during the early 1960s. Several learners hid their eyes during certain parts of the film, as the violence they had read about became real, and some of the more conservative learners agreed that the racism of the South could have only been mitigated through federal intervention.

Learners reacted similarly to *Three Days of the Condor* (1975), *All the President's Men* (1976), *Hair* (1979), and *Hamburger Hill* (1987), all of which illustrated how federal officials either trampled upon the Constitution of the U.S. and the rights of ordinary Americans or ignored public opinion and sent young men to violent and questionable deaths. From federal officials considering themselves above the law to drafting young, unwilling men into the military, learners became stakeholders in their own society, shrugging off their previous ambivalence or disdain for political issues. For the first time in many of their lives, they set aside their blind loyalty to the government in order to question the role of government in society. Thus, the history and film courses would have been successful as separate, uncoordinated entities— the honors learners would have learned a vast quantity of information regardless of the course structure — but the integration of primary and scholarly readings with film provided learners an opportunity to examine the human condition in multiple ways, allowing them to adapt and re-create a new reality and understanding of the Sixties, arguably the most well-known yet least understood period in U.S. history.

Charles Hamilton

My first meaningful film experience of the 1960s was *The Graduate*, a 1967 Mike Nichols film starring Dustin Hoffman as Benjamin, a disillusioned college graduate, about to enter graduate school and begin a business degree before a move into the business world, typically following in his father's footsteps. What is wrong with that? Actually nothing. The controversy here begins with the newfound philosophy of independent thought — of not robotically following in your father's footsteps, but taking the time to decide the future for yourself. The problem —from my parents' point of view — was that I was too young and inexperienced to make those kinds of decisions, so they were made for me. Benjamin stood as a symbol for me — I was about to enter college with no idea what I wanted to do in life, and trying my best to not blindly follow my parent's instructions, but to formulate some personal design for my own future.

This was also a time of political unrest, social conflict, and protesters marching in the streets— the war in Vietnam, the Kent State shootings, race riots in Watts, the Watergate break-in, President Nixon's resignation — but I was not part of what the world was seeing on television, I was Benjamin. I, too, was avoiding the security of a life planned by my parents, while going through the mental turmoil of trying to find my own personal path.

The idea of an "independent thinking" philosophy, which came to the surface for me in *The Graduate*, was not a popular one with my parents, or the public school and colleges I attended then, they wanted complacency and consistency (a sit, listen, and learn mentality). But, I did not want to become my parents—unless that was my choice. I only wanted to have the choice. Benjamin could have chosen "plastics"—I will never know—but I do know (or think I know) that whatever field he ended up in was his choice—not his father's. My position was similar to Benjamin's. My father wanted me to become a lawyer, something I did not want to study and failed at miserably. I, instead, chose to become a journalist, out to save the world, for which, puzzling as it was to me, my father gave his blessing, and I felt like the decision was mine.

So—entering the conversation as one who participated in the late 1960s and early 1970s as a college student, I had, and still have, the perspective of "being there" in analyzing that time period—and especially the films of the era (*Easy Rider, Five Easy Pieces, The Trip, The Graduate*, etc.)—as they represented my generation in revolt against the status quo of our parents. The main attributes I gained from experiencing one of the most exciting and controversial periods of American culture are senses of self-importance, self-awareness, self-confidence, and independence, which helped form my continually morphing ideology. Unfortunately, all those factors also caused me to appear self-centered, condescending, pompous, and dismissive to anyone who had opinions contrary to mine, or could not identify with the time period in the same way I could. Basically I was (and in some cases still am) the opposite of my "practice what you preach" philosophy I learned during my early college period—I had lost touch with Benjamin. But, being involved in a graduate class as a student in the 2000s, and undergraduate classes as an instructor during the same period, I began to see how I had been forcing my ideological philosophies on my graduate classmates and my students. In other words, I was using the same methods of indoctrination that my parents and teachers used against me earlier in life. When politics became part of the discussion I had a tendency to show my side of an issue as being superior to any other positions because of what I thought was a "special connection" to the events and time periods. The same tendency was apparent in discussions of literature, religion, or government control. Being in the class as a graduate student taught me to back off from my heavy-handed tactics and look at the events I had experienced first-hand from other perspectives—through the eyes of those who had only read about them, heard about them from parents or relatives, and seen them acted out on film in the forms of movies, documentaries, and film clips—or are only now reading about them in the multitudes of books about the films of the 1960s and1970s. Watching the documentaries *The Sixties* and *The Decade Under the Influence* in class generated discussions about the college learners who were seen on the television news throwing blood on soldiers returning from Vietnam, violently demonstrating in the streets, or smoking marijuana and using drugs openly, to cite only a few clips. Since I had been a part of the college population at that time I knew that these images represented only a small percentage of that population, and I began to understand that my job was to offer these learners, many of whom were seeing these images for the first time, a different perspective that was not meant to persuade, but only to supply them with information from a source close to them who had actually participated. My reasoning, again, was to offer more information in an attempt to give them more choices as they formed their personal opinions of the sociological events of that period and how films were affected by those events.

As we probably all remember from our early elementary school days, there is a game our educators used to show us how information changes as it is passed from person to person. You begin by telling one classmate a story, whispering it in his or her ear, and that classmate passes it to another, and so on until all have heard the story. The last person tells what they heard, which is, in many cases, far from the original. The same is true for remembrances of historical, social, and cultural experiences. My remembrance of the facts changed through my personal interpretation of those facts so that they now had become the truth—my truth. So, in a sense, my ideology was formed by my interpretation of the facts molded into what I thought they should be, and I could not tolerate those who did not agree. Listening to what others in my graduate class had to say about a certain film, how they reacted to the film's message and discussed its social and cultural importance within their current socio-cultural context, and the differences between their points of view and mine, made me realize (rightly or wrongly) that no one can completely understand the emotions associated with the events of a historical context with or without being there to experience them.

This experience of participating as a graduate learner, while also teaching a similar course to undergraduates, has also made me realize how valuable the proper method of information delivery and information use can be. The "I was there, and I know best" tactic is off-putting to me and to other learners. Somehow I began to hear myself speak, and I did not like what I was hearing. However, the use of anecdotal information through a 1960s and 1970s perspective as a sort of filling in the gaps methodology, and participating in open discussions using comparisons to modern-day perspectives, opened the thought processes from a variety of sides, with the point of providing incite that stimulated critical thinking. I now teach my classes without imposing my ideology on my students—and without the condescending nature of the "Know-it-all; I was there" mentality I had previously practiced.

If I had not participated in that 1960s and 1970s film course I might never have reflected critically on the influences those years had on my life and experiences. I can never completely convey what I gained from my experiences during the 1960s and 1970s to my students or classmates, or exactly the personal connection I feel when I watch and re-live the fear and mental tension of Benjamin in *The Graduate*, but, now I at least understand that the ideology of independent thinking I formed during those years continues as the basis of my adaptive processes, which are continually undergoing investigation and change. The processes of investigation, and the willingness to listen and possibly change, were essential elements of this class. As I listened to my instructor and classmates discuss *The Graduate* and Benjamin's rejection of his father's design for his future I realized I was interacting with independent thinkers like myself, and that I needed to open my processes and make some personal changes. As a result, I was able to add their viewpoints to mine and broaden my perspectives, something that might not have happened had I not been a part of this class.

Hayley Hasik

As second semester freshmen, the learners enrolled in the cluster courses of film and history of the 1960s (hereafter the Sixties) in the U.S. expected the classes to be like any other—that is, do the work and make the grades. The idea that the learners could learn something that they would remember and find applicable to their lives had not yet solidified in their minds. I was still in high school mode upon my enrollment in these courses, which is to say that I went to class to get a grade rather than to actually learn something.

Prior to enrolling in this history course, I had never taken a university history course and had despised history because of the emphasis placed on memorization and regurgitation. All of my history classes in high school were about memorizing people, places, and dates without actually fitting anything into the context of the time period or looking at how different events fit together. Because of my past experience with history, I had no reason to believe that this course would be any different from every other history class. The history and film courses were a packaged deal and to enroll in film, I had to enroll in history. The opportunity to study film, which I did not see as being difficult, motivated me enough to suffer through a semester in a despised history course.

My expectation that a film class would consist of watching films every day was spot on; I had no idea, however, that my perception of the film class could be so far from the truth. The amount of analysis and effort the film class required was something that many of my classmates and I were not prepared for. At the beginning of the film course, learners felt as though we were learning a foreign language with terms like auteur and *mise en scène* being used heavily but having very little applicable meaning due to our limited knowledge of film. Even the terms we knew and understood (lighting, camera angles, music and sound) were aspects of film that we had never considered in detail before. Discovering that every little detail can contribute to a film as a whole helped us to quickly adapt our perception of the class aims and objectives.

The film professor, in particular, challenged me to analyze what appeared on screen in order to become engaged in the film as a participant. My first film analysis, connecting a film to the Sixties, challenged me because I had no idea what to do; the process of analyzing film and connecting it to history was still very new and I was uncomfortable trusting that my analysis and interpretations were acceptable because I was still looking for the "right" answer. However, after doing a film analysis of Nicholas Ray's *55 Days at Peking* (1963), I was no longer worried about obtaining a high grade: realizing how far my abilities had advanced from the very first assignment, which required us to answer analytical questions about *American Graffiti* (1973). I had managed to use my knowledge from the history class and various other sources to make my own interpretations and support them. It was at this moment that I realized how much more these two classes had to offer other than simply memorizing facts and watching films.

Both of these classes relied heavily on individual as well as collaborative learning and I remember very few lectures given by either professor. Each learner was responsible for reading and knowing the same material, but the interpretation and connections made within the material, readings, films, and discussions, were up to each learner individually. With the freedom and opportunity to adapt our own opinions about the material, each topic made a different impression upon each learner; learning about women's rights and the various civil rights movements was intriguing for some learners but not for others. This independent process was important because it allowed the learners to form their own opinions from the information given, basing them in fact as well as personal experiences, beliefs, and interests. At the same time, however, both courses relied heavily on discussion, which tested learners' individual ideas and opinions. Class discussions allowed learners to share interpretations and work to understand how different people could adapt the same historical information in different ways, but learners could not expect to find a "right" answer about any topic or interpretation. Surprising to many learners, class discussions from the history course did not always end when the professor dismissed class; they continued at dinner, in someone's apartment, or even between classes and at times became quite heated, both in and out of the classroom. Not all discussions were directly related to the information at hand and most often reflected ideas and themes from a week's reading rather than specific details. During one class meeting, learners spent a significant time facing the "back" wall of the classroom, and a debate ensued over which direction constituted the back of the room and why we came to that conclusion. I can honestly say that I was confused by this entire debate and what it meant in reference to the Sixties; only later did I understand the entire discussion to be about perspective. It is not wrong to say that the back of the room is the front of the room or vice versa because it is all about perspective and interpretation, which was relevant to understanding the events of the Sixties, as well as understanding our own ideas about those events.

In studying for the mid-term and final exams in the film class, a group of learners formed a study group and attempted to develop a thesis and supporting evidence to answer each of the twenty questions that had been provided as a study guide. One question from the mid-term review asked learners to choose one topic from a list of BIG ideas from the Sixties and analyze how the topic was treated in three films. There were so many different topics and movie combinations that my decision to analyze violence in *Dr. Strangelove* (1964), *Bonnie and Clyde* (1967) and *Mississippi Burning* (1988) was completely different from someone else's assignment based on different films. The questions were intentionally vague and open-ended to allow for a variety of answers and, as long as the films used as examples could be explained and evidence could be given to support your answer, the answer was deemed appropriate. These situations enabled learners to realize that both classes became more about the learners supporting their interpretations and less about finding the "right" answer.

The university did not publicize that the film course would focus on the Sixties and, because of this, learners did not know about the connection between the film and history courses until they attended both classes. As a learner enrolled in both courses, the vast amount of information that was reiterated, expanded upon, and introduced through the conjoined courses was much greater than each course alone. Learners not enrolled in the film class were almost done a disservice because there was an element of understanding and realism that came with seeing ideas of the Sixties depicted on film. By bringing primary documents and films together, the courses combined to enhance our learning, although the history course provided most of the content. The film *Easy Rider* (1969) and its depiction of the counterculture and rebellious attitude often associated with the Sixties is one such example. Not only did the film depict the counterculture as being comprised of wild and free individuals, it also included elements of racism and discrimination. The combination of multiple elements, typically discussed separately in primary documents, helped to show how no single event stood on its own and how many of the big ideas of the Sixties were intertwined. This intellectually collaborative construction of the two courses allowed me to adapt myself into more than just a learner in search of grades; these classes shifted my thinking from the idea of just getting by in a class and doing assigned work as a means to an end, to actually learning the information and taking it beyond the classroom. If I had known how much I would learn, not just about the Sixties but about myself prior to signing up for these courses, I would have signed up without a negative thought toward either one.

Conclusion

Our understanding of films and history, like language, like perceptions, are constantly changing. What was popular or acceptable in the 1950s changed drastically in the 1960s, both in the United States and abroad, as historical and cultural events brought new ways of thinking about war, government, music, sex, drugs, religion, and the legal system. The demographics of movie audiences also changed radically in this period. As a result, screenwriters and directors targeted a younger (18–34 year old) audience, and producers financed films that reflected the changing times. But for many of today's students and instructors who did not live through that period, to get a sense of those times and how they influence us today requires reading deeply in primary sources, seeing documentaries and films that try to capture the ethos of those years, or interviewing those who lived through that decade. But each film, each written document, each interview is but a reflection of whoever is creating the text.

Works Cited

All the President's Men. Dir. Alan J. Pakula. Perf. Robert Redford, Dustin Hoffman. Warner Bros., 1976. Film.
American Graffiti. Dir. George Lucas. Perf. Richard Dreyfuss, Charlie Martin Smith, Ron Howard. Universal Pictures, 1973. Film.
Bonnie and Clyde. Dir. Arthur Penn. Perf. Warren Beatty, Faye Dunaway. Warner Bros/ Seven Arts, 1967. Film.
A Decade Under the Influence: The 70s Films That Changed Everything. Dir. Richard LaGrevenese and Ted Demme. IFC, 2003. DVD.
Dr. Strangelove. Dir. Stanley Kubrick. Perf. Peter Sellers, George C. Scott. Columbia Pictures, 1964. Film.

Easy Rider. Dir. Dennis Hopper. Perf. Peter Fonda, Dennis Hopper, Jack Nicholson. Columbia Pictures, 1969. Film.

55 Days at Peking. Dir. Nicholas Ray. Perf. Charlton Heston, Ava Gardner. Samuel Bronston Productions, 1963. Film.

Five Easy Pieces. Dir. Bob Rafelson. Perf. Jack Nicholson, Karen Black. Columbia Pictures, 1970. Film.

The Graduate. Dir. Mike Nichols. Perf. Dustin Hoffman, Anne Bancroft, Katharine Ross, Embassy Pictures, 1967. Film.

Hair. Dir. Milos Forman. Perf. John Savage, Treat Williams, CIP FilmProduktion GMBH, 1979. Film.

Hamburger Hill. Dir. John Irvin. Perf. Anthony Barrile, Don Cheadle. RKO Pictures, 1987. Film.

Mississippi Burning. Dir. Alan Parker. Perf. Gene Hackman, Willem Dafoe. Orion Pictures, 1988, Film.

The Sixties: The Years That Shaped a Generation. Dir. David Davis and Stephen Talbot. PBS Video: 2005. DVD.

Sorlin, Pierre. *The Film in History: Restaging the Past.* Oxford: Basil Blackwell, 1980. Print.

Three Days of the Condor. Dir. Sydney Pollack. Perf. Robert Redford, Faye Dunaway. Dino Di Laurentiis Company/ Paramount Pictures, 1975. Film.

To Kill a Mockingbird. Dir. Robert Mulligan. Perf. Gregory Peck. Universal International, 1962. Film.

The Trip. Dir. Roger Corman. Perf. Jack Nicholson, Susan Strasberg, Bruce Dern. American International, 1967. Film.

About the Contributors

Dunja **Dogo** obtained her Ph.D. in 2009 from the Department of Modern Literature and Sciences of Languages, University of Siena, presenting a dissertation titled "Icons of Martyrs and Fighters: Survival and Metamorphosis of Sacredness in Russian Propaganda Posters and Films Before and After 1917." She is co-director of the Russian section of the International Women Film Pioneers Project Online Encyclopaedia. Since 2006, she has been part of the editorial staff of the Italian academic peer-reviewed journal *Cinergie: Il cinema e le altre arti* (University of Udine), whose editorial board she joined in 2010.

Gerald **Duchovnay** is a professor of English and film studies at Texas A&M University–Commerce. The author of *Humphrey Bogart: A Bio-Bibliography*, editor of *Film Voices: Interviews from* Post Script, and co-editor (with J. P. Telotte) of *Science Fiction Film, Television, and Adaptation*, he is the founding and general editor of *Post Script: Essays in Film and the Humanities*, an international film journal.

Tanfer **Emin Tunç** is an assistant professor in the Department of American Culture and Literature at Hacettepe University, Ankara, Turkey. She holds a Ph.D. in American history from the State University of New York at Stony Brook, and specializes in women's studies and American cultural studies, with an emphasis on gender, race, and ethnicity. She is the author or editor of six books and more than fifty book chapters, reference book entries, reviews, and articles for such publications such as *Asian Journal of Women's Studies, Foreign Literature Studies, Women's History Review, Historical Journal* and *Journal of Women's History*.

Defne **Ersin Tutan** teaches in the Department of American Culture and Literature at Başkent University, Ankara, Turkey. Having earned her M.A. and Ph.D. degrees in cultural studies from Hacettepe University, she worked extensively on the intersection of postmodern and postcolonial discourses, with her dissertation titled "Postmodern Fabulation in the Postcolonial Novels of Salman Rushdie and Ben Okri." She teaches courses on American history and culture, as well as on semiotics and cultural criticism.

Clare **Foster**, after an undergraduate degree in classics, taught Greek literature as a Knox fellow at Harvard before attending the UCLA film school, where her award-winning short film and feature scripts launched a career as a screenwriter. She specialized in adapting literary and "true life" source material for the prestige/art house theatrical market, working on material by Sebastian Faulkes, John Updike, Flora Fraser and others. She is a Ph.D. candidate in the Faculty of Classics at Cambridge University.

Claudia **Georgi** studied English, French and German at the University of Göttingen, Germany, and the University of Exeter, England, and graduated in 2005. She is a lecturer on English literature and cultural studies in the English Department of the University of Göttingen and is working on her Ph.D. dissertation, "Liveness and Mediatisation in Contemporary British Theatre and Performance."

Marco **Grosoli** was awarded a Ph.D. in film studies from the University of Bologna for a dissertation concerning the integral corpus of writings (2600 articles) by André Bazin. His other research interests are French criticism, French New Wave, film theory and media studies. His essays have appeared in *Fata Morgana*, zizekstudies.org, *Film Comment* and several edited collections, and he regularly contributes to periodicals such as *Cinergie*, *La Furia Umana* and *Sentieri Selvaggi*.

Eric **Gruver** teaches U.S. history courses in the University Honors College at Texas A&M University–Commerce, and specializes in 20th century topics including the Great Depression and New Deal and war and popular culture. He taught history in public secondary schools for four years before becoming a member of the history faculty at A&M–Commerce in 1999.

Rose **Gubele**, a Cherokee mixed-blood, is an assistant professor of English at the University of Central Missouri where she teaches courses in rhetoric and writing. She received her Ph.D. in rhetoric and composition at Washington State University. Her research focuses on American Indian rhetorics, racism and Cherokee rhetorics.

Charles **Hamilton**, a professor of English at Northeast Texas Community College, is completing a Ph.D. in English with an emphasis in literature and film studies at Texas A&M University–Commerce. He has worked as a corporate and freelance photographer and writer in the Houston area, and as a photographic researcher, archivist and conservator at the Houston Metropolitan Research Center.

Hayley **Hasik** earned a full scholarship from the University Honors College at Texas A&M University–Commerce in 2010 and is pursuing a baccalaureate degree with a double major in history and English. She recently presented at the Southwest Texas Popular Culture Association conference on her experiences in film and history courses that focused on the 1960s.

Gülden **Hatipoğlu** received her M.A. in 2004 with her thesis on James Joyce's *Ulysses*. She is a Ph.D. candidate writing a dissertation on Flann O'Brien, transgression and Irish modernism. She teaches courses on the modern English novel and 20th century Irish literature at Ege University in Turkey. She has translated

The Third Policeman and *The Dalkey Archive* by Flann O'Brien into Turkish, and published articles on Joyce, O'Brien, and Irish Gothic.

Manjree **Khajanchi** received her B.A. (Hons) in integrated archaeology and anthropology from the University of Wales, Lampeter (now known as the University of Wales, Trinity Saint David), and completed an M.Sc. in human osteology and palaeopathology from the University of Bradford. Her research interests extend to genocide commemoration work, famine and starvation studies, and cultural fasting customs.

Anne **Klaus** was employed as a research assistant at the University of Osnabrück, Germany, from 2008 to 2011. Her research interests involve children's literature and the Victorian era. She is completing a doctoral dissertation on savior figures in fantasy fiction for children and young adults and is taking her second state examination to become a teacher in secondary education.

Walter C. **Metz**, chair and professor of the Department of Cinema and Photography at Southern Illinois University, is the author of three books: *Engaging Film Criticism: Film History and Contemporary American Cinema* (2004), *Bewitched* (2007) and *Gilligan's Island* (2012). He is writing a book about Dr. Seuss, Pixar Animation Studios and American culture.

Cynthia J. **Miller** is a cultural anthropologist specializing in popular culture and visual media. She is film review editor for *Film & History: An Interdisciplinary Journal of Film and Television Studies,* and has published in a wide range of journals and edited volumes. She is the editor of *Too Bold for the Box Office: The Mockumentary* and co-editor (with A. Bowdoin Van Riper) of the forthcoming *1950s "Rocketman" Television Series and Their Fans: Cadets, Rangers, and Junior Space Men.*

Sabelo J. **Ndlovu-Gatsheni** holds a B.A. (Hons), M.A., and a D.Phil. in historical studies from the University of Zimbabwe and is a professor at the University of South Africa (UNISA). He has published extensively on history and politics of Zimbabwe and South Africa. Two of his major publications are *Do Zimbabweans Exist? Trajectories of Nationalism, National Identity Formation and Crisis in a Postcolonial State* and the forthcoming *The African Neo-Colonized World.* He has also authored more than fifty academic articles and book chapters.

Heather **Norris Nicholson** has recently joined the Centre of Oral History at the University of Huddersfield as a visiting research fellow after six years working on film and on regional history at Manchester Metropolitan University. She has taught widely in areas of 20th century migration history, urban social change and the visual politics of cultural representation. She has written numerous chapters and articles on aspects of recreational cine use and a book *Amateur Film: Meaning and Practice 1927–1977* (2012).

Yuki **Obayashi** is a graduate researcher studying in the English Department at Japan Women's University, Tokyo. She graduated from a Master's program in Asian American studies at San Francisco State University. Her research interests include Asian American literature and transnational war memories.

Laurence **Raw** has published widely in adaptation studies. He wrote two books on adapting Henry James and Nathaniel Hawthorne, co-edited a volume (with Tanfer Emin Tunç and Gülriz Büken) on *Cultural Adaptation in American Film* as well as two volumes on teaching adaptations (*The Pedagogy of Adaptation* and *Redefining Adaptation Studies*, both with Dennis R. Cutchins and James Michael Welsh), and edited an anthology on *Translation, Adaptation and Transformation*. He is also the author of *Character Actors in Hollywood Horror and Science Fiction Films 1930–1960* (McFarland, 2012).

A. Bowdoin **Van Riper** is an independent scholar whose work focuses on the history of modern science and technology and historical memory on film. His work has appeared in *Film & History, New Scientist, Journal of Popular Film and Television,* and collections such as *Icons of Evolution* (ed. Mathew J. Bartowiak; McFarland, 2009) and *Too Bold for the Box Office* (ed. Cynthia J. Miller, 2012). He wrote *A Biographical Encyclopedia of Scientists and Inventors in American Film and TV since 1930,* and co-edited, with Cynthia J. Miller, the forthcoming collections *1950s "Rocketman" TV Series and Their Fans* and *Undead in the West: Vampires, Mummies, Zombies and Ghosts on the Cinematic Frontier.*

Index

227

232 Index

DISCARD